Charitable Choice
at Work

Other Titles in the Series

Charitable Choice at Work

Evaluating Faith-Based
Job Programs in the States

SHEILA SUESS KENNEDY &

WOLFGANG BIELEFELD

Georgetown University Press
WASHINGTON, D.C.

As of January 1, 2007, 13-digit ISBNs will replace the current 10-digit system.
Cloth: 978-1-58901-131-1
Paperback: 978-1-58901-132-8

Georgetown University Press, Washington, D.C.

This book is printed on acid-free paper meeting the requirements of the American National Standard for Permanence in Paper for Printed Library Materials.

Library of Congress Cataloging-in-Publication Data
Kennedy, Sheila Suess.
    Charitable choice at work : evaluating faith-based job programs in the states / Sheila Suess Kennedy, Wolfgang Bielefeld.
        p. cm. — (Public management and change series)
    Includes bibliographical references and index.
    ISBN 1-58901-131-7 (alk. paper) —
ISBN 1-58901-132-5 (pbk. : alk. paper)
    1. Church charities—United States. 2. Social service—United States. 3. Public welfare—United States.
I. Bielefeld, Wolfgang. II. Title. III. Public management and change.
    HV530.K395 2006
    362.5'840973—dc22
                                                    2006006683
13 12 11 10 09 08 07 06   9 8 7 6 5 4 3 2
First printing

Printed in the United States of America

Contents

Tables

Preface

In late 1999, when we began researching the effects of the Charitable Choice provision of the Personal Responsibility and Work Opportunity Reconciliation Act of 1996, we certainly did not foresee President George W. Bush's "Faith-Based Initiative" or the very contentious and polarizing political debate around efforts to involve greater numbers of religious providers in the provision of social services. As the environment surrounding our research has changed, so have our goals for this book. Initially, we intended to produce a fairly straightforward research report, but what follows represents a more ambitious effort. We do report the results of our research, but we also attempt to place these results within a broader context, thereby—we hope—illuminating the larger social trends and policy issues involved.

Our goals in this volume are to summarize what is known about faith-based contracting thus far, to explain what we think our research adds to that body of knowledge, and to use the combined information to draw conclusions about the larger philosophical issues and policy debates. Rather than a relatively restricted discussion of the conclusions reached in one particular study, we hope this book will provide readers with a more comprehensive, "holistic" overview of the subject at hand.

Acknowledgments

This book is the culmination of nearly five years of preparation, research, and writing. It would not have been possible without the generous support and assistance of many people and institutions. The Ford Foundation provided major funding for the research. The Joyce Foundation; the Center on Philanthropy at Indiana University–Purdue University, Indianapolis (IUPUI); and the Family and Social Services Administration of the State of Indiana all provided important seed money. The research was conducted under the auspices of IUPUI's Center for Urban Policy and the Environment (hereafter "the Center"), where we are faculty fellows. The Center's resources, support staff, and collegial environment were enormously helpful.

It is impossible to overstate the contribution of the colleagues whose research informs this book, beginning with the Charitable Choice Project research team: Laura S. Jensen, associate professor of political science at the University of Massachusetts–Amherst; Edward L. Queen, formerly at the Center for Philanthropy and now at Emory University; Partha Deb, formerly a faculty member at IUPUI and currently associate professor of economics at Hunter College of the City University of New York; Rachel Thelin, staff researcher at the Center; Laura Littlepage and Drew Klacick, also at the Center, and Dana Jones, the graduate assistant who spent a year and a half as the project's liaison with the Indiana Manpower Placement and Comprehensive Training program. Charitable Choice and its various progeny—including most significantly the President's Faith-Based Initiative—implicate a number of substantive scholarly areas, and any analysis, any effort to understand the policy's impact, requires a wide variety of scholarly perspectives and skills. Without that variety and the insights they provided, this book would never have been written.

We have also benefited enormously from the generosity of the practitioners and scholars of many disciplines whose names appear in the next paragraph. As members of our national Project Advisory Committee, they gave their time and lent their expertise throughout the course of the project, giving us valuable feedback on structure and methodology and helping us test the validity of research questions and conclusions. They were an invaluable resource.

The Project Advisory Committee included Michael Adams, deputy legal director, Lambda Legal; the Reverend Kevin Armstrong, senior pastor, North United Methodist Church, Indianapolis, and senior public teacher, the Polis Center; Mark Chaves, professor and Sociology Department chair, University of Arizona; Gary Cyphers, director of Human Services Research and Information Center, American Public Human Services Association; Sharon Daly, vice president for social policy, Catholic Charities USA; Fred Davie, vice president for faith-based programs, Public/Private Ventures; Arthur E. Farnsley, director of research, Project on Religion and Urban Culture, Polis Center; Omar McRoberts, assistant professor, Department of Sociology, University of Chicago; Martha Minow, professor of constitutional law, Harvard University; Stephen Monsma, professor and chair, Social Science Division, Pepperdine University; James Perry, distinguished professor, School of Public and Environmental Affairs, IUPUI; Brett Shankman, director of government relations, Jewish Community Federation of Cleveland; Drew Smith, scholar-in-residence, Leadership Center, Morehouse College; Steven Rathgeb Smith, associate professor of public affairs, University of Washington; Richard Steinberg, professor of economics, IUPUI; Melinda Story, project director, Faith in Action Wisconsin, and mentor, Robert Wood Johnson Foundation; Kirsten Grønbjerg, professor and Efroymson Chair in Philanthropy, Center on Philanthropy at Indiana University; Kara Heffernan, program officer, Ford Foundation; Thomas Jeavons, general secretary, Philadelphia Annual Meeting of the Religious Society of Friends; Irv Katz, president and chief executive, National Assembly of Health and Human Services Organizations; Stephen Lazarus, senior policy associate, Center for Public Justice; Jackie Bowie Suess, director, Children's Rights Project, Indiana Civil Liberties Union; Winnifred Fallers Sullivan, dean of students and senior lecturer,

Divinity School, University of Chicago; James Torke, professor of constitutional law, Indiana University; and Robert Walters, associate director, National Urban League.

Conducting research is expensive. Without the generosity and financial support of the Ford Foundation, the Center on Philanthropy at Indiana University, the Joyce Foundation, and the Indiana Family and Social Services Administration, this research simply would not have been possible.

People who work for government and for nonprofit providers of social services experience extraordinary demands on their time and attention. Nevertheless, those who were the subject of this study were uniformly generous with their time, talent, and insights. This study owes much to the willingness of those on the "front lines" to share their experiences and knowledge with our research team.

Finally, the authors thank Arthur E. Farnsley for reading early drafts of the book and providing valuable comments and suggestions.

To the extent that this book has value, it is in large part due to all these wonderful people and to many others too numerous to name. To the extent that there are errors or omissions, the fault lies entirely with the authors.

PART I
Setting the Stage

Chapter 1

Introduction and Background:

A New Faith in Faith

S ECTION 104 OF THE PERSONAL RESPONSI-
BILITY AND WORK OPPORTUNITY RECON-
ciliation Act of 1996 (PRWORA) was the first of a series of legislative measures that are often collectively referred to as "Charitable Choice" laws. They were, and are, legislative efforts to encourage greater numbers of religious, or "faith-based," organizations, including congregations, to bid on government contracts to provide social services to the needy. When George W. Bush was elected president in 2000, he announced that a Faith-Based Initiative expanding upon those legislative measures would be a centerpiece of his administration's domestic policy. Both the Bush Faith-Based Initiative and the various pieces of legislation that preceded it have triggered a number of policy debates and generated significant political opposition.

Although most critics of these initiatives have focused upon the First Amendment issues involved, Charitable Choice also raises a host of other equally thorny issues and implicates a number of other policy areas: the definition and design of social welfare programs; the practice of providing government services through third-party surrogates or intermediaries rather than through employees, and the management challenges attendant to such delivery mechanisms; methodological difficulties and resource constraints that complicate (or preclude) the evaluation of government program effectiveness generally, and social service delivery mechanisms particularly; and—not incidentally—stormy political, religious, and ideological debates over the causes of, and appropriate remedies for, poverty in America. Even more than most policy choices, this new outreach to religious social service providers simply cannot be

3

understood or evaluated without recognizing the religious, legal, and historical roots of those ongoing debates.

A commonplace criticism of policy in the United States is that it is driven more by ideology than evidence. This criticism, which is often leveled by the public administrators who must implement these policies, has been particularly prominent in arguments over social welfare policies. Proponents of policies placing a greater emphasis upon "personal responsibility" and more stringent work requirements describe opponents of such measures as "liberal-left" apologists ready to "throw money at problems." For their part, those opposing these approaches accuse supporters of mean-spirited unwillingness to assist the less fortunate and willful refusal to recognize systemic barriers encountered by those on welfare. These are not new arguments, but the introduction of faith-based initiatives exacerbated them, and added the potent element of religion to an already acrimonious public debate.

The goal of this book is to provide a comprehensive and critical overview of the *evidence* for and against this new approach to social welfare services ten years after passage of the initial Charitable Choice legislation, in order to inform future policy initiatives and provide guidance for public administrators charged with the oversight of welfare programs. That goal required that we engage in empirical research, and that we make every possible effort to substitute dispassionate analysis of evidence for ideological preferences. For that reason, we ignore (for purposes of our research and this book) the fairly copious polemical literature that arose in the wake of the first Charitable Choice legislation. Many of the authors of these essentially political articles were knowledgeable and persuasive, but our goal was not argumentation. It was evidence.

To obtain that evidence, we focused upon job training and placement services. Unlike several other social services, it is an area with very definite, objective goals and thus measurable outcomes. Our discussions of constitutionality, general management challenges, effects of government contracting on faith-based organizations, and the like, however, are not limited to those services but have broader applicability to the contracting out of government services. Our evidence was gathered from three states chosen because they represent three distinctive types of political culture and display different demographic characteristics, including religious demographics: Indiana, Massachusetts, and North Carolina.

The qualitative information about implementation from these three states was gathered by project researchers chosen for their familiarity with that state's social service landscape. Our team was based in Indiana. In North Carolina, data were collected by a member of our Indiana team with extensive contacts there. And in Massachusetts, data were collected by a social welfare scholar at the University of Massachusetts in Amherst. These researchers used several methods; they did a limited number of surveys of faith-based organizations and other nonprofits, they did quite a bit of face-to-face interviewing with faith-based providers, and they did literature searches and archival searches specifically targeted to those states. Their common assignment was to determine what the contracting environment was before Charitable Choice—including an analysis of the prior welfare programs, the degree of centralization or devolution, and the like—and the involvement of religious providers before and after the initiatives. Statistical data about percentages of faith-based participation before and after simply were not available, although there were anecdotal data. The researchers then analyzed the changes: That is, what did this state's system look like before and what did it look like after? What did the "folks on the ground" (faith based, secular, nonprofit, and government) think was working, and not? The information gained from this research informs this entire book.

The in-depth quantitative study of provider experience and comparative outcomes was done in only in Indiana, because—as we explain in more detail in chapters 2 and 3—Indiana was the only state of the three for which such data were available. Fortunately, Indiana's political culture has traditionally been considered representative of the country as a whole. Unlike Massachusetts and North Carolina, it is religiously diverse, with no single denomination having a majority. Though no one state can function as a proxy for a large and diverse nation, Indiana probably comes as close as any, and closer than most. The vast majority of Indiana's welfare population resides in Marion County and Lake County, so the available data included most of those providing job training and placement services under Temporary Assistance to Needy Families.

Part I of this volume consists of chapters 1 and 2. In this chapter, we describe faith-based initiatives and the various issues these initiatives raise, and we provide the legal, legislative, and historic context within which they must be understood. In chapter 2, we detail the literature we consulted, the process through which we chose our research questions, the practical and methodological challenges involved (and what those challenges imply for policy implementation), and the reasons we made the particular choices that we did.

Part II, by far the largest part of the book, summarizes our research results, both descriptive and statistical. The general descriptive material is based upon research findings from all three states in the study; the analyses of outcomes given in chapters 4, 5, and 6 are limited to research conducted in Indiana. Each chapter is organized around three questions: What questions were we asking? What did we find? And what conclusions did we draw? Chapter 3 describes the implementation of Charitable Choice legislation and the Faith-Based Initiative by the public managers "on the ground" in the three states chosen for in-depth study. Chapter 4 tackles the definitional issues involved—what are "faith-based" organizations? How will a public administrator know them when he or she sees them? How do they differ from each other? What does previous scholarship tell us about their characteristics? Chapter 5 looks more closely at the management of religious nonprofit organizations and the particular management challenges they face. Chapter 6 compares the objective effectiveness of the faith-based and secular social service providers in our study. What were the measurable outcomes for clients? Were there differences in performance success that could be attributed to a faith dimension? What did the empirical data show?

Part II concludes with chapter 7's discussion of the constitutional issues raised by these initiatives, including descriptions of litigation involving faith-based contractors and legal scholarship analyzing the constitutional issues involved. Part III has only chapter 8, in which we summarize our findings and highlight areas needing further study.

We turn now to the context of this particular debate.

Social Welfare in the United States

Charitable Choice and the president's Faith-Based Initiative are part of a movement that can be broadly described (depending upon the political viewpoint of the narrator) as either a backlash against, or a correction to, the creation of what has been called the "administrative state" during the latter half of the twentieth century. That changing governmental landscape was itself a response to rapid, dramatic changes in American society, especially the growth of both actual diversity and (thanks to communications technology) awareness of it. The rapidity of technological innovation, the increased mobility of populations, the nationalization and globalization of legal and economic systems, and the seemingly inexorable growth of government have all contributed to a sharpening of the tensions between America's historic individualism and the growing interdependence of its citizens.

The central question for liberal democratic regimes—what is the proper role of the state, and where should we strike the balance between communal obligations and libertarian values—has arguably been the central philosophical fault line across which the electorate has polarized into "red" and "blue" Americans. Charitable Choice emerged at the nexus of two of these arguments over the proper role of the state: the nature and extent of government's obligation to provide social welfare and the proper place of religion in the "public square." These concerns are interrelated, as is illuminated by the following brief overview of social welfare provision, religious charity, and church–state law in America.

SOCIAL WELFARE POLICY

Welfare policy disputes have an even longer pedigree than does the modern idea of the limited state; indeed, the origins of contemporary debates over government-funded social welfare programs can be traced at least as far back as 1349. In that year, England enacted the Statute of Laborers, prohibiting citizens from giving alms, or charity, to those who had the ability to work—that is, to "sturdy beggars" (Handler and Hasenfeld 1997). This first attempt to deal with what we would later call welfare was not about providing assistance; it was about forcing people to work. Not until

1601, in the reign of Elizabeth I, would a tax be levied to provide material assistance to the poor. The Elizabethan Poor Law established three categories of needy people: children without parents (or at least without parents who could care for them adequately); the able-bodied; and the incapacitated, helpless, or "worthy" poor. Vagrants, or able-bodied persons who refused to work, could be "committed to a house of correction, whipped, branded, put in pillories and stoned, or even put to death"(Indiana Department of Public Welfare 1985). Help—however meager—was limited to the deserving, or "worthy," poor.

The Elizabethan Poor Law thus incorporated a distinction between the "deserving" and "undeserving" poor that would eventually be carried to the British colonies and reproduced in the laws of virtually all American states. It was the model that settlers brought to the New World; it was the approach adopted by the original thirteen colonies; and as people moved west, it was the approach incorporated into the Ordinance of 1787, which prescribed rules for governing the Northwest Territory. To a significant extent, the distinction between the deserving and undeserving poor, the "categorizing" of people needing assistance, and the emphasis upon work have remained the primary framework within which the general public and federal and state policymakers view social welfare and poverty issues today.

This paradigm found considerable support in religion. The belief that poverty is evidence of divine disapproval—that virtue is rewarded by material success—was held in one form or another by a number of the early Protestants who settled the colonies; it is a theological perspective that has continued to influence American law and culture. In the early 1900s, moral opprobrium directed at the poor found an ally in science, and poverty issues were caught up in the national debate between Social Darwinists like William Graham Summer and their equally religious critics—notably, William Jennings Bryan (Walsh 2000). It was not until the Great Depression that blaming the poor for their own poverty would become a minority position and that American lawmakers would widely acknowledge the need for some sort of social safety net. Even then, it would be a mistake to assume that the dislocations of the 1930s or the passage of New Deal legislation changed Americans' deeply rooted beliefs about poverty, welfare, or their own history of self-reliance. As the social historian Stephanie Coontz has written, "Most Americans agree that prior to federal 'interference' in the 1930s, the self-reliant family was the standard social unit of our society. Dependencies used to be cared for within the 'natural family economy' and even today the healthiest families 'stand on their own two feet'" (Coontz 1992, 69).

Coontz and others have demonstrated that this widely held belief in self-sufficiency is inconsistent with the reality of the American experience. Pioneer families owed their existence to massive federal land grants and state economic investment in new lands. In the early twentieth century, western populations depended on government construction of dams and federally subsidized irrigation projects. During the Depression, government electrification projects and other government subsidies were critical to the survival of the family farm. In the 1950s, Coontz notes, suburban families were "more dependent on government handouts than any so-called 'underclass' in recent U.S. history" (Coontz 1992, 76), thanks to the GI Bill and the National Defense Education Act that subsidized the educations of a whole generation; and to the Federal Housing Authority and the Veterans' Administration, which allowed Americans to purchase homes with artificially low down payments and subsidized interest rates. Meanwhile, billions of dollars of government-financed inventions, production processes, and research enabled businesses to flourish, and by the 1970s, Social Security had virtually wiped out the historic tendency for the elderly to be the poorest sector of the population.

Many, if not most, of these programs benefited the middle and upper classes rather than those in need. Even between 1965 and 1971, during the height of federal Great Society antipoverty initiatives, 75 percent of American social welfare dollars went to the nonpoor. Nevertheless, despite the lessons of the Depression and the documented, pervasive reliance of middle- and upper-income families on a wide variety of government assistance programs, acceptance of poor relief or welfare continues to be viewed by many Americans as an entirely different matter, and as evidence of a moral or character deficit. Neither welfare reform nor Charitable Choice can be understood without recognizing both the persistence and widespread acceptance of that perspective, and the continuing vitality of religious doctrines that support and inform it. Opposition to those measures, conversely, cannot be understood without the recognition of equally significant, countervailing political and religious influences that have argued for social justice and greater governmental responsibility for the poor. As Mary Jo Bane, Brent Coffin, and Ronald Thiemann have eloquently reminded us,

> Indeed, these great religious traditions differ in their beliefs about
> ultimate reality, their approaches to community, and the types
> of institutions they foster. Yet for all their enduring differences,
> these traditions share central commitments: to the equal worth
> and sacredness of all men and women; to recognizing our shared
> vulnerability as finite creatures; and to our common needs for
> nurture and support to achieve our potential as creative participants
> in family, community and society. The Torah, Bible and Koran
> especially stress that the covenant community requires of its
> members a special obligation to the poor and vulnerable; by their
> treatment, the character of the entire community is measured. (Bane,
> Coffin, and Thiemann 2000, iii)

Although many religious communities do their charitable works through nongovernmental channels, many others have insisted that working for social justice and sharing responsibility for those less fortunate must be a shared obligation of religious communities and governmental institutions. As with so many other issues in a diverse polity, there has been no one "religious" or "faith-based" approach to social welfare issues. Contemporary social Darwinists and proponents of the Social Gospel both justify their policy preferences as expressions of Christian theology. One of the least edifying aspects of public debates over the Faith-Based Initiative and the proper place of religion in public life has been the virtually unquestioned assumption by people on all sides of the issue that "religion" is a distinct and undifferentiated (if not monolithic) commodity. Typical is a remark made by James Towey, then the director of the White House Office for Faith-Based and Community Initiatives, who told attendees at a White House Conference that support for the Faith-Based Initiative is a "flashpoint in the 'culture war' between people of faith and the secular world" (Wallsten 2004). In reality, there is no singular entity called "people of faith." Though many religious communities have a long history of outreach to the needy, both the nature and the extent of those efforts have reflected significant differences rooted in both doctrine and history.

RELIGIOUS CHARITY AND SOCIAL PROVISION

In the United States, social outreach programs grounded in religious belief date virtually from the arrival of the earliest European settlers, when Catholic missionaries from France and Spain combined their zeal for converting the native inhabitants with efforts to minister to their physical and human needs. However, it was not until massive waves of immigration in the sixteenth and seventeenth centuries brought English Christian settlers to the New World that significant outpourings of religiously inspired philanthropy began in earnest. Protestant missionary work had its genesis in attempts to convert Native Americans, but it soon developed an organizational and intellectual context that fostered the eventual emergence of many other forms of American philanthropy (Porterfield 2003). Historians have documented the religious values, traditions, and beliefs that so significantly contributed to the establishment of American social welfare. Religious ideals, particularly those focusing on the importance of brotherly love and altruism, had a significant intellectual influence on American welfare institutions in the nineteenth century, and they fostered the development of early sectarian welfare agencies (Tirrito and Cascio 2003).

In *Democracy in America*, Alexis de Tocqueville commented specifically on this influence of religion on social welfare institutions. De Tocqueville noted that

> A citizen's churches and voluntary groups reflected and reinforced his moral and spiritual values and imparted them to his children, surrounding him with a familiar, self-contained, breathable moral atmosphere. Voluntary social welfare associations ministered to the community's vulnerable according to the tenets of compassion and charity. A citizen's schools, whether publicly or privately funded, enshrined those values, and were run in accordance with them, with extensive citizen involvement and supervision. (quoted in Skocpol 2000, 21)

Even among the English Christians who originally populated the American colonies, spiritual and moral values and denominational approaches to charity differed widely—not only in their manifestation and expression but also in their theological roots. Teachings about poverty and other human afflictions varied significantly across the different faith traditions represented. From the early missionaries, to Puritan forms of outreach to the sick, disabled, and indigent, to the Calvinist formulation of social responsibility, these early settlers' understandings of when and how their faith required them to aid their neighbors were shaped—and often sharply differentiated—by the particularities of their theologies. In some cases, responsibility to care for the sick and poor was seen not as a requirement of Christian compassion but as an element of self-interest; in a frontier environment, the failure to take care of others could undermine the bonds of community and reciprocity, resulting in a lack of assistance when the donor needed help (Porterfield 2003).

In the nineteenth century, Catholics and Protestants who may all have agreed with the abstract proposition that "true Christian stewards" would share their talents and material resources with others to benefit society nevertheless had different perspectives on the reasons for stewardship, as well as significantly different beliefs about what such stewardship entailed. Protestants generally believed that they would be saved through faith, not works; they saw acts of benevolence not as a way to earn salvation but as a way to manifest the depth of their faith (Oates 2003). Some Protestant denominations believed that Christian duty included a requirement to remake society in God's image, that it required them to "build the City on the hill" (Marone 2003, 31). As an extension of that obligation, members of such churches often took up unpopular social causes, such as the abolition of slavery or temperance.

Catholicism taught that salvation rested on good works as well as faith, and that charity was a religious duty incumbent on all believers. Furthermore, Catholics believed that collective giving was preferable to individual charity because special spiritual benefits accrued to those who united with fellow believers in acts of charity and social compassion. (Oates cites as a typical example of the Catholic approach the establishment of a lay benevolent association, the Saint Aloysius Orphan Society, by German Catholics in Quincy, Illinois, in 1851. The society was founded to finance a parish home for children orphaned in the wake of a cholera epidemic.)

Catholic theology insists that the needs of the poor take priority among the church's good works, a distinctive spiritual value that has traditionally characterized Catholic philanthropy. That priority has also driven the Church's policy preferences; until the 1930s, Catholic leaders staunchly defended laissez-faire economics, on the belief that free markets would result in improved employment opportunities and living standards for all. The onset of the Great Depression greatly altered this perspective, and for the first time, Catholic religious leaders vigorously lobbied for social welfare programs, federal relief programs, and reform legislation. Within Catholicism, as within other religious communities, there have been significant internal disagreements over the appropriate methods for discharging the Church's duty to the poor. The Catholic Worker Movement, founded in 1934 in New York City by Dorothy Day and Peter Maurin, forcefully challenged the Church's acceptance of government funding, as well as its bureaucratic charity structure (Oates 2003).

Although Jewish immigrants arrived in this country much later than their Christian counterparts, they immediately began fulfilling their own religious charitable mandates. Because Jewish immigrants' faith placed them in a very small minority, their first priority was to care for each other—a priority that was both religious and prudential in origin. The religious motivation was clear: Judaism holds *Tzedakah* as one of its core tenets. *Tzedakah* requires that Jews give aid and assistance to the poor and elderly, and that they support other worthy causes. In Judaism, the highest form of giving is that which enables a person to become self-sufficient. Thus, many of the earliest Jewish social service agencies offered language, financial, and job assistance so that immigrants would be able to provide for themselves and in turn offer assistance to other immigrants who arrived after them. The prudential motivation for concentrating early philanthropic efforts on needs within the Jewish community itself grew out of culturally internalized lessons of Jewish history; if the Jews did not take care of their own poor and elderly, no one else would. And if the Jews were seen as a burden to others, if they were unable either to sustain themselves or to contribute to the larger society, they would suffer discrimination and possibly even expulsion.

More recent waves of immigration have added other religious traditions—notably Islamic and Asian—to the American philanthropic
landscape, and the beliefs of those immigrants will undoubtedly
continue to shape and reshape national attitudes about poverty,
charity, and the obligation of the state—just as, throughout American history, religious beliefs have motivated charitable giving and
prompted (sometimes radical) moral and political movements for
social change and equal justice (Skocpol 2000).

Aside from the particulars of their charitable convictions, it is
important to recognize how many of America's religious settlers
brought with them not only distinctive theological beliefs about
poverty and misfortune but also their own historical reasons to
distrust the power and motives of government. From the earliest
days of the country, the "dissenting" churches that had come to
America to find religious liberty were skeptical of governmental
involvement with religion and fearful of state overreaching. From
early settlers like the Baptists to later groups like the Jews, many of
America's religious communities have insisted on the separation
of church and state and been fiercely protective of their religious
autonomy. Those beliefs persist and continue to inform opposition
to the acceptance of government dollars for faith-based social service programs, even while many religiously affiliated programs, including many operated under the auspices of those same religious
groups, have increasingly come to depend upon those dollars.

As noted above, large-scale government efforts to combat poverty did not exist before the Depression; by that time, many religious organizations had been providing services to the indigent
and the elderly for decades. Government partnerships with established charitable institutions that had been providing social welfare
were thus inevitable, and were—and have remained—largely un-
controversial. Most—although certainly not all—of the long-time
religious social service providers are separately incorporated nonprofit charitable organizations like Catholic Charities, Lutheran
Social Services, and Jewish Family Services that offer both employment and assistance on a professional, nondiscriminatory basis.
Often, too, the structures of government programs have operated
to minimize concerns about church–state violations. In many cases,
government funds follow the individuals entitled to the benefits
involved. For example, Medicaid patients may choose a nursing

home or hospital, which then receives payment from the government. Though these and similar benefits are not generally referred to as vouchers, they are functionally indistinguishable from vouchers, and they have long been an accepted part of the social service landscape. Direct contracts and other collaborations between government units and pervasively sectarian organizations, including individual congregations, have been much less common, although even they have been far from unusual.

Government financial support for religiously affiliated organizations providing social services has thus been a long-standing feature of most public welfare programs. In a 1969 study of findings from a 1965 survey of 406 sectarian agencies in twenty-one states, Bernard J. Coughlin reported that 70 percent of them were involved in some type of purchase of service contract with the government. A 1982 study by F. Ellen Netting, focusing on government funding of Protestant social service agencies in one midwestern city, found that some agencies received between 60 and 80 percent of their support from the government and that approximately half of their combined budgets were government financed. In 1994, government funding accounted for 65 percent of the nearly $2 billion annual budget of Catholic Charities USA and 75 percent of the revenues of the Jewish Board of Family and Children's Services. These and similar studies provide evidence that—whatever the merits or flaws of current faith-based initiatives—it is simply inaccurate to suggest that government partnerships with religious providers are something new.

CHURCH AND STATE

Although the First Amendment to the U.S. Constitution forbids the "establishment" of religion in the United States, the precise dimensions of the metaphorical wall separating church from state have been a source of dispute through most of American history, and debates over the appropriate relationship between religion and government have been a feature of the American landscape since the Pilgrims first landed at Plymouth Rock. However, for a variety of reasons, these debates became considerably more acrimonious following passage of the Fourteenth Amendment, as the Supreme Court decided, in a series of cases stretching over a number of years, that the amendment's language—and more specifically the phrase "No State shall make or enforce any law which shall abridge the privileges or immunities of citizens of the United States; nor shall any State deprive any person of life, liberty, or property, without due process of law; nor deny to any person within its jurisdiction the equal protection of the laws"—required the "incorporation" of fundamental civil liberties into state law. For the first time, state and local units of government were obliged to respect the fundamental rights that had been protected against federal government infringement by the first eight amendments.

As scholars have amply documented (Lowi 1995; Amar 1998), the consequent nationalization of the Bill of Rights, and in particular the First Amendment's religion clauses, meant that state and local governments were no longer free to pass laws privileging religious beliefs held by the majority of their citizens. Constitutional provisions that had hitherto been experienced as abstract principles applicable only to a distant federal government suddenly became all too real. The ensuing struggles have involved virtually all the institutions of government at one time or another. Citizens continue to debate whether behaviors deemed sinful by theologians, from gambling and prostitution to shopping on Sundays, should be prohibited by the state; they argue about the propriety of using tax dollars to support parochial schools; and they demonstrate for or against the posting of religious symbols or texts on public buildings. Currently, impassioned efforts to avert legal recognition of same-sex marriages are grounded almost entirely in religious doctrine.

As government at all levels has grown, multiplying the points of contact between citizens and their governing agencies and institutions, these conflicts over when it is appropriate to give religious beliefs the imprimatur of the state have likewise increased. The courts have been obliged to decide, among other things, what sorts of religious displays can be erected on public property, what sorts of public services can be provided to students in parochial schools, and what sorts of holiday observances are too sectarian to be permissible in public schools.

Interestingly, in contrast to the frequent challenges to public religious displays, and persistent, vocal opposition to public funding for religious elementary and secondary schools, the long-standing allocation of public tax dollars to religious social services providers has gone virtually unchallenged. There are two major Supreme Court precedents: *Bradford v. Roberts*, an 1899 case permitting the flow of public dollars to religious hospitals, and *Bowen v. Kendrick*, decided in 1988. *Bowen* involved a challenge of the First Amendment's establishment clause to the Adolescent Family Life Act, which provided funding to a variety of local organizations, including religious organizations, to support counseling of teenagers about premarital sex and teenage pregnancy.

In *Bowen*, the Court acknowledged a danger that counseling services might be delivered by sectarian groups in a manner that violated the establishment clause, but it declined to find the act facially unconstitutional merely because that danger existed. According to the majority, a successful challenge would have to rest upon the particulars of a specific program; the mere inclusion of religious contractors in the program was held not to constitute a per se establishment clause violation. Funding for religiously affiliated schools, conversely, has generated a significant jurisprudence, and many efforts to direct public funds to such schools have been struck down.

Despite this seeming inconsistency between the cases involving social welfare services and those involving schools, the courts have actually been quite consistent—and virtually unanimous—in their insistence that, whatever else the establishment clause may mean, it absolutely forbids government funding of religion. What the case law in both areas has also recognized is that the mere payment of tax dollars to a religious organization is not the same thing as funding religion. Government may constitutionally purchase services from sectarian sources or enter into other partnerships that involve the transfer of tax dollars to such entities, so long as the funds are used to purchase secular, rather than religious, goods or services.

Historically, the relative lack of litigation over government support for religious social services might be explained at least in part by the fact that the secular nature of those services is so readily apparent. Hospitals and nursing homes are providing medical care; day care facilities are supervising children; job placement counselors, drug treatment facilities, and the like have secular counterparts engaged in providing similar, if not identical, programs. Though economists remind us that dollars are fungible, so that support for one activity frees up funds that can then be used elsewhere, it is relatively simple to calculate the costs of nursing services or child care, and it is reasonable to argue that if the payment of government dollars is only sufficient to cover those determinate costs, public money is subsidizing only the secular activity. In the school context, where litigation of First Amendment issues has been copious, direct funding programs that have passed constitutional muster have generally been those involving an identifiably secular benefit available to all citizens—immunization, speech and hearing testing, transportation—where the exclusion of children attending religious schools was deemed to burden the free exercise rights of parents opting for religious education.

When such aid has been disallowed, the Supreme Court has pointed to the "pervasively sectarian" nature of parochial schools, where religion is interwoven into all aspects of the school day, making it impossible to ensure that only secular programs benefit from the expenditure of public funds. If public money does flow directly to a pervasively religious institution, the courts have consistently held that any benefit accruing to that institution must be incidental to a secular purpose.

For many years, these legal and constitutional issues were salient primarily to large, sophisticated, religiously affiliated providers and their lawyers. Their current prominence is in large measure a result of the transformation of American governance during the past century and, more recently, the exponential growth of government contracting, sometimes (incorrectly) referred to as "privatization."[1] Not only has the scope of government action increased at all levels; the mechanisms through which government addresses public problems and delivers public services also have changed radically. As we shall see, the issues raised by this fundamental shift in the way government does business are central to the concerns over Charitable Choice and the president's Faith-Based Initiative.

Law, Public Management, and the Evolving State

Public services originally were delivered primarily by state actors—government employees. Later, they were delegated to closely related agents of the state. Today, discretion over the day-to-day operation of public programs routinely rests not with the responsible state or federal government agencies but with a host of nongovernmental, "third-party" surrogates or "proxies" that provide programs under the aegis of loans, loan guarantees, grants, contracts, vouchers, and other new mechanisms for taking public action. This exercise of core governmental authority by non- and quasi-governmental entities is perhaps the most distinctive feature of America's "new governance" (Jensen and Kennedy 2005; Salamon 2002, 1–2; Kettl 1988, 1993).

The substitution of new forms of collaboration and public–private partnerships for historically hierarchical, bureaucratic chains of command has raised a number of administrative and legal concerns about public accountability. Public administration scholars have worried whether public managers can ensure that services provided by intermediaries are delivered in accordance with traditional American constitutional commitments to liberty, equality, and fairness—not to mention transparency and fiscal accountability—and have produced a substantial public management literature (Salamon 1993, 2002; Kettl 1988, 1993; Gilmour and Jensen 1998; Richie and Kennedy 2001) dealing with the management challenges and accountability issues raised by such significant reliance on contracting.

For their part, legal scholars have focused upon the problems that arise when boundaries between "public" and "private" become blurred or indistinguishable as a result of public–private collaborations. Public actors are obligated to meet constitutional and public law standards for government behavior—as Donald Kettl has observed (1993, 40), the government "is not just another principal dealing with another agent"—but contracting has made it increasingly difficult to know when any particular action can properly be attributed to government. Because the concept of "state action" is central to protection of individual rights in the American constitutional system, where we define liberty as freedom from government interference, it is essential that we know when the state has acted. As chapter 7 discusses in more detail, the proliferation of partnerships between government agencies and for-profit, nonprofit, and faith-based partners has made that determination increasingly difficult, raising well-founded concerns about a loss of constitutional accountability.

For their part, scholars studying nonprofit and voluntary organizations have warned that these organizations' increasing dependence upon government funding may be weakening the independence and vitality of the sector (Smith and Lipsky 1993; Chambré 2001; Alexander, Nank, and Stivers 1999) and that an eventual consequence of "privatization" and government "reinvention" may be the inadvertent transformation of the nonprofit sector into an unrecognized arm of the state. Privatization advocates argue that contracting for services increases efficiency and reduces the size of government; critics respond that what such arrangements really do is extend the reach of the state while decreasing its visibility and accountability (Kennedy 2001).

Critics also point to significant differences between the age-old practice of procurement—the purchase by government of pencils, computers, or asphalt paving from for-profit vendors—and the purchase of drug-counseling services or parenting classes from nonprofit or religious providers. The latter arrangements are more complicated than the relationship between buyers and sellers, and require different and more sophisticated management tools; many public management scholars argue that we have not adequately mapped the contours of such relationships nor traced their consequences for either partner.

When the nonprofit partner is a religious organization, these concerns take on added dimensions. In particular, representatives of faith communities worry that significant growth in faith-based contracting—particularly among smaller, more "grassroots" organizations—will lead to the co-option of religion or to a muting of religion's distinctive "prophetic voice." As one pastor in Indiana memorably put it, "With the government's shekels come the government's shackles" (Kennedy and Bielefeld 2002, 4). Others worry about the dangers of becoming dependent upon income from government contracts and the attendant risk of "mission creep," a term describing the gradual alteration of a nonprofit organization's original mission to meet changing state priorities and keep government contract dollars flowing.

Faith-Based Contracting

Charitable Choice can justifiably be seen as a natural outgrowth of the long-standing involvement of religious organizations in social welfare, and these changes from direct government provision of services to so-called third-party government. Indeed, it is reasonable to ask: What's new? Government agencies in the United States have paid religious organizations to house, clothe and counsel the poor since the earliest days of state involvement in social welfare programs. Religious organizations providing government-financed social services range from tax-exempt affiliates of denominational entities under International Revenue Service Code Section 501(c)(3), like Catholic Charities and Lutheran Social Services; to "pervasively sectarian" organizations like the Salvation Army; to individual congregations.

In fact, many proponents of "Charitable Choice" legislation and President Bush's "Faith-Based Initiative" describe those policies as simply an attempt to level a playing field that already includes significant numbers of religious players. They argue that fear of overzealous application of the First Amendment has kept religious providers from bidding on government contracts, and they characterize the legislation as merely an effort to ensure that government officials do not inappropriately require participating "faith-based" contractors to diminish or eliminate the religious components of their services. Whatever the merits of that claim, the fact is that public tax dollars are routinely used to purchase social services from sectarian providers—and have been so used for decades.

If we try to answer the question "What is new?" by reading the legislative history of Charitable Choice, we find that it is not as illuminating as we might wish. Nevertheless, a review of that history does shed some light on the initial purposes of the legislation, the assumptions that motivated it, and the changes that occurred as various proposals moved through the legislative process.

Congressional action on Charitable Choice began on January 31, 1995, when Representative Joe Knollenberg (R-Mich.) inserted in the *Congressional Record* remarks in favor of the "Common Sense Welfare Reform Act" then being introduced. Among the provisions of that proposed act was a "Choice-in-Welfare Tax Credit," which was described as a measure giving "individual citizens a voice in how this country fights poverty." The proposal gave taxpayers a credit for contributions to nonprofit organizations working to fight poverty, and it allowed nonitemizers as well as those who itemized deductions to claim it. The tax credit enjoyed widespread, bipartisan support; 70 percent of taxpayers—approximately 85 million Americans—do not itemize, and a study conducted by the organization Independent Sector estimated that the credit would cost the federal government approximately $20 million in forgone tax receipts but could generate as much as $80 billion for charitable organizations (A. Sullivan 2004).

The tax credit was not enacted as part of the Personal Responsibility and Work Opportunity Reconciliation Act of 1996, but it reappeared shortly after George W. Bush took office and was included in the "Community Solutions Act" the White House sent to Congress early in 2001. Though the more controversial elements of the bill stalled, the tax credit provision was included in a tax bill that was quickly passed, in somewhat different form, by both houses of Congress. However, as Amy Sullivan has reported,

> When congressional and White House negotiators sat down to iron out the differences in the two separate tax cut bills that had been approved by the House and Senate in the spring of 2001, they were faced with a price tag that topped $1 trillion. Fiscal conservatives started to balk, protesting that the cost was simply too high. Something had to go. Sitting next to each other on the potential chopping block were reductions in the tax rate, the repeal of the estate tax, and the charitable giving proposal. The choice for Republicans was, in the end, simple. (A. Sullivan 2004)

Charitable organizations not only failed to receive the anticipated income boost; the repeal of the estate tax—which was, according to an administration spokesperson, a higher priority—was expected to cost them an estimated $6 billion a year from bequests. Though the tax credit proposal has been reintroduced, current fiscal and budgetary realities make its passage unlikely.

The tax credit proposal was not the only measure proposed as a way of increasing nonprofit and religious charitable activities. On May 23, 1995, then-senator John Ashcroft introduced the "Communities Involved in Caring Act," the precursor to Section 104 of PRWORA. According to Ashcroft's testimony, the act was predicated on three fundamental beliefs: that states need the maximum flexibility possible if they are to reform their welfare systems; that intermediary organizations—especially private and religious charities—need to be involved in the welfare system; and that those intermediary organizations need "not only money, but volunteers":

> The CIVIC Act also provides explicit authority for States to contract with nongovernmental organizations, including private and religious charitable organizations, and other institutions, in the effort to help

solve the welfare problem. . . . We have all heard the stories of small organizations that are hugely successful in helping America's poor. Unfortunately, many of these programs have been constrained from receiving Federal funds because all too often those Federal funds would require radical changes in their beliefs, their structure, their facilities, their program or their organization—changes that would rob these programs of the very characteristics and attitudes that make them successful. (U.S. Senate, Committee on the Judiciary 2001)

As the massive welfare reform bill proceeded through the legislative process, comparatively little attention or debate centered upon Section 104. What discussion found its way into the *Congressional Record* tended to reiterate Ashcroft's central themes: the need to level the playing field in order to encourage charitable and faith-based organizations to participate in social welfare efforts, the inability of government acting alone to address issues of poverty, and—almost always—the greater effectiveness of religious organizations. Representative Jon Kyl (R-Ariz.), among others, took the House floor in August to argue that "no government program can replace private sector charities" and to remind his colleagues that most Americans "know" the private sector is more effective at service delivery.

Section 104, as enacted, prohibited discrimination against religious providers by federal or state government agencies ("Neither the Federal government nor a state receiving funds under such programs shall discriminate against an organization which is or applies to be a contractor . . . on the basis that the organization has a religious character"), and explicitly safeguarded the religious character of such organizations ("Neither the Federal government nor a State shall require a religious organization to [A] alter its form of internal governance; or [B] remove religious art, icons, scripture or other symbols, in order to be eligible to contract"). In response to First Amendment concerns, Section 104 also prohibited discrimination by religious contractors against beneficiaries of services, and it required that alternative providers be made available to recipients who objected to the religious character of the provider offering services. Many, if not most, legal analysts considered these provisions little more than an affirmation of existing First Amendment jurisprudence.

The one provision of Section 104 that was indisputably new was subsection (f), which read:

> A religious organization's exemption provided under section 702 of the Civil Rights Act of 1964 (42 USC 2000(e-1a) regarding employment practices shall not be affected by its participation in, or receipt of funds from, programs described in subsection (a)(2).

Religious organizations have always enjoyed an exemption from civil rights laws allowing them to use religious criteria when hiring and firing certain employees.[2] Such an exemption would seem to be required by the free exercise clause of the First Amendment; it would be a patent infringement on religious autonomy to require a Baptist congregation, for example, to hire an assistant pastor or Sunday school teacher who was not a Baptist. Prior to passage of subsection (f), however, when religious organizations contracted with government, they usually had to agree that any positions funded with tax dollars would be filled in accordance with applicable state and federal civil rights laws. Section 104 specifically allowed religious contractors to apply religious criteria to jobs that would be funded with tax dollars. Chapter 7 will analyze the legal arguments for and against that change; but for purposes of this discussion, it is sufficient to note that this was a change from prior practices and politically the most controversial provision of Section 104.

Following the passage of PRWORA, Charitable Choice provisions modeled on Section 104 were included in other legislation. During testimony on the "Effective Substance Abuse Act"—an act to amend the Public Health Service Act to permit faith-based substance abuse centers to receive federal assistance, then-senator Spencer Abraham revisited the issue of effectiveness, saying "I believe we owe it to our citizens and particularly those addicted to drugs or alcohol to make the most effective treatment available to them. That treatment is provided by faith-based charities. . . . It is very simple, Mr. President, where most treatment centers fail, those that are faith-based work" (U.S. Congress 1997). Similar justifications—the greater effectiveness of religious providers and the need to combat bureaucratic discrimination against them—led to the inclusion of Charitable Choice provisions in welfare-to-work legislation, the Community Services Block Grant Program, and the Children's Health Act.

On January 29, 2001, President Bush announced the creation of the White House Office of Faith-Based and Community Initiatives and the establishment of Faith-Based and Community Centers in five Cabinet agencies: Education, Health and Human Services, Housing and Urban Development, Justice, and Labor. The Faith-Based Initiative was described as an effort to broaden the reforms effected by Charitable Choice legislation. The administration vowed to help faith-based providers overcome unnecessary barriers to their participation, including government managers' reluctance to contract with providers whose programming was infused with religious doctrine. The White House announcement stressed the proven superior effectiveness of religious providers, and the president repeatedly referred to the "Armies of Compassion" waiting in America's religious communities for a signal that they were welcome to enlist in the national fight against poverty.

By this point, however, political opposition was sufficient, and sufficiently motivated, to block passage of further legislation. Critics of the initiative leveled a number of charges. Civil libertarians argued that the proposal was a further effort to erode the separation of church and state. Democrats described it as an effort to play to evangelical Christians, an important part of the president's core constituency, and to make inroads into the African American community by "buying" the allegiance of inner city black clergy. Similar concerns were voiced by several in the African American community (Blake 2005). Leaders of Unitarian, Jewish, and liberal Protestant congregations joined evangelicals like Jim Wallis of Sojourners to oppose the measures.

The one element of the Community Solutions Act of 2001 that enjoyed wide support, the tax credit, was not a White House priority and, as discussed above, was allowed to die in committee in exchange for the repeal of the estate tax. The more controversial parts of the bill stalled. Eventually, the president implemented most of his program through a series of executive orders—a strategy that raised still other constitutional and policy concerns. Indeed, the one thing that public and nonprofit managers, welfare scholars, lawyers, and policymakers could all agree upon was that there were many unanswered questions.

Unanswered Questions

Scholars, policy analysts, and political scientists have raised a large number of questions about the Faith-Based Initiative and the various Charitable Choice provisions that preceded it. Some of those questions are overarching, philosophical ones: What are the dynamics—historical, ideological—of this debate? What does it tell us about the ongoing tensions of democratic governance and policy-making for a diverse citizenry? Other questions focused upon more pragmatic and immediate concerns, many of which were raised by the ambiguities in the legislation: What do these laws require of government managers? How will Charitable Choice and the Faith-Based Initiative affect welfare clients and services? How do the First Amendment and other constitutional provisions affect program administration? The broad issues—and some of the specific questions raised by each—can be categorized as follows:

- *Definitional issues.* Government has contracted with religious organizations ever since it has provided social services. Furthermore, there are enormous variations among religious organizations. How are the faith-based organizations targeted by these measures different from Catholic Charities, Lutheran Social Services, the Salvation Army, and government's many other long-time religious partners? What are "faith-based" organizations, and how do they differ from other nonprofit organizations? What do we mean by "programmatic success" and "efficacy"?
- *Funding issues.* The effort to recruit new faith partners has not been accompanied by additional funding for social services. To the contrary, the amount of money budgeted for social services has declined. With no new money, what will prevent Charitable Choice and the Faith-Based Initiative from operating simply to shift funds from one set of religious providers to another—presumably, from government's traditional religious partners (who generally operate in accordance with applicable professional norms) to providers more focused upon the "personal transformation" of clients? What will happen to small, grass-roots, faith-based organizations if diminished public resources make funding streams unreliable? Will government funding af-

fect the character or mission of small religious organizations new to the contracting regime? If so, how?

- *Constitutional issues.* The First Amendment does not prevent government from doing business with faith-based organizations, but that does not mean that any program run by a religious provider will pass constitutional muster. There is a constitutionally significant distinction between programs that are offered by a religious provider or in a religious setting and programs in which religious observance or dogma is integral to service delivery. What mechanisms are proposed to ensure that services are delivered in a constitutionally appropriate manner? What is the capacity of public managers to ensure constitutional accountability, and what resources will be made available to them for monitoring compliance? Can we avoid government favoritism for certain religious providers over others or privileging of either religious or secular providers? How can we ensure constitutional accountability?

- *Evidence issues.* John DiIulio, the first director of the White House Office of Faith-Based and Community Initiatives, readily admitted the absence of credible research supporting the assertion that religious providers are more effective, quoting the academic adage that "the plural of anecdote is not data." DiIulio expressed his hope that future studies would provide answers to such questions. One can recognize that many faith-based and religious organizations do important, often exemplary, work without taking that indisputable fact as evidence that religious organizations as a category are more effective than secular ones. At the time the White House implemented its initiative, no evidence for such an assertion existed. (It is also worth noting that religious sociologists have criticized this emphasis upon efficacy, suggesting that to focus on religion's "effectiveness" is to profoundly misunderstand the nature of religion—that such instrumental approaches to religion are self-defeating. As Reinhold Neibuhr has reminded us (Neibuhr 1993, 12), the instrumental value of faith for society is dependent upon faith's conviction that it has more than instrumental value (Althauser 1990).

- *Management issues.* The public officials whose job it is to manage faith-based contracts were faced with many ambiguities and unanswered questions. The question for them is not, for example, whether government should partner with religious organizations to provide social services. It always has, and undoubtedly it always will. The question is, "Under what circumstances are such partnerships appropriate, and when they are, how should they be structured and monitored?" Similarly, the question is not whether, in the abstract, religious programs or secular approaches are preferable. The questions for government program managers are, "What organizational characteristics are most likely to predict successful program delivery, and how can I determine which of the bidders for this contract possesses those characteristics?" and "How will I define and measure accountability?" Complicating these management questions is the likelihood that in a federalist system, different states will approach implementation of Charitable Choice differently. Those differences will also pose management challenges. Finally, contracting with government presents nonprofit managers with challenges of their own: managing cash flow and absorbing transaction costs, responding to government monitoring and reporting requirements, and compliance with constitutional restrictions and government program regulations. These management challenges can be particularly onerous for small organizations unaccustomed to a contracting environment.

In the following pages, we detail efforts made by our research team over a period of three years to choose from this multitude of open questions those capable of being empirically studied and to provide at least preliminary answers to them.

Notes

1. Strictly speaking, privatization is the outright sale of a governmental operation to a private-sector purchaser, which thereafter owns and manages it and pays taxes on any profit accruing to it. In the United Kingdom, Prime Minister Margaret Thatcher sold off railroads, steel mills, and other enterprises because her administration did not believe government should own them.

2. Melissa Rogers has provided an excellent history and analysis of the exemption. See "Federal Funding and Religion-Based Employment Decisions" (Rogers 2005).

Chapter 2

Asking the Right Questions

*A*S CHAPTER 1 DETAILED, CHARITABLE CHOICE LEGISLATION RAISED MANY MORE theoretical, legal, and policy issues than one research project could address. All legislative proposals—indeed, all programmatic or policy responses to perceived problems, whether public or private— are based upon multiple assumptions: about the nature and extent of the problem to be solved, about the choice and feasibility of appropriate or desirable solutions to the problem, and about the best way to implement the solutions selected. (Different lawmakers will also have different reasons for supporting or opposing particular policies; at times, as we have noted, those motives may have more to do with political or ideological predispositions than with policy considerations.) In that sense, at least, Charitable Choice legislation was business as usual.

Section 104 of the Personal Responsibility and Work Opportunity Reconciliation Act of 1996 (PRWORA) grew out of a number of beliefs—some articulated, some implicit—about the causes of poverty, the effects of welfare dependence, the presumed efficacy of interventions that incorporate religious elements and values, and the reasons for government's historic preference for larger, more professionalized contracting partners, whether religious or secular. Among those assumptions was the belief that faith-based organizations (FBOs) do a better job at lower cost; a conviction that a significant number of FBOs would act on a desire to participate in government welfare programs but for the existence of "unnecessary and burdensome" institutional barriers; and a belief that FBOs had been discriminated against by public managers excessively concerned with First Amendment issues. In an analysis of press releases and statements issued by the Bush administration, one researcher identified several other assumptions as well:

that larger, more traditional service providers have failed to deliver effective services; that smaller organizations, and particularly congregations, are able to be more flexible and responsive than established providers; that small FBOs and congregations are better able to enlist and employ volunteers; and that such organizations are inherently more trustworthy (Gibelman and Gelman 2002).

Our first task was to analyze these assumptions in the context of the broad areas of inquiry we had identified and to then choose from among those that had not been adequately researched: the ones we felt were both important and capable of being empirically tested. Existing research, some of which is described below, challenged the assertion that religious providers had been discriminated against, and it cast significant doubt on the thesis that significant numbers of FBOs were eager or able to become government contractors providing sustained services to needy populations. Credible evidence for other assumptions—pro or con—was skimpy or nonexistent. Some simply did not lend themselves to empirical investigation.

Before we could refine our research questions and determine how we would approach them, we needed to consult the existing academic literature, to find out what evidence for the legislative assumptions already existed and what existing scholarship could tell us.

The State of the Evidence in 2000

A review of the literature available in 2000 quickly underscored the unexamined nature of several of the assumptions we had identified. It turned out that very little was known about the efficacy of religious social services in general, or whether there were outcomes or other differences between religious providers who accept government contracts and those who do not. For that matter, there had been relatively little evaluation of the efficacy of *any* social service programs. No empirical studies had compared faith-based contractors' outcomes to secular ones. Government agencies rarely evaluated their contractors to determine the utility of the programs being funded or to compare the performance of contractors. Existing government partnerships with religious organizations had generated very little constitutional litigation or commentary.

What information existed tended to be descriptive: how many religiously affiliated organizations were government contractors and what percentage of contractors' budgets came from government (Netting 1982, 1984); and the extent of congregational (as opposed to religiously affiliated nonprofit organizations) interest in providing social services under such contracts and the capacity of such congregations to deliver those services (Chaves 1999; Grettenberger 1997). To suggest that faith-based social services of the sort contemplated by Charitable Choice were "understudied" would be a considerable understatement.

Although research directly on point was sparse, studies having varying degrees of relevance to the inquiry at hand did exist. Several articles by Mark Chaves were particularly helpful, given Charitable Choice's new emphasis on outreach to congregations in addition to religiously affiliated social service agencies (and the president's later assertions that "Armies of Compassion" represented significant untapped resources that could be made available to help fight poverty). Chaves mined the National Congregational Study to provide a wealth of information about American congregations, including information relevant to the question of congregational capacity to provide social services. His data suggested that most congregations are severely limited in their capacity to operate formal programs. Only 12 percent of the congregations in his study operated social service programs under their own auspices—that is, using their own staff and financial resources. It was far more typical to find congregations supporting programs delivered by others. Chaves found congregations to be adept at mobilizing small groups of volunteers to conduct well-defined, periodic tasks. Churches and synagogues are particularly well suited to providing short-term responses to immediate needs and were much less able to sustain long-term programs requiring consistent staffing and supervision (Chaves 1999). An earlier study by Susan Grettenberger, limited to United Methodist congregations in Michigan, had come to similar conclusions; she found that these congregations provided services primarily in response to emergencies and that they simply did not possess the necessary resources to implement programs requiring more sustained service delivery (Grettenberger 1997).

In a later article, Chaves once again used data from the National Congregational Study to assess the prospects for Charitable

Choice and the Faith-Based Initiative. He noted that only 3 percent of congregations surveyed in 1998 received government funding; that larger congregations—those having more than 900 regular attendees—were more likely to operate social service programs; that ethnic composition was the single most important predictor of willingness to partner with government; and that congregations in the South were less willing than congregations elsewhere to apply for government funding. He also found that "secular integration" (defined as the extent to which a congregation operates within a relatively more secularized institutional environment) was a factor in its willingness to work with government agencies. Chaves noted that Catholic churches and liberal Protestant denominations expressed significantly more willingness to enter into government contracts than did more conservative, or evangelical, churches (Chaves 1999).

Also helpful was a 1998 policy paper by Stephen Monsma that was issued by the Center for Public Justice, in which Monsma referenced the long history and currently widespread practice of government cooperation with religious social service providers—a history and practice that he characterized as "largely positive." He based his findings on a national survey of religious agencies providing services to children and families, which he had conducted in 1993–94. Ninety percent of his respondents reported receiving at least some public funding. Of those who characterized themselves as "clearly religious," 82 percent got government money, and a strong majority of those reported no problems with government officials over religious practices. Most that had experienced such problems had been requiring religious participation as a condition of receiving the service involved—a clear violation of the First Amendment (Monsma 1998, 5–6).[1] Monsma's results have been recently confirmed by other scholars (Kramer, De Vita, and Finegold 2005).

In 1999, McCarthy and Castelli published a summary of the literature on religious social services then available. *Religion-Sponsored Social Service Providers: The Not-So-Independent Sector* was issued as part of their working paper series by the Aspen Institute's Nonprofit Sector Research Fund. Their introduction noted that "political leaders are . . . making dramatic proposals and even enacting new laws without the benefit of an understanding of the extent and nature of existing religion-sponsored social service providers" (McCarthy and Castelli 1999, 3). Their review of available research reinforced Chaves's finding that religious social services primarily take the form of emergency interventions and that congregations most likely to provide services are those that are ideologically liberal and large, high-income, suburban, or black. They found that religious social services were almost exclusively local and were typically provided without reference to the religion of the beneficiary. They also found that government agencies and religious providers worked together in a number of noncontractual contexts (e.g., by providing referrals, consultations, and facilities). With respect to the issue of comparative effectiveness of faith-based and secular providers, they flatly stated: "We have been unable to locate a single credible study assessing the relative effectiveness of religion-sponsored social services" (p. 5). In language anticipating the belief that "Armies of Compassion" were waiting to help government provide for the needy, they were similarly blunt, saying "We do not believe, given the evidence we have examined, that it is possible for America's religious institutions to dramatically expand their provision of social services" (p. 6).

Even those who did hope for increased congregational participation in social service delivery as a result of faith-based outreach efforts recognized that religious congregations would not and could not replace the nonprofit and religious organizations that have traditionally provided the bulk of American social services. In 1996, in the wake of PRWORA, several scholars published articles that addressed that issue and looked specifically at the capacities of nonprofit and religious providers to succeed in the expanded role envisioned for them as a result of the various Charitable Choice measures being enacted.

In 1999, John Bartkowski and Helen Regis published *Religious Organizations, Anti-Poverty and Charitable Choice: A Feasibility Study of Faith-Based Welfare Reform in Mississippi*, which surveyed religious involvement in social services in that state. Their study analyzed the strengths and weaknesses of the organizations involved; they found that religious providers tended to be more "holistic" but also noted limits on such organizations' capacity imposed by inadequate resources, as well as a "potential for exclusivity and insularity" (Bartkowski and Regis 1999, 6).

Also in 1999, Jennifer Alexander published an analysis of the effects of devolution on nonprofit organizations in Cuyahoga County, Ohio—the heart of the Cleveland metropolitan area. She concluded that the capacities of community and FBOs to fulfill the expectations raised by Charitable Choice were severely limited by a lack of human and financial resources. She also noted that many of those working at nonprofit agencies believed they had already begun to absorb added costs as a result of welfare reform and "load shedding" by government (Alexander, Nank, and Stivers 1999).

Similar results were reported in a study of faith-based service providers in the city of Washington; in that study, a majority of respondents said they lacked adequate resources, facilities, staff, and funds to meet increases in need (Prinz 1998). (The survey also found that large numbers of nonprofit service providers could not account for the resources they had, or for their income and expenditures, because they did not keep records.)

Many of the articles and pamphlets published in the wake of PRWORA saw Charitable Choice as an opportunity. One of those was aptly titled "The Charitable Choice Opportunity." Issued by the Center for Public Justice, it described the old rules (i.e., before PRWORA) as "restrictive" and the new ones as "inclusive," and it cheered passage of the law for "clearing away barriers to full involvement by faith-based organizations" (Carlson-Theis 2000, 2–3). Others—including many who were supportive of participation by faith-based providers in welfare programs—raised red flags.

In 1997, the Nonprofit Sector Research Fund sponsored the report *Government Promotion of Faith-Based Solutions to Social Problems: Partisan or Prophetic?* by Thomas J. Harvey, president emeritus of Catholic Charities USA. Harvey's experience, he wrote, led him to "believe that religiously affiliated agencies, other voluntary agencies, and the public at large" should assess Charitable Choice efforts carefully, in the context of government's unique role in promoting the general welfare (Harvey 1997, 5–6). Among his concerns was the "values" rhetoric frequently employed by proponents of the measure—rhetoric that tended to characterize poverty as a spiritual deficit rather than a material one. In that formulation, people in need lacked jobs not because the local factory had closed, or because educational requirements had changed, or because day care was unavailable, but because they possessed an inadequate work ethic or otherwise lacked the "middle-class values" demanded by the job market:

> Interpreting the problems of the poor as spiritual also subtly perpetuates a centuries-old interpretation that the poor are lazy and without worth. . . . This prejudice implies that government assistance to help them will only perpetuate the problem. This bias represents a form of social Darwinism—survival of the fittest— which has been well documented and analyzed by historians and social commentators as being deep-seated, but without foundation. (Harvey 1997, 9)

Harvey also advised the religious community to resist the temptation to see public programs as evidence of altruism rather than as evidence of "a political process [that] often reflects vested interests more than a commitment to the common good" (p. 21).

Several articles addressed the issue of load shedding, warning that nonprofit agencies, whether faith based or secular, lack the resources to substitute for the eroding public safety net (Edin and Lein 1998). Other writers focused upon the potential effects of government contracting on religious and community-based organizations. Alexander, Nank, and Stivers investigated the impact of welfare reform generally on nonprofit agencies in Cuyahoga County and concluded that smaller nonprofits simply lacked the capacity to adopt the organizational and business practices required by government agencies (Alexander, Nank, and Stivers 1999). Their research confirmed several earlier articles, including a 1994 study by Kearns, who had found "public sector conceptualizations" (i.e., business practices) "ill-suited" to nonprofit agencies (Kearns 1994, 185). In "Black Churches' Involvement in 'Charitable Choice' Programs: The Promise and Peril," Ryden endorsed the effort to direct added resources to urban African American churches but warned that such churches would have to learn to walk "a fine line" to avoid a number of legal pitfalls (Ryden 2000, 2). Chambré studied four faith-based AIDS organizations in New York and found that the religious identity of the providers had become attenuated in the course of the contract relationship; two of the organizations she studied became secularized, while the other two adopted more "ecumenical" forms of faith. Though she did not attribute these changes solely to the organizations' receipt of government funds, her research suggested that such funding was a significant element driving the documented shift (Chambré 2001).

Arthur E. Farnsley was an early, acute observer of Charitable Choice efforts, and his work on the subject has since grown to include two books.[2] In 2000, the Polis Center published his *Ten Good Questions about Faith-Based Partnerships and Welfare Reform.* Among the questions he identified as important and at that point unanswered were "How will this work?" "Do congregations have the necessary administrative capacity to use public funds?" "Will congregations change individuals' values, and are we comfortable with that?" and "Who will benefit, and who will lose?" (Farnsley 2000).

Ten Good Questions was followed by an article in *The Christian Century,* in which Farnsley pointed out that "many interested parties have different goals" for Charitable Choice and that it is difficult if not impossible to decide whether a program is successful when there is no agreement on what that program is intended to do or what "success" might look like. He identified four interest groups with highly disparate agendas that had supported Charitable Choice legislation: (1) advocates of privatization, who believed outsourcing would save money, and whose motives were largely economic; (2) social service and foundation professionals, frustrated with social service failures and the seeming intractability of poverty, who saw Charitable Choice as a "bold social experiment" that might work; (3) "reformers" for whom the separation of church and state has gone too far, who wanted government to be more "accommodating" to religion and religious expression; and (4) "Salvationists," who saw an opportunity to press a Christian mission agenda with money from the government (Farnsley 2001).

These wide differences in perspective explain the equally different approaches to Charitable Choice in the scholarly literature. Romzek and Johnston offered an explanatory model of accountability mechanisms and focused on problems likely to be faced by public managers operating in the "hollow state" described by Milward (1994) and others (Romzek and Johnston 2001). Nank and Stivers also explored public administration issues arising out of the "hollow state" (Nank and Stivers 2001). Monsma, whose work is perhaps closest to ours and is discussed later in this chapter, continued to produce careful descriptions and case studies of partnerships between religious organizations and government and to catalogue their approaches to service delivery (Monsma and Mounts 2002), while others brought social work and social service network perspectives to bear (Cnaan and Boddie 2002; Wineburg 2001). Still other research efforts focused upon particular faith communities or on specific social services (Choi and Tirrito 1999; Thomas et al. 1994). The picture that emerged from these and later studies, although far from complete, was of a wide variety of nonprofit and religious social service organizations engaged in a daily struggle to stretch limited resources and meet existing demands while assessing the pros and cons of closer relationships with government.

As shown by this brief and necessarily incomplete summary, much scholarship was relevant to aspects of our project and helpful in formulating our inquiries, even if very little of it was directly on point. It was when we looked for empirical research comparing the performance of secular and faith-based nonprofits, however, that we came up dry. Once we excluded anecdotal reports and public relations efforts by agencies promoting their own programs, we found—as McCarthy and Castelli had predicted—only four articles of even arguable relevance. All four involved substance abuse programs; and two, though not actually involving comparisons of religious and secular treatments, did explore the role of religion in these programs.

One of the two investigations of religious elements in substance abuse treatment was a 1978 evaluation of a Salvation Army alcohol treatment program. The researchers concluded that the "social climate" and "treatment approach" of the Salvation Army contributed to the success of treatment for those participants who actively participated, and they further concluded that the Salvation Army's program was as successful as (but not more successful than) other, similar programs (Moos, Mehren, and Moos 1978). The other investigation was a study titled "Individual Religiosity, Moral Community and Drug User Treatment," reporting the results of research to examine the relationship between reductions in alcohol and drug use and religiosity. Despite the authors' original hypotheses that such connections existed, and despite some evidence suggesting that participation in a "religious moral community" could positively affect use, they could establish no "obvious relationship" between dependent behavior and individual religiosity (Richard, Bell, and Carlson 2000).

Two studies compared secular and religious programmatic effectiveness. A 1981 article by David Desmond and James Maddux reported on research involving programs for heroin addicts. Eighty-seven percent of the addicts who participated in the study were Hispanic. Over a twelve-year period, 11 percent of them had entered religious treatment programs, and 10 percent had participated in a methadone program that also had a religious component. The rest had gone to providers offering traditional treatment modalities. Those addicts who willingly joined the religiously intensive programs were more successful than those who participated in conventional programs; however, the religious methadone program was less successful than the secular programs. (The researchers theorized that many of those who signed up for the methadone program did so only to obtain the substitute drug, not to reduce their drug dependence.) The researchers concluded that the variable most likely to predict success was personal motivation—that those who entered programs with positive attitudes and openness to the treatment approach were more likely to succeed. The evidence did not support a determination that effectiveness was attributable to the religious character of the programs. Such a conclusion would be particularly problematic, according to the researchers, because Hispanic clients were likely to self-select religious treatment programs (Desmond and Maddux 1981).

The other comparative study was a 1993 report on church-based smoking cessation programs. The authors compared the efficacy of "intensive, culturally relevant and spiritually based church interventions" to the effectiveness of a "self-help, cold turkey" approach. The church interventions used sermons, testimony, volunteer counselors, and follow-up evaluations; these mechanisms—not surprisingly—were found to be more effective than the "tough it out" approach (Stillman et al. 1993).

This was the state of the empirical research when we began our research in 2000. Since then, of course, there has been additional work—most notably, a 2004 book by Stephen Monsma, *Faith in Partnerships*. Monsma examined welfare-to-work programs in Los Angeles, Chicago, Philadelphia, and Dallas during 2001 and 2002. He included all organizations in those four cities with programs to help welfare recipients achieve economic self-sufficiency—a total of 1,559 organizations. His conclusions were based on 493 completed surveys returned by those organizations; his sample included government agencies, secular and faith-based nonprofits (of the 120 that were religiously affiliated, he determined that 48 were strongly faith based), and for-profit providers. He then asked about the nature of the services each provided.

For purposes of analysis, Monsma divided these services into eight "job-oriented" categories and three "life-oriented" programs. Job-oriented programs were those geared specifically toward obtaining employment: education and literacy, job search and placement, and the like. Life-oriented services included mentoring, work preparedness, and similar life skills. He found that all of the providers offered a similar number of life-oriented services but that faith-based providers offered fewer job-oriented services. Approximately 40 percent of the FBO services in his sample fell into the "life-oriented" category, while the corresponding percentage for secular providers ranged between 25 and 32 percent.

Selecting Research Questions: Implementation, Organizational and Management Capacities, Performance, and Accountability

After reviewing the relevant history and background, and surveying existing literature, we narrowed the universe of open questions to five that we felt we could answer and that we believed would illuminate the broader areas of concern we had previously identified:

- *In a federalist system, what will emerge as differences in state implementation approaches?* One of the frequently cited virtues of a federalist system is the freedom such systems afford individual states to act as "laboratories of democracy"—to take different, hopefully innovative, approaches to the national agenda from which the country as a whole can learn and benefit. However beneficial such experimentation may prove to be, however, federalism poses a considerable challenge to congressional lawmakers, whose efforts to create national policy must contend with significant variations in state and local implementation. It was inevitable that states would approach Charitable Choice and the Faith-Based Initiative differently; we wanted to examine those differences and see what policy conclusions, if any, we might draw. Because our resources were limited, we chose three states to serve as a primary focus for that part of our inquiry, although we did monitor publications, news items, and lawsuits from all of the states. (The criteria we used to choose states to study are discussed in chapter 3.) Federalism also provides a lens through which broader issues of funding and public management can be explored.

- *What are the distinctive characteristics of FBOs?* For-profit and nonprofit organizations that work with government agencies exhibit a variety of adaptations as a result of these partnerships (Smith and Lipsky 1993; Kettl 1993; Frumkin 2002) A significant concern voiced by religious critics of Charitable Choice and the president's Faith-Based Initiative has been that small FBOs accepting government funding would thereby lose independence—that they would eventually be co-opted, and the distinctive and important "prophetic voice" of the church would be muted. If, as some proponents of Charitable Choice assert, the larger religiously affiliated providers that have worked with government for decades have become "too secularized" as a result of those partnerships, what are government agencies doing to ensure that smaller FBOs will not experience the same organizational and behavioral metamorphosis (e.g., see Alexander, Nank, and Stivers 1999; Chambré 2001)? Answers to these questions will be important to policymakers, public managers, and others, but before those questions (among many others) can be asked, we need to define the characteristics that differentiate faith-based from other nonprofit organizations. (That is the issue addressed in chapter 4.) Unless we know what an FBO looks like, it will be hard to know whether it has changed.

- *What organizational characteristics and management capacities correlate with effectiveness, and what are the public management challenges of faith-based contracting?* The success of any government program depends significantly on the organizational and management capacities of those in charge; in the case of Charitable Choice, successful implementation depends on the fiscal, programmatic, and constitutional capacities of both government agencies and the faith-based service providers with whom they contract. Analysis of these capacities requires answering several questions: How do the states define and locate FBOs, and what criteria do they use to assess their ability to deliver the necessary services? Are small, grassroots FBOs able to absorb the transaction costs associated with government contracting (Grønbjerg 1997)? What about their access to the accounting and legal resources needed to assure compliance? (These and other organizational and institutional challenges faced by non-profit managers are addressed in chapter 5.) If FBOs do not have these resources, are states assisting with "capacity-building" measures? If not, should they be? What about the states' own capacities to manage contracts and to monitor for fiscal, programmatic, and constitutional compliance? These narrow questions go to the broader issues of public management, how to define terms, and funding.

- *Is there a measurable difference in performance efficacy between faith-based and secular services?* A significant part of the political justification for faith-based initiatives was the often-articulated belief that religious providers are more effective, that religious providers do a better job than their secular counterparts. We proposed to look at faith-based services provided to recipients of Temporary Assistance to Needy Families—specifically, job training and placement programs—to determine whether FBOs were, in fact, more successful in meeting observable, objective benchmarks: Were their clients more likely to obtain and hold employment? Did they earn more? And if so, if there were measurable differences in performance between faith-based and secular organizations providing government services, was faith the variable that accounted for those differences? (Our answers to these questions—and the methodology employed to find these answers—are the subject of chapter 6.)
- *How accountable are public managers and contractors?* Outsourcing generally, and Charitable Choice specifically, implicate important issues of constitutional, programmatic, and fiscal accountability. What are the capacities of grassroots religious organizations and their government partners to provide the required services, account for government funds, evaluate program outcomes, and adhere to constitutionally mandated

boundaries?[3] Accountability requires clarity of definition, implicates funding and management issues, and is at the very core of concerns over the constitutionality of Charitable Choice programs. (We tackle these issues in chapter 7.)

Methodological Challenges

Methodology in the social sciences presents a number of difficulties, and research on welfare populations is notoriously challenging. The issues involved in the study of faith-based organizations raised still other methodological questions.

DEFINING "FAITH BASED"

In many ways, the most difficult research issue to be resolved was the most basic: in order to compare "faith-based" and secular programs, it is necessary to have a clear description of the characteristics that differentiate them. To examine the implementation of Section 104 of PRWORA, it is necessary to know what it had changed; that is, we needed to know how the "faith-based organizations" targeted by the legislation differed from the many religious providers that had partnered with government for decades.

Most public discussion of Charitable Choice and the Faith-Based Initiative simply assumes the interchangeability of terms like "religious," "sectarian," and "faith based." There has been and is, however, enormous variation among the entities so labeled, and certain of those variations are both constitutionally significant and politically relevant to Charitable Choice. Many of the religious social welfare providers with the longest histories of government contracting are "faith based" in a very literal sense—that is, the provision of (essentially secular) social services is motivated by their specific religious beliefs. For such organizations, feeding and clothing the poor, tending to the sick, and housing the aged are essentially secular manifestations of religious duties rather than tasks imbued with inherently religious meaning or opportunities for proselytizing or transforming the individuals served. The religious dimension of service in such organizations is not immediately apparent from the program's content. Religious providers rooted in other faith traditions, however, do see their role as transformative;

they believe that ameliorating the problems of drug and alcohol dependence or joblessness must begin with spiritual renewal. Religious observance and doctrine play a role in—indeed, may be integral to—the delivery of social services by those organizations, and they are immediately visible in their programs.

Congress did not include a description of what it meant by "faith-based" organizations for the purposes of Section 104 or subsequent Charitable Choice legislation. It did not address whether or how the FBOs targeted by Charitable Choice differed from the many religious social service providers with a long history of governmental contractual relationships. It did not define the barriers to their participation in social service delivery (although the White House subsequently issued a report in which it attempted to do so[4]). Nor did it indicate to what extent those barriers might be constitutionally required. The challenge was clear: If we were to measure the difference "faith" made, we would first need to define "faith," and that definition should correspond to the legislative intent insofar as that intent could be determined.

The term "faith based" was new to the legislative lexicon, and though it may simply have represented an effort by its congressional authors to be inclusive of all religious traditions, it was seen by some members of more "works-based" religions like Catholicism and Judaism as evidence of a specifically Protestant religious paradigm. The suspicion that the language of "faith" was intended to privilege certain religious approaches over others was also rooted in the fiscal and organizational realities of the social service landscape. Well before passage of the first Charitable Choice legislation, a significant percentage of the providers working with government were religiously affiliated nonprofits; furthermore, there was no new money being appropriated for social services. This led several observers to see Charitable Choice as an effort to redirect existing funds from Catholic Charities, Lutheran Social Services, and similar long-term providers to evangelical organizations that might be expected to focus their services on "transforming" clients into citizens possessing more desirable values. Seen from this perspective, to the extent that Charitable Choice and the Faith-Based Initiative were efforts to expand help to the nation's needy, they were efforts to do so by encouraging evangelical and explicitly transformative approaches to program delivery. In the view of these critics, because the question was not *whether* religious providers would be included (they always had been), it had to be *which* providers would be favored.

Whatever the merits of that analysis, political reality—not to mention the dictates of the Constitution's equal protection doctrine—requires government to treat all religious providers equally, and state and federal agencies subsequently charged with the implementation of faith-based outreach could not and did not overtly distinguish among religious traditions in their regulations or bid practices. However, the fact that government did proceed to treat all religious providers as essentially fungible for purposes of implementation (at least ostensibly—there are anecdotal reports that individual public managers may have indulged their own preferences in some agencies) brought us back to our original dilemma. If no legal or theological distinction was being drawn between longtime contractors like Catholic Charities, Lutheran Social Services, the Salvation Army, and Jewish Family Services on the one hand and Pentecostal or urban American Methodist Episcopal churches on the other, what was the legislative intent? Which "faith-based" providers were federal agencies and state governments being told to include? How would public managers know how to proceed?

A review of the *Congressional Record* and other speeches by members of Congress eventually led us to the conclusion that the primary beneficiaries of Charitable Choice were intended to be small community-based, grassroots religious organizations. These were the organizations that had presumably encountered difficulty entering into the contracting regime (a presumption based upon their underrepresentation in the contractor pool). They were also the religious providers that most closely resembled the picture painted by proponents of greater outreach; they were less professionalized and thus less "secularized" than the larger religious social service agencies, their programming tended to be more explicitly infused with religion, and they lacked the prior experience and organizational capacity that government managers can be expected to reward in the bid process. That these were the organizations being courted was made more explicit in 2001, with the establishment of the White House Office of Faith-Based and Community Initiatives.

Identifying the desired beneficiaries of the legislation did not, however, solve the methodological problem. To test the assumption that faith or religion was a key variable leading to more positive results, faith still had to be defined. Furthermore, it is impossible to consider "faith" or religious identity as either/or attributes; organizations fall on a continuum of religiosity, and there are significant differences among organizations that might all be categorized as "faith based." The YMCA and Teen Challenge are not analytically interchangeable. (On a theoretical level, there is also the issue posed by so-called mission-driven nonprofits. Those who volunteer at Planned Parenthood clinics or shelters for battered women are often passionate about their efforts and driven by political or social beliefs that can be quite as fervent as any religious doctrine. Indeed, some of those beliefs grow out of religious tenets and teachings. Might passion and commitment rather than theology define "faith-based" organizations?)

We eventually resolved the definitional issue as other researchers have subsequently done: by adopting a template allowing us to distinguish among organizations along the dimension of religiosity. One of the best known of those typologies emerged from the deliberations of the Working Group on Human Needs and Faith-Based and Community Initiatives, coordinated by Search for Common Ground and convened in 2001 for the purpose of "clarifying areas of confusion." Noting that "Americans need a better understanding of the variety of faith-based and other nonprofit organizations, and participants in public discussions and debates need to be attentive to the reality that the current vocabulary of public discussion can serve to confuse and divide," the Working Group developed six organizational categories, ranging from "faith saturated" to "secular," and listed the attributes of each (Wofford et al. 2002).

As helpful as that highly sophisticated typology was for defining the terms of public discourse, however, we determined that the number of categories identified, and the relatively nuanced distinctions between them, could lead to somewhat subjective—even arbitrary—identification of providers in the course of an empirical research project. We relied instead upon a descriptive analysis of religious organizations developed by Thomas Jeavons (1998) as the basis for distinguishing between religious and secular organizations and among organizations having varying degrees of religious affiliation or identity. The specifics of the definitions we adopted are described in detail in chapter 4. But essentially we distinguished between organizations that we categorized as "strongly" faith based, "moderately" faith based, and essentially secular. These categories reflect the degree to which specifically religious elements operate within the organizational structure and program delivery of the provider in question.

Merging Legal and Social Science Discourse

Finding adequate and meaningful definitions was by no means the only methodological challenge. The issues raised by Charitable Choice and its progeny crossed disciplinary barriers and required a research team that was similarly multidisciplinary. The principal investigator was a lawyer with a background in constitutional law and civil liberties; the senior scholar was a sociologist who had done significant research on nonprofit sector organizations. Rounding out the team were an econometrician, a political scientist whose prior work had focused upon welfare and federalism, a law student with a doctorate in religious studies, and several research assistants with varied academic backgrounds and credentials.

There are significant differences in approach and language among these disciplines and even more significant differences between social science methodologies and legal research. These differences required explanation and accommodation. Legal research, for example, tends to look argumentative to social scientists—that is, the examination of precedent and scholarship will often lead the legal scholar to decide that a particular law or action is or is not consistent with the law and/or the Constitution. Law review articles tend to argue for acceptance of the researcher's contention that precedent requires this, rather than that, result. Empirical research, conversely, is appropriately reluctant to generalize outcomes of small samples. Good social science scholars take care not to prejudge, so as to avoid misreading the evidence they are collecting; they take similar care not to claim more for their results than those results can reasonably explain. These disciplinary differences meant that it was more important than usual to employ careful language and draw relevant distinctions—especially after the president's announcement of the Faith-Based Initiative and the ensuing politicization of the issues involved—if we were to avoid having our conclusions appropriated or misrepresented by political partisans.

ACCESS TO RELIABLE DATA

Overcoming the language problems created by the researchers' disciplinary differences was a relatively minor issue. The availability—or, more accurately, the lack of availability—of good data presented us with far more significant challenges—so significant, in fact, that two of the project's researchers eventually dubbed the effort to find reliable information "the Quest for the Holy Grail" (Klacik and Jones 2001). We soon realized that our initial goal of studying comparative efficacy in all three of the states we had chosen was too ambitious, given the magnitude of the data problems involved. States rarely evaluate their social programs; they do not have the resources to do so. What data they collect tends to be that which is necessary for management purposes—evidence supporting claims for payment, or statistics required by other government agencies—and depending upon the state, it may be collected by ninety or more county offices, by regional state offices, or by a central state agency. Providers are not identified as "faith based" or secular (indeed, prior to passage of Charitable Choice, the states in our study had not attempted to identify the existence, let alone the nature, of a faith element); performance and outcome measures, to the extent that they exist, vary widely. Many systems do not track clients by provider. The confidentiality of the client must be protected, which means that names cannot be used to track clients. Welfare recipients are notoriously difficult to track in any event—poor people move frequently, have their telephone service disconnected more often, and are less likely to have steady employment.

We soon discovered that, of the three states we had chosen to study, in only one—Indiana—would we be able to access the data required to conduct a meaningful comparison of outcomes. Accordingly, though we examined implementation in all three states—the policy environment generally, the implementation mechanisms chosen, the policies adopted, the public management and legal challenges that emerged, and the state's general experience with the new emphasis upon FBOs—we limited the in-depth study of provider experience and comparative outcomes (reported in chapters 4, 5, and 6) to Indiana, where we could be confident that we had access to the necessary data.

As daunting as the data problems were, they were exacerbated by outsourcing, a situation that is increasingly common (and for public management researchers, increasingly frustrating). In Indiana, the state had contracted with a consultant to design and implement the computer program used by the Family and Social Services Administration (FSSA). The system was difficult to use for our purposes, and attempts to modify the program to help with data collection ran up against proprietary and contract concerns. Other consulting arrangements meant that a number of people were involved in data collection, management, and reporting, with the result that the data flow from entry to reporting was unclear. At least five offices within the agency produced reports using the same data, but people responsible for analysis were not necessarily familiar with the input process, and vice versa. State analysts sometimes could not explain the meaning of the variables they worked with. Overlapping agency structures required rationalizing different data formats. Data were often incomplete or contradictory (e.g., the simple misspelling of a name or identifier, or the transposition of a number, created many problems). And our research effort came at a time that Indiana—like most other states—was experiencing a severe budgetary crisis.

Although the FSSA's directors and managers were more helpful than we had any right to expect (they even provided $15,000 in early "seed money" for the project, recognizing the usefulness of program evaluation to their own future efforts), the agency was too understaffed to allocate personnel to our project. We eventually placed a full-time research assistant at the agency to gather and enter information. She was able to "clean" much of the data and to work with FSSA employees to resolve reporting issues and discrepancies. After significant negotiation with the information technology consultant, modifications to the computer program were eventually made. But it was an extraordinarily difficult process—far more difficult than we had initially (naively) anticipated. We would later learn that our experience was not an anomaly; there is a reason for the dearth of quantitative evaluation of social service efficacy, a reason that all of the other studies of Charitable

Choice that we are aware of have employed case studies and qualitative and descriptive methodology. Objective comparisons of outcomes require reliable data reflecting those outcomes. Such data are virtually nonexistent, and creating it is incredibly expensive and time consuming. (It should be noted that this absence of reliable data is not simply a problem for academic researchers; it creates a genuine dilemma for public managers, because it deprives them of accessible benchmarks and the ability to learn from the experiences of others.)

THE CONTEXT OF GOVERNMENT CONTRACTING AND THE SERVICE PROVIDED

The final methodological challenge was to avoid too narrow a focus—to remember that the accuracy and usefulness of any research will depend upon an appreciation of the multiple variables involved and the significance of the context in which the research is done. For example, comparisons of the efficacy of religious and secular providers that do not contract with government may yield valuable insights; but such comparisons do not tell us whether Charitable Choice works, because contracting with government may change organizational behavior and affect outcomes. Comparisons of faith-based and secular government contractors providing job training and placement tell us very little about the comparative performance of faith-based and secular organizations providing substance abuse services or day care. Any conclusions drawn must reflect such realities and include those caveats.

What We Learned—and What We Did Not Learn

The chapters that follow detail the results of the discrete elements of our research project and the respective methodologies employed. A general introduction to those specifics, however, is necessary if both the contributions and limitations of the research are to be adequately appreciated. All analysis begins with initial framing of the inquiry, and the way in which a question is framed will very often dictate the conclusion that is reached. Before presuming to test legislative assumptions, or critiquing them as ideologically based, we should make our own research assumptions and hypotheses explicit.

When we began the project, in 1999, Charitable Choice meant Section 104 of PRWORA. Few people other than "policy wonks" had ever heard of it, and it certainly was not the high-profile issue in the American culture wars that it subsequently became. Our collective interest in the legislation grew out of our respective research agendas. One such agenda had focused upon the effects of contracting-out—often referred to as privatization—by government agencies. That prior body of research had focused on concerns about the legal and constitutional accountability of government agencies when these agencies deliver services through third-party providers (the "state action" problem described more fully in chapter 7). Another researcher had studied organizational behavior and viability in the nonprofit sector; still another came to the project with an interest in the interaction of federalism and social welfare programs.

The project's research questions were informed by those prior interests, rather than the more ideological and political questions that subsequently emerged. As a result, we did not frame our research as an either/or, should-we or should-we-not inquiry; instead, we asked a series of "how" questions: How does national policy translate to state and local practice? How can government managers ensure fair (and constitutionally appropriate) bid practices? How do the tools used by those same managers to ensure accountability change when services are delivered through religious surrogates or contractors? How can we devise measures to help government choose the best providers from among the third-party intermediaries available? How can the managers of faith-based nonprofits evaluate the risks and rewards of a contract relationship? How can they ensure that they have the tools to meet the management challenges that inevitably accompany such a relationship?

These are large questions, and no single study, including this one, will provide definitive answers to them. But they provided the context within which more specific questions could be addressed: What are the states actually doing? What are the elements of legally and constitutionally appropriate processes? What does effective service delivery look like, and what are the organizational characteristics of effective service providers? Among providers found to be effective, is the dimension of faith a significant variable? What direction can we offer public managers who must choose among competing providers?

Number of New Providers

Some of our findings seem straightforward. Relatively few new religious providers have responded to the invitation of Charitable Choice, despite the widespread publicity and encouragement that accompanied President Bush's Faith-Based Initiative, the establishment of Faith-Based and Community offices in federal agencies, and the commitment of significant resources to capacity-building intermediaries. A number of reasons have been offered to explain the paucity of new faith-based contractors: the fact that most social services are contracted at the state level, and states have experienced fiscal pressures requiring retrenchment, rather than growth, in social programs, and as a result have seen increased competition for fewer state dollars (Gais and Burke 2004; De Vita and Palmer 2004); the skepticism of much of the clergy (DeVita and Palmer 2004); lack of capacity and the complexities of working with government (DeVita and Palmer 2004), among others. As we hypothesized, and as chapter 3 describes in more detail, different states have responded differently to the legislation and the president's executive orders. Some of those differences can be attributed to state-level political and religious cultures, some grow out of different state histories (particularly with respect to the administration of social welfare programs), and others are the effect of differently constituted governing institutions.

Relative Effectiveness

Our evidence did not support the hypothesis that faith-based contracting organizations were more effective than secular ones; we were surprised to find that, in our sample, clients of FBOs fared somewhat more poorly than did their secular counterparts. However, our research was limited to job training and placement agencies. Studies of contractors delivering other social services, or studies of job placement services in other states, may yield different results, as might comparisons of faith-based and secular providers that do not contract with government. Much more research is needed, not only into the identification of organizational characteristics most likely to correlate with successful results but also on the characteristics of organizations most likely to contract successfully with government agencies and those most likely to be changed by that experience, whether for good or ill.

Public Management Challenges

Perhaps the most worrisome of our findings were those that dealt with issues of public management and accountability. When government delivers a service, it retains ultimate responsibility for that service, whether it is being provided by its own employees or by a third party. At a minimum, it is responsible for ensuring that public funds are spent for the intended purpose, and that the services purchased are properly designed and delivered—that the taxpayers are getting what they are paying for. When government delivers services to highly vulnerable populations, it must be especially vigilant to ensure that the rights of recipients are respected and that the services provided are appropriate and effective. The management challenges presented by outsourcing have been widely documented in the public administration literature, and these challenges apply whether the provider is faith based or secular. When the applicable legal and regulatory constraints include those required under the First Amendment, however, government agencies assume added responsibilities for compliance.

Our research suggests that public managers simply do not have adequate resources to ensure more than the most minimal accountability; they do not have the tools, the time, the management depth, or the funding to monitor for compliance with any but the most basic fiscal and programmatic requirements. Nor do they have sufficient resources to evaluate programs and providers, so that they can learn from the successes and failures, and make future contract awards on the basis of indicators that have previously demonstrated an association with provider competence. As a result, it is not just that we do not know much about the comparative effectiveness of faith-based and secular contractors; we know far less than we need to about the effectiveness of most contractors. Accountability for constitutional compliance suffers not only from these systemic accountability problems but also from widespread constitutional illiteracy exacerbated by the uncertainty of some aspects of current law. Several of the legal issues raised by Charitable Choice and discussed in chapter 7 will not be resolved until cases being litigated in the lower courts eventually find their way onto the Supreme Court's docket. Until the Court acts, these ambiguities will remain.

The good news is that many capable scholars of public management and nonprofit and voluntary organizations have turned their attention to these issues. Important empirical work is being done by Stephen Monsma, Stephen Rathgeb Smith, Robert Wineburg, Arthur Farnsley, and many, many others. Robert Tuttle and Ira Lupu have produced an impressive body of legal analysis. Little by little, their research, and that of many others, will help policymakers and public managers ask the right questions and make informed choices among policy options.

Notes

1. A fuller description of that research is contained in Monsma's book *When Sacred and Secular Mix: Religious Nonprofit Organizations and Public Money* (1996).

2. His most recent book on the subject is *Rising Expectations: Urban Congregations, Welfare Reform and Civic Life* (2003).

3. In "Should We Have Faith in Faith-Based Social Services?" Gibelman and Gelman (2002) searched press reports of instances of FBO wrongdoing during the period 1995–2001. They concluded that religious organizations were just as likely to engage in financial and sexual misconduct as other organizations, and that religion was frequently employed as a "ruse" or shield enabling such behavior. They note that "these cases point to a problem with public funding of self-governing groups when the funded group fails to institute appropriate accountability mechanisms and public oversight is lacking" (p. 56), and they express concern over the efforts of the Bush Faith-Based Initiative that are intended to decrease regulation and oversight.

4. In August 2001, the White House issued "Unlevel Playing Field: Barriers to Participation by Faith-Based and Community Organizations in Federal Social Service Programs." The specifics of that report are addressed more fully in chapter 7, but its allegations of "widespread bias" against religious providers displayed a significantly flawed understanding of the contracting processes involved, the nature of "bias," and the requirements of the First Amendment. The report found that a distressingly small percentage of funding had gone to FBOs; however, subsequent analysis has found that assertion to be factually inaccurate, no matter what the criteria used by the White House to categorize organizations. The administration did not indicate the basis upon which it defined providers as "faith based" or secular; furthermore, the claimed percentages did not include state-level regranting decisions, and most social

service funds are spent at the state level. It is also likely that the administration has not applied consistent criteria to the categorization of providers; early in 2005, when the White House issued press releases purporting to show that its Faith-Based Initiative had generated a substantial increase in the percentage of funds going to FBOs, a number of organizations identified in those later releases as "faith based" specifically disputed their placement in that category. In the absence of clear and consistent definitions, such pronouncements cannot be considered to have empirical value.

PART II
What We Have Learned

Chapter 3

The Implementation of
Charitable Choice in the States

---

*T*HE DIVISION OF POWER BETWEEN FED-
ERAL AND STATE LEVELS OF GOVERNMENT
in the United States has historically been contested and ill defined.
The one constant has been the steady growth of central government authority, the reasons for which are multiple: As indicated in
chapter 1, the Fourteenth Amendment required states to protect
the basic civil liberties of their residents, thus nationalizing most
of the Bill of Rights; federal measures like Prohibition were enacted
to deal with moral evils perceived to be extensive (or at any rate,
not localized); the states lacked resources sufficient to deal with
the challenges of the Depression; and continuing advances in science and technology—particularly communication and transportation—increasingly necessitated uniform federal standards for
interstate commerce, environmental protection, food safety, and
numerous other aspects of our interrelated activities.

For sixty years following the New Deal, Congress and the Supreme Court accepted the necessity of federal responses to such
challenges, and they were "energetic proponents of centralization"
(Conlan and de Chantal 2001). More recently, the Supreme Court
under Chief Justice William Rehnquist signaled its concern that
the central government may have acquired too much power, and
it decided a series of cases intended to limit the reach of Congress
and uphold the prerogatives of the states. The Court's change of
direction has been sufficiently dramatic that an article in *Governing* magazine (appropriately titled "Governor Rehnquist") asserted
that the Court had ushered in "the most fundamental debate over
federalism since the 1930's" (Kettl 1999).

Nevertheless—whatever the merits or consequences of the Supreme Court's newly protective stance toward states' rights, and however heartfelt the promises of numerous political candidates to return power to the local level—centralization of power has continued virtually unabated. If there are situations in which Congress cannot simply require states to follow federal rules, other powerful enforcement mechanisms are available and enthusiastically employed; as one scholar has noted, longstanding federal court doctrine permits conditional offers of funds to circumvent most if not all of the restrictions imposed by the U.S. Constitution on the government's authority to regulate the behavior of citizens or the states directly (Jensen and Kennedy 2005). The federal government transfers more than $300 billion to the states each year, and those funds come with numerous restrictions: Highway trust fund money is used to exact laws reducing speed limits; education funds require adherence to the No Child Left Behind Act and a host of other federal requirements; and social welfare payments are conditioned upon compliance with volumes of federal regulations. In many cases, state "autonomy" has been reduced to the right of the state to reject federal dollars.

Yet despite this seemingly inexorable centralization of legal authority, states remain strikingly distinctive in their responses to, and application of, federal mandates. Some of the differences are simply the inevitable consequences of any chain of command; much like the childhood game of "telephone," the message that is first communicated often becomes garbled or changed by the time it reaches the final repetition. Other differences grow out of systemic variations in governing institutions—variations rooted in the histories and political cultures of the individual states. The choice of states for this research project began with our hypothesis that states with different political cultures and religious landscapes would respond to Charitable Choice directives differently, and that those differences might yield useful insights into the process through which policy prescriptions are translated into actual government programs.

Questions Asked: Differences among States

As a threshold matter, we were interested in gauging the response of faith-based organizations (FBOs) that had not previously participated in governmental contracting regimes to the invitation of Charitable Choice. But we also hypothesized that a federalist system would be characterized by differences in state implementation approaches, and that those differences would reflect differences in the political cultures and religious landscapes of the various states. Because one of the frequently cited virtues of a federalist system is the freedom such systems afford individual states to act as "laboratories of democracy"—to take different, and it is hoped innovative, approaches to the national agenda—we hoped to (1) test that hypothesis; (2) describe the nature of and probable reasons for such differences as emerged; and (3) provide sufficient data on state responses to allow researchers and managers to draw conclusions about effective public management and policy implementation.

To analyze Charitable Choice implementation in each of the different states, we asked a series of common questions: What was the contracting "culture" of the state prior to Charitable Choice? What was the previous level of participation by faith-based contractors? How did state program managers interpret Charitable Choice legislation, and how did they implement those interpretations? What efforts, if any, have they made to encourage additional participation by faith-based providers? What effect, if any, has there been on the rate of participation by religious contractors? How did each state's unique history and culture affect its approach to implementation?

Methodology

Resource limitations meant that we could not take a national approach, and that the states chosen to study would necessarily be less than fully representative of the broad federal landscape. We needed to determine the criteria for making those choices.

SELECTING REPRESENTATIVE STATES

The first task was to choose states for in-depth study. We wanted states that would be as broadly representative of national differences as possible, recognizing that three states would not give us a full picture of these differences. Accordingly, we looked for states representing diverse, but it was hoped representative, political cultures.

Political Culture

The term "political culture" can mean many things. Given the nature of our inquiry and the data available, the most useful theoretical and descriptive analysis of political culture was constructed by Daniel Elazar in *The American Mosaic: The Impact of Space, Time and Culture on American Politics* (Elazar 1994). Reminding readers that political culture is by its nature fluid and evolving—a product of particular times, places, and cultures—Elazar traced the movements of native and immigrant populations over the country's geography and history. He described how three major subcultures had overlapped and joined, and how the synthesis of those distinctive subcultures had produced America's national political culture. Overlap and synthesis are not, needless to say, homogenization, and substantial regional distinctions remain. In *The American Mosaic*, Elazar demonstrated that each of the three distinct subcultures he identified—individualistic, moralistic, and traditionalistic—has remained tied to specific geographic regions of the country. (It should be noted that, as he uses them, these descriptive terms do not translate into the conservative–moderate–liberal framework used in popular media, although there are some parallels.)

An "individualistic" political culture, in Elazar's formulation, sees the polis as a type of marketplace. Individualistic cultures emphasize the centrality of private concerns, look askance at most government interventions, and see political activity in quite "transactional" terms. Political success is achieved by mutual accommodation; the art of politics consists in giving the "buying public" what it wants. Party regularity is valued, and the politics of the subculture are characterized by a "quid pro quo" mentality, in which patronage is considered a natural attribute of political life.

"Moralistic" political cultures, conversely, see political activity as the way communities conduct their search for the good society. Politics is considered noble, a "calling" rather than a job, and holding political office is viewed as public service, not as simply another way to make a living. Government is considered a "positive instrument" through which communitarian goals can be met, and party affiliation and regularity are less important than in individualistic states.

A "traditionalistic" political culture, in Elazar's formulation, is "rooted in an ambivalent attitude toward the marketplace coupled with a paternalistic and elitist conception of the commonwealth"

(Elazar 1994, 235). It functions to confine power to a relatively small group of people, and one's place in the power structure is determined through family and other ties to the elite. In traditionalistic cultures, political systems tend to be dominated by a single party, and political leaders play a "conservative and custodial" role. (Elazar notes that traditionalistic political culture, which was largely an outgrowth of the southern agrarian plantation system, has diminished and can be expected to continue to diminish.)

Because of the ways in which settlement and migration of religious and ethnic groups have occurred throughout American history, different political cultures are dominant in different areas of the country. *The American Mosaic* includes a "political culture" map of the United States, distinguishing areas of the country on the basis of the subcultures identified. On that map, Massachusetts is shown as primarily moralistic, with a lesser current of individualistic culture. Indiana is virtually all individualistic. In North Carolina, the predominant culture shown is traditionalistic, although moralistic culture provides a lesser influence. The three states chosen for our study each reflected one of the three political subcultures, and these differences might be expected to influence how those states approached the implementation of federal programs.

Religion
In addition to the role played by religious worldviews in shaping political culture generally, populations of the states chosen for the study display contemporary religious differences that might be expected to affect the implementation of a policy with religious dimensions more directly. There is a strong Catholic influence in Massachusetts. In North Carolina, Baptists are the dominant religious tradition. Indiana is more religiously diverse than the other two states and no one religious influence predominates, although the state is overwhelmingly Protestant. To the extent that dominant religious perspectives shape local institutions and attitudes, and contribute to the differences in political cultures, we expected those religious differences to also contribute to different approaches to implementing Charitable Choice. On a more practical level, the preponderance of a particular religious community was likely to be reflected in the composition of the state's nonprofit sector, and thus in the pool of potential faith-based contractors.

Demographics

Finally, the states we chose were characterized by different demographic characteristics (income, education, and especially race), factors that could be expected to contribute to other differences in state responses. The uneasy relationship between welfare policy and race has been widely noted; our sample included three states with very different histories of race relations and minority demographics. Though the relationships between those historical realities and contemporary political culture are not amenable to quantification, a sample that represented the disparities should further support the generalizable nature of our findings.

Findings: The States before and after PRWORA

Any effort to analyze a state's implementation of a new policy must occur in the context of the state's particular policy history. Thus, our first efforts were directed toward historical differences and similarities in states' social welfare programs and approaches.

MASSACHUSETTS: LEADING IN WELFARE REFORM AND PRIVATIZATION

The history of welfare in the Commonwealth of Massachusetts is a history of "firsts." In 1797, Massachusetts enacted the new nation's first law designating insane people as a special group of dependents; in 1836, it enacted the first restrictive child labor law; and in 1850, it established the first school for "idiotic and feeble-minded" youth. The YMCA was organized in Boston, and the first State Board of Charities (charged with oversight and administration of state charitable and penal institutions) was established in the Commonwealth. The state also established the first permanent state board of health and vital statistics, and it was the first state to send "agents" to supervise placements of children in foster homes. The first college course on social reform was taught at Harvard University in 1885, and the Federation of Jewish Charities was established ten years later in Boston. During the 1950s, Brookline, Massachusetts, was the site of the first urban transitional residence, and in 1972, the state's Youth Services Department replaced juvenile reformatories with community-based work and education programs. Massachusetts hospitals and universities claim author-ship of a number of innovations in medical and psychiatric social work (Alexander 2000).

Despite the liberal and moralistic political culture reflected in its history, however, Massachusetts had made a commitment to more restrictive standards and other welfare reforms well before the pas-sage of the Personal Responsibility and Work Opportunity Rec-onciliation Act of 1996 (PRWORA). In February 1995, the Mas-sachusetts legislature had passed legislation that was hailed widely as "one of the most sweeping welfare reform bills in the nation" (Jensen 2003, 9). Relying upon waivers from the U.S. Department of Health and Human Services, the legislation (chapter 5 of the Acts of 1995) transformed the sixty-year-old federal/state entitle-ment program Aid to Families with Dependent Children, renam-ing it "Transitional Aid to Families with Dependent Children." The act's benefit cuts, work requirements, strict time limits, family cap, requirements for pregnant and parenting teens, and sanctions an-ticipated many of PRWORA's key features. The then-governor (Re-publican William Weld), members of his administration, and leg-islators had spent several years working toward a consensus on the shape of welfare reform, and they were determined to transform a system that fostered dependency into one that promoted self-suf-ficiency (Jensen 2003; Buis 1998). By 1996, the new policies were firmly in place.

Massachusetts was also committed to privatization in the form of contracting out well before Section 104 of PRWORA was en-acted. Far from being a recent phenomenon, contracting in Mas-sachusetts can be traced to the late 1960s, when the state took over responsibility for the administration of public assistance from lo-cal welfare offices. Since that time, under Democratic and Repub-lican governors alike, Massachusetts has steadily increased its re-liance upon nongovernmental entities to deliver publicly funded programs and services. According to former governor Michael Dukakis, the primary incentive for privatization was not the po-tential for cost savings; rather, contracting out for human service programs was a response to a growing conviction that "large insti-tutions had failed, that there was a need to get out from under civil service requirements in order to allow some program experimen-tation, and that putting people in community settings might work better." Massachusetts hoped that the purchase of services would protect "the promise of community based care" (Jensen 2003, 10).

Between 1971 and 1988, the cost of the Commonwealth's purchase of service agreements with nonprofit agencies rose from $25 million to $850 million (Smith and Lipsky 1993). And in the early 1990s, the Weld administration made further expansion of privatization a high priority. Although there was serious opposition to many of the Weld initiatives from the Democratic-controlled legislature, Massachusetts legislators authorized the administration's privatizing proposals in 1993 (Wallin 1997; Jensen 2003). In 1996, procurement reform legislation was passed to make it easier for a broader range of organizations and firms to access information on state contracting opportunities and to simplify the competitive bidding process. The state's processes were thus already consistent with most of the dictates of PRWORA.

In addition, as Jensen has emphasized, the Commonwealth's contracting for social services had historically been characterized by the presence of religious organizations. FBOs routinely bid on, and received, social service contracts. This undoubtedly reflected the politically and theologically liberal disposition of the Massachusetts faith community, where congregations and religious organizations have historically engaged with their communities (Chaves 1999). Massachusetts shelters, youth programs, and employment and training programs for welfare recipients have long been run by such organizations as Catholic Charities, the Jewish Vocational Service, and the Salvation Army. As of May 2000, the Department of Transitional Assistance had contracts with thirty different FBOs (Jensen 2003); Catholic Charities, the largest provider of contracted social services in the state, has been a force in shaping welfare policy in Boston since the early nineteenth century (Brown and McKeown 1997; Jensen 2003), and Catholic beliefs about the nature of poverty and the requirements of social justice are clearly reflected in many of those policies.

Massachusetts is the most administratively centralized of the three states in our study. Unlike most states, it has no functional county government. Larger cities and towns play a part in providing social welfare services, but the authority for social service contracting and the responsibility for administering state and federal public assistance programs lie with the state. Even ostensibly local welfare offices are run by the Commonwealth; the Department of Transitional Assistance maintains thirty-three regional offices, to which Massachusetts residents in need of aid must go to apply for federal or state benefits (Jensen 2003).

Indiana: Work First and Personal Responsibility

Indiana's welfare history was quite different, although, like Massachusetts, the state had adopted a number of reforms prior to passage of PRWORA in 1996. Indiana had been among the first states to emphasize "work first" and "personal responsibility" approaches as a strategy for increasing employment and encouraging economic self-sufficiency. The state had imposed strict sanctions for failure to comply with program requirements, and it had also made those requirements more stringent, by imposing a twenty-hour-per-week job search rule, by employing a "Personal Responsibility Agreement" (a contract detailing the recipient's responsibilities under program regulations), and by setting time limits (twenty-four months) on eligibility for cash assistance. The state established a family cap, denying additional benefits to families that had more children while they were on welfare; and it imposed sanctions on clients who did not meet program requirements and/or parental responsibilities (Thelin 2003).

These relatively draconian reform efforts were an outgrowth of Indiana's historic approach to social welfare, an approach that reflected its political culture as well as generally mirroring the policies of the nation as a whole. The correspondence with national norms should not be a surprise; the publication of *Middletown* by Robert and Helen Lynd in 1929 put Muncie, Indiana, on the map as the "typical" American community, and other studies have used Indianapolis as a similar example of the quintessential American city. Furthermore, since the 1930s, welfare policies in all the states largely have been responsive to federal mandates, leading to a certain amount of standardization. However, some of the elements that characterized the state's welfare system prior to the reforms of the early 1990s can best be understood in the context of the state's particular legal and political culture and history.

Although America as a whole is religiously very diverse (albeit overwhelmingly Christian), many if not most regions of the country have been shaped by a majority religious culture. Indiana, as noted above, is more religiously diverse; virtually none of its political subdivisions has a dominant religious culture, and no one theological perspective on issues of poverty has predominated. Indiana's system has thus remained firmly rooted in the language of the Northwest Ordinance, itself an outgrowth of early English poor law distinctions between the "deserving" and "undeserving" poor. Poor relief in the state was originally part of the criminal justice system, a circumstance that continued until 1936. (The very first institutions established in Indiana were county jails and county poor asylums; the jails consisted of two apartments, one for debtors and another for lawbreakers; Kennedy 2006).

Even after 1936, poor relief was largely left up to local township governments, whose responses varied considerably. As a consequence, at the beginning of the Depression, Indiana's only resources for meeting the needs of the unemployed were the township trustees and private philanthropy. In its Acts of 1933, the Indiana legislature created a Governor's Commission on Unemployment Relief; the commission would eventually assume responsibility for determining which counties were entitled to federal aid and for ensuring compliance with the federal rules that came with the money. That same year, as part of a reorganization of Indiana government, the Board of State Charities became part of the executive branch, under then-governor Paul McNutt, and was renamed the State Department of Public Welfare (Kennedy 2006).

With passage of the Welfare Act of 1936, Indiana vested authority for welfare at the state level, but it made county governments responsible for administration—an allocation of duties that persists today, along with the (increasingly criticized and dysfunctional) Township Trustee system. (This trustee system has survived primarily because patronage remains the essential element of Indiana's political system [Kennedy 2006] and the trustees are one of the last remaining sources of that patronage. The importance of patronage in the state tends to confirm Elazar's categorization of Indiana's political culture as individualistic.)

From 1936 until the welfare reform efforts of the 1990s, the State Welfare Department administered state and federal legislative initiatives and responded to the shifting priorities they represented. State participation in Medicaid, which Congress enacted in 1965, required especially significant financial and administrative resources. (Indiana, characteristically, was among the last states to participate in the program.) Periodically, the department reorganized, regrouped, and added or subtracted program responsibilities. Probably the most significant reorganization occurred in 1991, during the Evan Bayh administration, when programs that had been scattered throughout state government were consolidated with the Welfare Department into a massive new agency, named the Family and Social Services Administration, an agency which the current Indiana governor, Mitch Daniels, has begun to dismantle once again. Governor Bayh also moved aggressively to obtain federal waivers allowing him to institute a number of pre-PRWORA reforms.

Benefits for a typical Temporary Assistance to Needy Families (TANF) recipient in Indiana when we began our study included a maximum monthly cash benefit of $288 for a family of three, food stamps, health insurance, and child care. To receive this assistance, applicants were required to sign "Personal Responsibility" contracts, in which they agreed to participate in work activities, and to adhere to child school attendance requirements, immunization and preventive health requirements, drug and alcohol restrictions, teen-parent living arrangements, and cooperation in the development of an individual self-sufficiency plan. Failure to comply with any of the provisions of the Personal Responsibility contract could result in the imposition of sanctions and the loss of benefits (Thelin 2003).

A key element of the Bayh reform philosophy—an element that foreshadowed many elements of PRWORA—was to shift the focus of welfare away from an education and job training model to a vigorous work-first approach and an emphasis upon placing clients in jobs suitable to their existing education and skills. The state increased resources for job search and job readiness activities and required all clients to be formally assessed for job readiness when they first applied for assistance. Those found to be job ready were to be placed in programs with specific policies aimed at strengthening work incentives. The only persons exempt from participating in work activities were individuals caring for children under the age of one year, disabled persons, persons suffering from temporary illness or incapacitation, those caring for a disabled household member, those over the age of sixty years, domestic violence victims, and pregnant women (Thelin 2003).

North Carolina: Decentralized Services

In 1868, when North Carolina established a Board of Public Charities, lawmakers cited language from the state's Constitution that
"beneficent provisions for the poor, the unfortunate, and orphaned
are one of the first duties of a civilized and Christian state." In 1917,
the General Assembly required each county in the state to employ
at least one part-time welfare worker, and it established a program
of social services to be carried out on a county basis under state
supervision—a decision that was not met with uniformly enthusiastic responses. (When the commissioners of one county voted
to hire a full-time superintendent of public welfare, the minutes
reflected that the decision had been made to do so "since the Legislature had ordered it.")

In 1937, North Carolina adopted legislation required under the
Social Security Act to make the state eligible for federal assistance,
and it began administering the program through county agencies
in each of its 100 counties. Subsequent activity was also responsive
to federal program requirements: The Housing Act of 1937 created
local public housing authorities and provided federal funding to
build locally owned, nonsubsidized public housing; in 1946, the
National School Lunch Act authorized federally subsidized school
hot lunches; and in 1964, the Food Stamp Act established national
nutrition programs for low-income households. Other federal
programs followed, with North Carolina continuing to implement
them through county governments, in a highly decentralized management structure.

If the state demonstrated a lack of enthusiasm for some of the
federally mandated programs it implemented, it displayed a troubling alacrity about other welfare "interventions." In 2003, the
Winston-Salem Journal ran a series devoted to the excesses of the
state's eugenics program, established by the General Assembly in
1929. That legislation authorized the sterilization of any patient or
inmate of any penal or charitable public institution, upon application by the individual's next of kin or guardian. The program was
not discontinued until 1977, and between 1929 and 1977, nearly
8,000 people were sterilized for their own or "the public good." Toward the end of the program, those sterilized were "mostly poor
and black." Ninety-nine percent were female, and a disproportion-

ate number were homosexual. According to the report, "Though more than 30 states had eugenic sterilization programs, North Carolina's record of dramatically expanding the program after 1945 and targeting blacks in the general population was different from most" (Railey and Begos 2003).

At the state level, North Carolina's social welfare services are currently centralized in its Department of Health and Human Services (DHHS), a state agency with 19,000 employees, although actual contracting decisions and administrative responsibilities remain vested at the county level, making North Carolina's actual management structure the most decentralized of the three states in the study. Beginning in the early 1970s, the state began a process that would eventually result in the consolidation of the more than 300 agencies then providing social services. In 1971, the legislature passed the "Executive Organization Act of 1971," creating a Department of Human Resources; in 1973, it repealed that act, replacing it with the "Executive Organization Act of 1973." The 1973 version required the transfer of a wide variety of divisions or agencies to "more appropriate" departments. In addition to this shuffling of existing agencies, the Legislature added several new ones: the Office of Rural Health (1974), the Division of Aging (1977), the Division of Medical Assistance (1978), the Division of Services for the Deaf and Hard of Hearing (1989), and the Division of Public Health (1989). In 1997, most related services were transferred into the Division of Public Health, which was renamed DHHS. North Carolina has remained to a significant extent a rural state, and its service history reflects both its rural character and its predominantly Baptist religious landscape. Because contracting decisions are made primarily at the county level, statewide data about the character of contractors are difficult to obtain (and what exists is considered to be of dubious reliability); however, anecdotal reports and case studies suggest that a significant number of those contractors have been religious or religiously affiliated (Queen 2003). Certainly, the informal collaborative networks of public and nonprofit organizations that have long characterized social service delivery in the state have included many FBOs (Wineburg 2001).

North Carolina's response to welfare reform was a program called Work First. Work First began in 1995, and it operated under waivers from the federal government until the passage of PRWORA in 1996. As with similar efforts in the other states, Work First was designed to move families off welfare and toward sustained self-sufficiency. Although Work First is a statewide plan, it includes adaptations to North Carolina's decentralized and "devolved" administrative structure; for one example, counties are allowed to "opt-out" and implement their own local plans. In July 2002, 18 of North Carolina's 100 counties exercised that option and operated as "electing" counties, functioning with their own block grant plans, including responsibility for distributing cash assistance (Queen 2003).

Responsibility for outsourcing the delivery of welfare services in North Carolina varies depending on the type of services. Most TANF programs are state supervised but county controlled. The state releases to the counties a set portion of the monies North Carolina receives as part of its federal block grant, and the counties then contract with providers of its choice. DHHS and its Division of Social Services (the unit directly responsible for TANF programs) have little direct knowledge of the providers with whom the various counties contract, or the programmatic approaches those providers employ. State oversight is provided by a single annual audit, and not every program is audited each year. Field representatives are responsible for monitoring specific programs, but there are only eight field representatives for Work First, whose responsibilities include overseeing issues related to program eligibility, children's services, adult services, and food stamps. Unlike Indiana, North Carolina has not moved to performance-based contracting; providers are paid a fixed price for services delivered, and there are no performance incentives or payments linked to specific goals achieved by the individuals served (Queen 2003).

The decentralized nature of the system in North Carolina—sometimes described as "second-order devolution"—means that decision making is made by local officials who, according to much current public administration theory, are closer to the problems involved and are better able to choose among the providers competing to serve them. This "belief in the salutary effects of market competition and local decision making on public services" was tested in North Carolina in a 1996 analysis of the state's contracting for substance abuse services. The researchers concluded that "government purchasing officials—contrary to the competitive market model—rely heavily on trust and long-standing relationships with private service agencies to guide contracting decisions," and that both evaluation and innovation are impeded under the system. The authors also found a lack of concern about equity of access to services, and a weakening of advocacy efforts and accountability measures (Smith and Smyth 1996, 277–78).

Findings: The States' Responses to Charitable Choice

These were the state histories leading up to Charitable Choice and the new efforts to involve faith-based groups more fully in the provision of social services. As these histories would suggest, implementation approaches differed.

Massachusetts: Compliance via a Level Playing Field

As we had anticipated, the responses of the three states to Charitable Choice varied considerably. Massachusetts was essentially unmoved by the enactment of Section 104 (Jensen 2003). In the years following its passage, the Commonwealth did little to alter the processes through which nonprofit and religious organizations compete for contracts. Massachusetts's lack of response to Section 104 has been attributed to a number of factors, not the least of which is the ambiguity of the statutory language itself. State officials who studied the statute after its passage concluded that it required "a level playing field," but that it lacked any other substantive, affirmative commands that the Commonwealth was required to obey. The Attorney General's Office analyzed Section 104 and found no discrepancies between its terms and existing Massachusetts law and procedure. So, too, did the legal staff of the Department of Transitional Assistance, the state welfare agency, which concluded that Massachusetts was already in full compliance with its requirements. State officials in Massachusetts interpret Section 104 to guarantee religious organizations the right to compete for social service contracts, or a right to equal access in procurement processes, on the same grounds as any other provider. In their view, Massachusetts was committed to a level playing field well before Section 104 was enacted. General statutes demanding fairness in procurement have long governed the Commonwealth's extensive purchase of service system. Moreover, in 1996, state lawmakers had reformed the procurement system to make it easier for a broader range of organizations and firms to find out about contracting opportunities and to engage successfully in competitive bidding processes. Bid solicitations are not targeted, but are open to all organizations, including religious ones (Jensen 2003).

Officials point to Massachusetts's actual performance in procurement as an additional justification for the state's belief that no affirmative steps to comply with Section 104 were required. Religious organizations historically have played significant roles as social service contractors in the Commonwealth. Virtually all the agencies located within the Executive Office of Health and Human Services have "purchase of service contracts" with religiously affiliated organizations, and that is especially true of public assistance programs. Having FBOs bid on social service contracts, and having contracts awarded to them, has long been "business as usual" in Massachusetts. Because there is no record of religious organizations being disadvantaged or systematically discriminated against in procurement processes, there is no sense that the state is obliged to do anything affirmative (Jensen 2003). The system was not broken, and therefore it did not require fixing.

When questioned, Massachusetts officials noted that Section 104 neither defines religious organizations nor requires that states partner with any particular type of religious organization. This lack of specificity means that the states remain free to rely upon their own interpretations of the statutory language. If a state takes a broad view of what constitutes a religious organization, as Massachusetts does, then the significant amounts of TANF funds already going to established, nonprofit, religiously affiliated charities like Catholic Charities, Lutheran Social Services, and the Salvation Army for the purpose of administering public social service programs may continue to flow. Whether or not these nonprofits are inherently different from the kind of small, street-level, faith-involving, holistic groups many charitable choice advocates hoped to involve in social service contracting, they should nonetheless "count" as religious organizations under Section 104. Massachusetts officials also noted that Section 104 does not directly command the states to alter the nature or content of existing public programs so as to include faith-related elements. Instead, the statute requires states to collaborate with religious organizations on the same basis as they collaborate with other nonprofit organizations, and it protects religious contractors against demands to alter or diminish their religious character. Absent a congressional mandate for programmatic change, Massachusetts officials felt justified in considering themselves compliant (Jensen 2003). Massachusetts approached Charitable Choice through the lens of its moralistic political culture and hierarchical governing structures. The state's policymakers and administrators simply added an awareness of provider religious affiliation to its existing system.

INDIANA: PRAGMATIC CAPACITY BUILDING

In Indiana, partnerships between the public welfare sector and private voluntary organizations (many of which have been religiously affiliated) are also not new. As with systems in most other parts of the country, formal and informal cooperation between the two sectors has been common, if less pronounced than in Massachusetts or North Carolina. Nevertheless, in contrast to Massachusetts, Indiana's response to Charitable Choice was bipartisan and enthusiastic. In 1997, in the wake of PRWORA, Indianapolis' then-mayor, Stephen Goldsmith, a Republican, generated national media attention with a program called the Front Porch Alliance, billed as a mechanism through which FBOs could partner with city government to improve inner city conditions. In 1998, the administration of Governor Frank O'Bannon, a Democrat, followed suit and began to explore the possibility of expanding the faith community's involvement in service delivery. Indiana officials made clear that they hoped to capitalize on the benefits being widely claimed for such partnerships, by leveraging FBOs local ties in communities, their proximity to potential clients, and their assumed ability to generate a greater level of trust (Thelin 2003). Most of the people who remained on the welfare rolls in Indiana in 2000 were facing a laundry list of barriers to self-sufficiency: lack of high school diploma or general equivalency diploma, low or nonexistent skills, child care problems, children's health problems, lack of transportation to job sites, depression and other mental illness, disability or other health problems, substance abuse, domestic violence, and other family health problems. If faith communities could fill a void by offering holistic services to these "hardest-to-serve" populations, the state was eager to work with them (Thelin 2003).

In 1999, Indiana's Family and Social Services Administration issued a request for proposals for a contractor to administer a technical assistance program, named FaithWorks, aimed at recruiting and educating FBOs. Crowe Chizek, a private consulting firm, was the successful bidder for a two-year, $500,000 contract that was subsequently extended for an additional year. The FaithWorks initiative was designed to reach out to FBOs by providing technical assistance and capacity building, thus equipping them to bid for available state funds. The long-term objective was the establishment of networks that would allow the faith community to sustain an effective presence in the area of social service delivery, especially delivery of job training and placement services to PRWORA recipients (Thelin 2003).

Six informal meetings were held around the state in February 2000 to gather information from and about the state's faith community and to gauge its interest in applying for government funding. More than 9,000 FBOs across the state received invitations to attend the public forums, and approximately 1,000 attended one or more of the sessions, which were held throughout the state. FaithWorks subsequently conducted technical assistance workshops around the state for those organizations expressing an interest in applying for state funding as well as for existing contractors. The workshops focused on explanations of Charitable Choice legislation, state procurement procedures, the contracting process, and effective proposal development. Four hundred religious organizations received technical assistance through FaithWorks in 2000 (Thelin 2003). In 2002, the state also designated 75 employees as "community service liaisons" at local county offices. Liaisons are to serve as points of contact for the faith community and as information resources for other Department of Family and Children staff and local providers. The election of Governor Mitch Daniels (previously the George W. Bush administration's director of management and budget) in 2004 intensified the state's commitment to faith-based outreach; the new governor created a state Office for Faith-Based Initiatives as one of his earliest official acts. Indiana's embrace of faith-based initiatives reflects its pragmatic political culture. Privatization and outsourcing are quite consistent with an individualistic, "quid pro quo" political culture, and Indiana policymakers were already fairly enthusiastic proponents of contracting out for services. Charitable Choice offered another opportunity to extend that approach.

North Carolina: Faith Communities Lead the Way

During the mid-1990s, prior to passage of PRWORA, North Carolina governor James Hunt had also been a vigorous proponent of both welfare reform and the greater involvement of FBOs in meeting the needs of the poor. His Governor's Task Force on Community Initiatives on Welfare Reform had focused extensively on the potential of FBOs to help the state address those needs. North Carolina has been—and after PRWORA remains—a state with very significant participation by religious contractors. That participation has not been the result of state-level outreach efforts (which have been comparatively minor) but are largely an outgrowth of its history and structural characteristics: North Carolina's highly decentralized approach to contracting, and its reliance on pilot projects established and managed by the North Carolina Rural Economic Development Center.

The Rural Center had long been a partner of DHHS; it had managed contracts for the agency and had helped amass data required under various federal reporting requirements. It also had worked well with faith communities around the state. For these reasons, the Rural Center was "viewed as an ideal organization" to direct the envisioned pilot project (Queen 2003), and it received a $3.5 million contract with the North Carolina Division of Social Services, to be used by its Communities of Faith Initiative (COFI), an alliance of rural North Carolina churches established in the early 1990s. COFI in turn funded five faith-based projects with Faith Demonstration Awards. Project awards were given to programs that promised to develop and implement strategies to assist families living in poverty (Queen 2003). The first grantees were the Asheville-Buncombe Community Christian Ministry, a welfare-to-work program focused upon three western North Carolina counties; the Christian Women's Job Corps, a group operating one-to-one mentoring programs in several sites around the state; Catholic Social Ministries, for a Working Families Partners Program; the Jobs Partnership, operators of an "innovative technology training program" at twenty-one sites; and the TANF Faith Collaborative, a network of primarily African American churches offering computer-assisted instruction at a number of sites throughout the state. In addition to acting as a regranting agency, COFI was to provide technical assistance to the service providers on a wide range of skills: financial accountability, eligibility assessments, case management, and reporting.

The term of the original contract between the state and the Rural Center ran until June 30, 2001; at the conclusion of that term, COFI spun off from the Rural Center and renamed itself Faith Partnerships, Incorporated. During fiscal year 2001–2, it received $266,250 to continue its work; $100,000 of that amount was applied to the Faith Demonstration Awards, with the balance supporting technical assistance and capacity-building efforts (Queen 2003).

In North Carolina, unlike in Indiana, much of the response to Charitable Choice was initiated not by government agencies but by the state's faith communities, which had been alarmed by the passage of PRWORA and the probable effects of welfare reform on the state's poorest citizens. Two of those responses deserve mention: Jubilee, a project of the North Carolina Council of Churches, responded to the new legislation with "Families First," an effort to assist congregations in forming "faith teams" and to provide a variety of educational and technical assistance. Jubilee also engages in advocacy on behalf of the poor. It was Project Jubilee that created the faith-community coordinator positions that now exist in many North Carolina counties. The role of coordinator "has many variations"; approximately half are employees of their county department of social service, while the rest are employed by local faith-based or community agencies. Some are full time, some not. They all engage in efforts to coordinate educational and programmatic efforts within their counties (Wineburg 2000). The Welfare Reform Liaison Project was a creation of the Reverend Odell Cleveland and the Greensboro Mount Zion Baptist Church. It is a widely praised and emulated welfare-to-work program.

Because programs in North Carolina are so often initiated by faith communities, rather than by government agencies, they tend to deal with a wider range of issues than those addressed by TANF and to focus "on meeting the needs of the poor and impoverished rather than merely providing a contracted service" (Queen 2003, 23). Again, we found the North Carolina experience consistent with its traditionalist political culture. The state's highly decentralized welfare system left implementation of Charitable Choice largely to local power brokers and responded predictably to traditional centers of influence over that state's governance.

Conclusions

Our investigation of program implementation in these three states demonstrated the existence of the differences we had anticipated. The nature of these differences was also consistent with the thesis that political culture and religious landscape operate to influence the approach taken by a given state. In an era of increasing homogenization, local variations clearly retain their power to shape local applications of national policy.

Variation in a Federal System

We chose to conduct in-depth analyses of state implementation efforts to answer rather specific questions about the ways policy implementation is affected by local cultural idiosyncrasies. One clear conclusion that we drew—that political culture matters—is consistent with the work of other scholars looking at this issue. In his study of the effect of political culture on PRWORA implementation generally, Lawrence Mead also referred to the Elazar categories, summarizing them as follows:

> Moralistic politics stresses problem solving, not partisan rivalry. In the individualistic style, goals are less high-minded, but there is also more tolerance for disagreement, and often more willingness to compromise. Both moralistic and individualistic states tend to have well-developed bureaucracies. In the traditionalistic style, social policymaking and administration are less well developed. (Mead 2004, 276)

Mead analyzed state implementation of PRWORA, looking at political performance (whether the state framed its own policies, achieved a measure of consensus, and devoted adequate resources to its reforms) and at administrative performance (the commitment of senior administrators to the proposed changes, coordination of agency efforts, general capacity). Mead found significant differences among the states that correlated with Elazar's political culture categories. Those differences were consistent with the Charitable Choice implementation differences we observed.

Massachusetts approached Charitable Choice pragmatically, with a minimum of partisan rivalry. Elected and appointed officials analyzed the statutory language, determined the criteria to be employed, and concluded that the state was in compliance. In Indiana, there also was little partisanship involved in implementation. The Democratic administration decided to embrace Charitable Choice, but—in a spirit of compromise and pragmatism characteristic of individualistic cultures—limited the state's involvement to job training and placement programs, services unlikely to implicate constitutional issues or passions. Outreach in Indiana was consistently framed in classic individualist terms; as the interim Family and Social Services Administration director, Katie Humphreys, explained during an interview, the state was open to any contractor, secular or religious, that could do the job. In North Carolina, where policymaking "appeared to be casual and personalized" (Mead 2004, 282) and where government has historically had difficulty recruiting capable people, reflecting "the low prestige and low pay of public service in traditionalistic cultures" (Mead 2004, 284), implementation efforts occurred largely outside state and local government agencies, either through pilot projects funded by the state but managed by nonprofit agencies or in response to initiatives of religious organizations themselves.

These differences confirmed the original hypothesis that implementation approaches will vary in a federalist system, and that the variations will be consistent with differences in political culture. On the one hand, if states are to be "laboratories" for policy, their disparate cultures provide assurance that local approaches to national mandates will continue to vary in significant ways, allowing policymakers to draw comparisons and conclusions. On the other hand, they remind us that efforts to prescribe national norms will inevitably confront the limitations on central authority that federalism and state differences represent.

Unanticipated Findings: Few New Faith-Based Contractors

Confirming the influence of political culture was one conclusion, and answered the question we had originally asked. Another conclusion, however, was less expected, and it led us to widen the scope of our inquiry in an effort to see if that particular finding was replicated elsewhere. Charitable Choice may have been prompted by multiple (and occasionally unclear or conflicting) goals, but almost certainly it was intended to increase the numbers of FBOs contracting with federal and state government agencies to provide social services. Thus, the first question that arises from any study of the states is whether, in fact, an increase at the state level occurred, and if not, why not. Though the ambiguity of the statutory definition of "faith based" is distinctly unhelpful in answering that question, it seemed quite clear that, in our states, the hoped-for armies of compassion failed to materialize.

In Massachusetts, where larger and more professionalized religiously affiliated contractors have been a significant part of the contracting pool for decades, the state continues to do business with those providers, but there is little evidence that smaller, more "grassroots" FBOs have entered the system in any numbers (Jensen 2003). In Indiana, despite a genuine (and relatively costly) effort to recruit such grassroots religious organizations, and an initial increase in the contract dollars awarded to such providers, very few new faith-based providers have continued to contract with the state (Thelin 2003). North Carolina actually had one of the highest percentages of religious providers of any state prior to the enactment of PRWORA, and undoubtedly it still does; however, the radically decentralized nature of its contracting regime can lead to erroneous conclusions about the composition of its contracting pool. For example, in 2002, the U.S. General Accounting Office (GAO) reported that North Carolina spent only 2 percent of its TANF funds on contracts with nongovernmental entities; that number, however, was based upon contracts with state-level agencies. The GAO was unable to determine the extent of county contracts going to FBOs, and counties do the vast majority of the state's contracting (Queen 2003).

Other States' Experiences

It seemed fair to ask whether these results were an anomaly. Certainly, we thought we had chosen a representative sample. But what if our states were not really representative? To answer that question, we compared the experiences of our three states with available data about other states, and our findings supported our conclusion that, "on the ground," very little has changed. In 2003, the Roundtable on Religion and Social Welfare Policy, a Rockefeller Institute of Government project supported by the Pew Charitable Trusts, issued reports on the implementation of Charitable Choice in five states: New Hampshire, Oklahoma, Montana, Florida, and Texas. A brief review of those reports supports the conclusion that the practical impact of Section 104 and its progeny has been relatively minimal.

In New Hampshire, where "participation in organized religion . . . is much lower than the national average," and where religious providers have always been eligible to compete for contracts, state officials "have seen no need to change practices in response to Charitable Choice," and legislators have not called for such changes (Merrow 2003, 7).

In Oklahoma, despite the state's frequent characterization as "the buckle of the Bible Belt," contractual opportunities for new FBOs "have been relatively limited" (Sharp 2003, 1). Despite a major overhaul of its welfare system well before PRWORA, Oklahoma's system remains "a patchwork of agencies and programs" (Sharp 2003, 3), making accurate estimates of contracting participation difficult. (As with many states, data in Oklahoma are not tracked in a manner that allows for the identification of FBOs.) In 1998, the state established an Office of Faith-Based and Community Initiatives, and in 2001, the governor issued an executive order directing state agencies to actively engage with FBOs; nevertheless, the report finds that "beyond the more longstanding charitable organizations and the highly visible Oklahoma Marriage Initiative, new financial relationships in the state of Oklahoma appear minimal" (Sharp 2003, 12).

At the time the 2003 Montana report was issued, the state had "one high-profile faith-based project—the Montana Faith-Health Demonstration Co-Operative—and it is financed through the Bush administration's new Compassion Capital Fund" (Miller 2003, 2). Montana officials had displayed little interest in Charitable Choice, and the Faith-Based Initiative is controversial there. Furthermore "special challenges of Montana's geography and the complex interplay of its governmental jurisdictions, social service regions and Indian Reservations present even greater obstacles" (Miller 2003, 3).

If participation by FBOs in social service provision might be expected to show an increase anywhere, Florida and Texas would seem to be the most likely venues. Florida channels the great majority of its social services through third-party providers, and Governor Jeb Bush has been an active and enthusiastic proponent of faith-based participation. Furthermore, "among non-profit organizations, faith-based entities have—*for as long as anyone can remember*—been an integral part of the social service delivery system" (Crew 2003, 1; emphasis in original). However, the state's social service delivery system is very decentralized, and administrative complexities have deterred smaller contractors, including smaller FBOs. As a result, little in Florida has changed. "Given their long-term and widespread use in the delivery of these services in the state, the on-the-ground difference between the uses of FBOs today and in the years prior to 1996 can be characterized as modest" (Crew 2003, 2).

Texas, under the leadership of then-Governor George W. Bush, was the first state to make a really aggressive effort to include FBOs in service provision, and the state's strong support for faith-based initiatives has been consistent since 1996. During the Bush administration, executive orders were issued, a task force was convened, and a series of legislative initiatives were passed, "aimed at achieving Gov. Bush's two-pronged goal of deregulating faith-based agencies and increasing the financial resources made available to them" (Ebaugh 2003, 2). Faith-based liaisons were designated in each of the twenty-eight regional workforce boards overseeing welfare-to-work programs. The Texas Department of Human Services distributed instructions to contracting agencies, emphasizing their responsibility to protect the religious character of contracting organizations, reminding them of the state's commitment to provide contracting opportunities to FBOs, and requiring them to include, in all published notices of requests for proposals, language explicitly encouraging applications from community- and faith-based bidders (Ebaugh 2003). The upshot of these and related efforts is unclear, because data are not maintained at either the state or county level that identify contractors' religious affiliation or lack thereof. "In general, the faith-based liaisons in both TWC [Texas Workforce Commission] and TDHS [Texas Department of Human Services] have the sense that awards to FBOs have increased since 1996, but could provide no hard data to substantiate their perception" (Ebaugh 2003, 9).

More recently, researchers with the Urban Institute studied responses to Charitable Choice and the President's Faith-Based Initiative in three cities—Denver, Birmingham, and Boston—and concluded that "in all three block grant programs, contracting levels represent little change in the three sites since the enactment of Charitable Choice. Program administrators reported that the scope of contracting with FBOs was unaffected by the Charitable Choice provisions and that contracts with FBOs were with existing contractors" (Kramer, De Vita, and Finegold 2005, 52).

Why the Tepid Response?

Many researchers have wondered what happened between the enthusiasm for "faith-based" solutions to poverty at the federal level and the essentially unchanged landscape of social service delivery at the local level. Certainly, a failure to appreciate the complex realities of social service delivery "on the ground" is one element. In all likelihood, the refusal to put any additional funding into the services themselves was another. And as the foregoing descriptions of state responses have demonstrated, Charitable Choice responses were shaped by local political cultures that were more or less receptive to the federal directive.

Other factors have also played a role. Ironically, widely publicized lawsuits stemming from the zealous approach taken by Texas may explain at least some of the caution about Charitable Choice displayed by public administrators elsewhere. Texas has provided a number of examples of what can happen when enthusiasm for a programmatic approach is coupled with inadequate accountability mechanisms. In one case that received widespread publicity, a challenge was mounted to the Alternative Accreditation program established by Governor Bush in 1997 to exempt faith-based child care centers and residential children's homes from state licensure requirements. Rather than having to demonstrate compliance with existing state standards, faith-based facilities were to be accredited by the Texas Association of Christian Child Care Agencies (TACCCA).

In the 1970s, radio evangelist Lester Roloff had founded Roloff Homes, and—according to a report in the *Washington Post*—had made those homes a "focus of his 'holy war' against the state. When teenage girls complained of being whipped and denied food, he refused to let the state inspect the facilities. After a showdown with the attorney general, Roloff Homes left Texas in 1985" (Rosin 2000). Wiley Cameron Sr., who assumed control of the Roloff Homes after Lester Roloff's death, lobbied then-governor Bush for the 1997 alternative accreditation law. Cameron was also appointed to serve on the board of directors of TACCCA.

After the law exempting faith-based children's homes from standard licensure restrictions was passed, Roloff Homes came back to the state and opened five facilities, which were duly accredited by TACCCA. In 2000, Texas authorities substantiated reports of physical abuse at several of the facilities, including frequent beatings and what one teenager characterized as "sadistic" punishments. In one case, young boys were roped together and forced to run barefoot through the woods, then made to stand and dig in a sewage pit for twelve hours (Rosin 2000). The state obtained criminal convictions against the Roloff Homes administrators in 2001. Teen Challenge facilities, also exempted from state licensing by Governor Bush, were cited for numerous health and safety violations, including, in 1998, allegations of sexual abuse by a drug counselor working for Dallas Teen Challenge. Other suits involved the Texas InnerChange Prison Program and the use of tax dollars by Jobs Partnership of Washington County, a faith-based contractor, to purchase Bibles (Ebaugh 2003).

A number of other local factors may also help to explain the tepid response to Charitable Choice seen thus far. Certainly state fiscal difficulties have played a major role. During the early 2000s, most state governments experienced quite drastic budgetary problems, necessitating painful cuts in services—including welfare services. In the states we studied, especially Indiana and North Carolina, the lack of funding operated to restrict state spending on precisely those services that were the target of faith-based initiatives.

State-level politics also (predictably) complicate faith-based efforts, just as they complicate the implementation of many other policies. Those politics range from the routine disjunctions and changes of priorities that occur between administrations—especially if the transition involves a shift in partisan control—to the more subtle, and arguably more difficult, ethnic and racial tensions

that often characterize states' political cultures in our multicultural
nation. In North Carolina, racial politics shaped by the state's history and exacerbated by its racial and urban/rural divisions required everyone involved to make fairly constant accommodations,
although state officials and faith organization representatives alike
were uncomfortable discussing those tensions other than obliquely
(Queen 2003).

Even when power struggles were not grounded in racial and ethnic identities, however, as Chaves and others have shown, the responses to Charitable Choice and faith-based participation in government programs vary along racial lines. In Mississippi, a 1999
survey of pastoral attitudes toward Charitable Choice showed that
14 percent of white clergy familiar with the program were favorably
disposed toward it, while the proportion of black pastors aware of
the approach and approving of it was 73 percent (Bartkowski and
Regis 1999, 19).

The differences in attitudes of black and white clergy are only
one manifestation of the widespread—and nonlocalized—am-
bivalence with which clergy and religious communities regarded
Charitable Choice, and especially the Bush Faith-Based Initiatives.
If some pastors were enthusiastic at the prospect of money for
street-level missions, others—black and white alike—were deeply
suspicious of the motives and probable effects of Charitable Choice.
Some worry that government funding will co-opt the church. Others recall the scandals of the Model Cities programs during the
days of the War on Poverty, and they draw comparisons to the lawsuits in Texas and to an embarrassing incident in Oklahoma, where
a suburb of Oklahoma City contracted with two local churches to
provide day care and pre-kindergarten facilities and services. The
school district counted the students as its own, received a state financial distribution based upon the inflated number, and split the
windfall with the churches. (In addition to the financial impro-
priety, the students were subjected to intensive religious instruction—paid for with tax dollars; Sharp 2003.)

Still other objections center on civil rights issues. In the Montana case study, clergy interviewed "expressed skepticism and/or
disagreement with policies that might permit the hiring of co-
religionists, and that would permit certain religious practices to
continue if a faith-based organization provided services that had

a secular purpose" (Miller 2003, 9). Though the salience of any of these concerns varied, depending upon the religious history and landscape of particular states, they were apparent everywhere.

In 2002, the GAO identified some of these same factors as barriers to increased collaboration between states and FBOs. A report prepared for Senator Joseph Lieberman (D-Conn.) and Representative Elijah E. Cummings (D-Md.) listed as key factors a lack of awareness and understanding of Charitable Choice, the unwillingness of some FBOs to partner with government, theological and/or philosophical beliefs of FBOs that preclude such relationships, complexities of the contracting processes in many states, the limited administrative and fiscal capacities of many FBOs, and the limited human resources—staff and volunteer—of many FBOs. It is likely that those factors remain significant.

Charitable Choice was frequently justified on the grounds that a law was necessary to correct discriminatory practices in the various bid and contracting processes used by government agencies to choose contracting partners for service delivery. Chapter 7 considers what sort of government actions constitute discrimination, and what constitutes evidence of discriminatory practices, but it may be appropriate to end this chapter by noting that the states we studied offered an instructive empirical window into the processes used by different public managers operating in different political environments to solicit bidders and choose providers. There may be public agencies that are inappropriately concerned with the religious identities of potential providers, but we saw no evidence of them in the course of our study, or in the empirical literature. In the three states we studied in depth, religiously affiliated providers had been part of the social service system for many years. In no state did any provider, faith based or secular, suggest to our researchers that religion was a negative factor in selection. (Some did suggest that, after passage of Charitable Choice, it had been a positive factor.) No public managers we interviewed knew how many providers were religiously affiliated, and that included those who were charged with outreach to FBOs, because the states do not keep data that would allow them to calculate that number.

In most situations we encountered, and most studies by other researchers looking at other states, state officials overseeing the bid processes had overwhelmingly chosen from among a very limited number of qualified bidders based on evidence meant to assess their capacity to deliver the services in question. To the extent that allegations of favoritism existed, they consisted of the age-old assertions of political patronage and influence peddling, not religion. If FBOs are "underrepresented" (and in the absence of an agreed-upon definition of FBO, and reliable data, it is by no means clear that they are), devoting additional resources to capacity building would seem to be the most useful strategy for remedying that underrepresentation.

Chapter 4

The Role of Faith-Based

Service Providers

*T*HE PASSAGE OF THE CHARITABLE CHOICE
LAWS USHERED IN A SUSTAINED, LIVELY,
and occasionally acrimonious discussion about the capacities
of faith-based organizations (FBOs) to provide social services.
Proponents of Charitable Choice and the president's Faith-Based
Initiative made a number of claims about the benefits that would
accrue if more faith-based service providers were encouraged to
participate. They argued that broader inclusion of FBOs would
increase the diversity of service delivery systems, and thus enhance
government responsiveness (Wilson 2003). They claimed that
FBOs are more efficient—that they make better use of resources
and achieve better outcomes—than secular organizations (for sum-
maries, see Sherman 2003 and White House 2001). They suggested
that the inclusion of organizations "rooted" in their communities
would give government program managers increased access to the
infrastructures, volunteers, and existing service networks in those
communities.

There were a number of assumptions implicit in these claims:
that smaller, "grassroots" organizations would be less bureaucratic
and more "rooted" in the communities needing services; that organizations with a "faith factor" would be better, more effective, and
more humane service providers than their secular counterparts;
and that FBOs would be more holistic in their approach to individual clients, and thus more likely to promote the transformation
of clients, than secular organizations. These organizations were described as more likely to establish personal, caring, and enduring
relationships with clients than secular providers; more likely to include mentoring relationships; and more likely to provide clients

with positive role models and ongoing support networks. Some proponents suggested that FBOs would have more motivated staff and more access to motivated volunteers. All these hypothesized characteristics would enhance the effectiveness of their service delivery, and taxpayers would get better results for less money.

Those rosy predictions were countered by the quite different picture painted by those who were skeptical about Charitable Choice. Opponents of expanded faith-based participation argued that indiscriminate government support of FBOs would erode the separation of church and state, promote employment discrimination, and result in favoritism for faith-based providers (Chaves 2003). And they pointed out that there was no conclusive evidence that faith-based providers as a category—either congregations or 501(c)(3)s—perform better or even differently than secular providers (Chaves 2003; Johnson, Tompkins, and Webb 2002; Nilsen 2002).

Research Questions: What Is a "Faith-Based" Organization?

To test the accuracy of these very different pictures of faith organizations, it is first necessary to define them. What are the differences between "faith-based" and secular organizations? What organizational characteristics differentiate religious providers from each other and from secular organizations, and do those characteristics include the strong community ties and holistic approach to service delivery that proponents describe? Does the capacity to offer effective services correlate with the dimension of faith? Can we even define the "faith factor," and will we recognize it when we see it? What, in short, do social service organizations that contract with government look like?

Methodology and Data

To answer these questions, we first surveyed the literature on faith-based service providers. We found significant limitations in previous studies and sought to design our research to take them into account.

Selecting Organizational Characteristics

There is a considerable body of work on the service activities of religious congregations (Chaves and Tsitsos 2001; Cnaan and Boddie 2002; Hodgkinson et al. 1993; Scott 2003; Wineburg 1994). This research has concluded that social services provided by congregations have generally been focused on short-term or emergency needs of recipients; and that congregations generally do not have the resources or capacity to manage programs that require systemic, sustained social services geared more toward significant or long-term problems (Chaves 2003). Research on noncongregational faith-based social service providers is spottier, and systematic evidence regarding differences in service approach is not yet available. Much of the discussion to date has been descriptive or theoretical. A number of researchers have offered descriptive reports of the scope and scale of faith-based social services, and a number of articles have posited theories of how "faith" and its consequences might be conceptualized and operationalized (see the review in Scott 2003). There is far too little recognition in the literature of the wide diversity of providers who might all be classified as faith based. Some sectarian agencies, like the Salvation Army, have provided services for many years and have well-established track records, whereas others lack capacity, professional qualifications, or relevant experience (Gibelman and Gelman 2002; Nilsen 2002).

In a handful of studies, researchers have discussed the operational differences between faith-based and secular providers and the possible consequences of those differences (Scott 2003). Generally, these researchers have used secondary data (e.g., from the Internal Revenue Service) to classify providers. Unfortunately, such data have limited utility. Organizations are usually classified as faith based or not according to their names or other similarly limited descriptions. In addition, the organizational characteristics included in the data may be incomplete or irrelevant to the questions at hand. For example, the Internal Revenue Service collects information returns only from larger nonprofits, and these returns include only a limited number of characteristics. Survey data can overcome these limitations but will, of necessity, include smaller samples of organizations. As a consequence, many studies will need to be done before all the disparate findings can be reconciled and overall conclusions drawn. Scholars are only beginning this process.

A few examples may demonstrate the difficulty. Ebaugh and others (2003) examined homeless services and found that FBOs made more use of volunteers and delivered the same range of services as their secular counterparts. Conversely, Goggin and Orth (2002) also surveyed service providers for the homeless and concluded that secular providers are different from some, but not all, FBOs and that FBOs vary widely among themselves in service delivery approaches. Pirog and Reingold (2002) surveyed a range of social service agencies and found that FBOs provide more health and human services than do secular providers but that both provider types have similar capacity levels as defined by their networks. Kearns, Park, and Yankoski (2005) compared faith-based and secular community service organizations in the Pittsburgh area. They found them to be similar in size, funding, program capacity, and management sophistication. FBOs in that study, however, made more use of volunteers, got less government funding, and engaged less in policy advocacy and lobbying. In work that is closest to our own, Monsma (2005) and Monsma and Mounts (2002) examined the types of welfare-to-work services provided by government, for-profit, secular nonprofit, and faith-based welfare-to-work agencies in four cities. They found that compared with secular providers, a higher proportion of the services of the FBOs in their sample were life oriented (which they designated as "holistic") rather than job oriented.

As this brief review demonstrates, there is much more work to be done. Furthermore, the research that has been done thus far is of limited utility for a number of reasons. Some studies have included only FBOs, precluding comparisons with non-FBOs. Very few have distinguished between FBOs that contract with government and those that do not. If studies are not genuinely comparative, they will have very limited utility to scholars and policymakers trying to answer the specific questions raised by Charitable Choice and the various faith-based initiatives that are its progeny. Worse still, many samples of FBOs in these studies have included both congregations and freestanding faith-based service providers—organizations with dramatically different origins, missions, and capacities. Combining these very different organizational types in studies inevitably limits the utility of the results. Other, probably inevitable difference in approach makes comparisons between research studies more difficult. Researchers take different approaches and use different criteria in measuring the degree of influence that faith may have in a particular organization. Finally, many studies have paid little or no attention to nonfaith organizational dimensions that have been shown to correlate with efficiency and effectiveness.

In formulating our research instruments, we tried to address each of these points. We framed our question as an exploration of the degree to which faith influences providers and the services they offer, and the consequences of such influence for both providers and clients. We focused our inquiry on a sample of government, for-profit, and nonprofit providers in a narrowly defined service area, to enhance comparability. All the nonprofit providers in our study were 501(c)(3)s. To measure the degree to which faith influenced any given provider, we developed a scale based upon organizational dimensions used in previous studies. Applying that scale, we identified a number of nonprofit FBOs; in addition—and to our surprise—we also identified a number of for-profit providers that were faith based. No one, to our knowledge, has previously documented the existence of for-profit FBOs; there is certainly no literature examining their operations. The first question raised by the existence of such organizations was thus the degree to which they are similar to or different from their nonprofit counterparts, and our data allowed us to address that question.

To assess the role providers played in the overall social service delivery system, we used a variety of organizational measures that have been correlated with the efficiency and effectiveness of service provision, including size, "holistic" orientation, use of volunteers, involvement in community networks, and what we refer to as "embeddedness" in the relevant community. Our goal was to enhance understanding of the characteristics specific to faith-influenced providers and to illustrate how those characteristics may affect their participation in government social service delivery systems.

Surveying Indiana Administrators

Our analysis in this chapter focuses on Indiana, specifically on the Indiana Manpower Placement and Comprehensive Training program (IMPACT). IMPACT is funded by the Temporary Assistance for Needy Families (TANF) block grant, and it contracts for employment-based services, including assessment; education; job training; job readiness; and job search, development, and placement. IMPACT contracts with newly formed and traditional faith-based providers as well as with non-faith-based providers to deliver these services.

As part of our research, we conducted interviews in person and by mail with IMPACT provider administrators in 2001 and 2002 to assess a variety of organizational dimensions. We designed the provider questionnaire to provide data on factors that have been identified as important indicators of efficacy in service provision. The factors we chose were based upon the scholarly literature and taken from conference presentations on organizational structure and processes, Charitable Choice and faith-based service provision, and other ongoing nonprofit surveys. Before finalizing our questionnaires, we sent them to those members of our national advisory committee familiar with research methodologies, and we requested their comments and suggestions.

The questionnaires (reproduced in appendix B) included questions about basic organizational factors such as the size and sources of the organization's revenues, the dollar amount of the IMPACT contract, and the number of agency and IMPACT employees and volunteers. To measure the degree to which faith influenced the providers, we developed a series of questions based upon a faith-influence scale that we constructed. (This scale is described in more detail below.) If an organization was determined to be faith based on that scale, we asked the respondent a further series of questions intended to help us measure the organizational and programmatic consequences of the faith orientation. In addition, we used a set of questions about the types of services provided, meant to assess the degree to which the organization manifested a holistic approach to clients and service delivery, and we measured the degree to which the organization was involved in community or other networks using questions about formal organizational affiliations, IMPACT-related contacts, and community involvement. Finally, we measured the degree to which clients served by the organization came from the immediate neighborhood.

The IMPACT Program

For this project, our sample included all IMPACT providers from three Indiana counties (Lake, Marion, and Miami). In each of these counties, some IMPACT providers had been designated by the state as "faith based" according to either (1) their participation

in a program designed to reach out to FBOs by providing technical assistance and capacity building (FaithWorks), or (2) their self-
identification as faith based. As table 4.1 shows, there were a total of
thirty-four IMPACT providers in the three counties. We were able
to obtain interviews with thirty of them: three in Miami County,
thirteen in Lake County, and fifteen in Marion County. These
interviewed providers included twenty-two nonprofits, five for-
profits, and three government agencies. One nonprofit and three
for-profit IMPACT providers would not agree to be interviewed.

DIMENSIONS OF RELIGIOSITY AND TYPES OF ORGANIZATIONS

In the emerging research on Charitable Choice and FBOs, a major
issue—perhaps *the* major issue—has been how one defines "faith"
and "faith based" (Chambré 2001; Jeavons 1998; Wofford et al.
2002; Smith and Sosin 2001). As noted above, the state of Indiana
classifies providers as faith based or not according to two factors:
self-identification (the chief method) and/or participation in the
FaithWorks program. This simple binary distinction is obviously
inadequate and arguably misleading; a number of researchers have
pointed out that it is more useful to think in terms of degrees of
religiosity (Green and Sherman 2002; Jeavons 1998; Monsma and
Mounts 2002; Wofford et al. 2002; Smith and Sosin 2001). Accordingly, we compared the twenty-four dimensions included by several
other researchers in their efforts to classify organizations by the degree to which faith influences their service provision (see table 4.2).

Table 4.1. 2000–2 IMPACT Providers

Type of Organization	County	Interviewed	Declined	Total
Nonprofit	Lake	9	1	10
	Marion	11		11
	Miami	2		2
For-profit	Lake	2	1	3
	Marion	2	2	4
	Miami	1		1
Government agency	Lake	2		2
	Marion	1		1
	Miami	0		0
Grand total		30	4	34

Source: Indiana IMPACT Provider Survey.

Table 4.2. A Comparison of Dimensions and Indicators Used in Identification of Faith-Based Organizations

Dimension or Indicator	Jeavons (1998)	Smith and Sosin (2001)	Wofford et al. (2002)	Green and Sherman (2002)	Monsma and Mounts (2002)	Bielefeld, Littlepage, and Thelin (2002)
Formal/informal religious affiliation						
Religious name	X					
Religious authority coupling		X				
Affiliated with religious agency			X			X
Founded by religious organization			X			
Religion in mission/governance						
Mission statement is explicitly religious			X	X		
Establishing separate 501(c)(3) would be a problem			X			
Religious criteria for board	X		X	X		
Senior management/other staff share faith	X		X	X	X	X
Religion in funding						
Financial support/resource dependency	X	X	X			X
Receives reimbursement for providing "entitlement" services			X			
Religion in structure and/or process						
Percent of participants in organization holding religious conviction	X					
Religious culture		X				
Religious symbols or pictures			X		X	X
Opening or closing sessions with prayer					X	X (meals)
Prayer or texts guide decisions	X					X

Table 4.2. Continued.

Dimension or Indicator	Jeavons (1998)	Smith and Sosin (2001)	Wofford et al. (2002)	Green and Sherman (2002)	Monsma and Mounts (2002)	Bielefeld, Little-page, and Thelin (2002)
Faith criteria used to assign staff	X			X	X	X
Uses religious values to motivate staff					X	
Partners with religious organizations	X					
Religion in services to clients						
Religion or faith is a part of services	X		X	X		X
Voluntary religious exercises for clients				X	X	X
Requires religious exercises for clients					X	X
Uses religious values to encourage attitude change			X	X	X	
Encourages clients to make religious commitments				X	X	X
Gives preference to clients who are in religious agreement				X	X	X

On the basis of previous research, especially the typology created by Jeavons, we developed six screening questions about funding, affiliation, shared belief, services, decision making, and staff assignment to ask our respondents. (They are shown in the first six rows of table 4.3.) These were questions from which we hoped to determine the relative influence of faith on their organization and operations.

As expected, we found substantial variations in the degree to which faith influenced the providers. Of the thirty providers we surveyed, seventeen gave no affirmative responses to the screening questions. Accordingly, we categorized these as not influenced at all by faith or explicit religious belief, and designated them as

Table 4.3. Dimensions Used in Measuring the Influence of Faith

Dimension	Question
Funding	Organization provides funds or support to any religious organizations
Affiliation	Organization affiliated with any religious organizations or faith traditions
Shared belief	Desired, requested, or required that staff and volunteers share the same religious belief or faith
Services	Religion or faith part of any services provided
Decision making	Organizational decisions guided by prayer or religious texts, documents, or periodicals
Staff assignment	Religious or faith criteria used to assign staff to positions
Visible religiousness	Yes to any of these: religious leader on staff, efforts to encourage clients to make personal religious commitments, required religious exercises, and spoken prayers at meals
Implicit religiousness	Yes to any of these: religious symbols/pictures in the facility, generalized spirit of love among staff, voluntary religious exercises, informal references to religious ideas by staff to clients, and staff that are members of the congregation

Source: Indiana IMPACT Provider Survey.

non-faith-based (NFB) providers. We categorized the remaining thirteen organizations as faith based and awarded them 1 point for each affirmative response to the six screening questions. These FBOs were then given a series of follow-up questions to measure two additional dimensions—visible religiosity and implicit religiosity (these are shown in the last two rows of table 4.3). An organization was given 1 point for each question to which it answered "yes" on the questions in the visible dimension group, and 1 for each question to which it answered "yes" on the implicit dimension list. Our scale thus ranged from 0 to 8.

We categorized organizations having 1 to 4 points as moderately faith based (MFB) and organizations with more than 4 points as strongly faith based (SFB). Of those initially found to be influenced by faith, six were classified as MFB and seven as SFB. It should be noted that our categorization of faith influence depends on the current director's responses to these questions, and that those responses are inevitably based upon that person's own practices and

Table 4.4. Faith Orientation of IMPACT Providers by Type of Organization

Type of Organization	Faith Influence		Number of Organizations	Average Age of Organization (years)	Average Number of Full-Time Employees
Nonprofit	NFB		13	37	39
	MFB		3	64	292
	SFB		6	10	2
		Total	22	33	63
For-profit	NFB		1	6	20
	MFB		3	3	5
	SFB		1	23	1
		Total	5	8	7
Government agency	NFB		3	62	250
	MFB		0		
	SFB		0		
		Total	3	62	250
Grand total			30	62	126

Note: NFB = non-faith-based (score of 0 on faith-influence questions)
MFB = moderately faith-based (score of 1–4 on faith-influence questions)
SFB = strongly faith-based (score of 5–7 on faith-influence questions)
Source: Indiana IMPACT Provider Survey.

perceptions of the organization. Thus the categorization was dependent upon leadership, and it could change if that leadership changed. As an example, a provider with a historically religious affiliation and several locations in Indiana was categorized as MFB at one location but as NFB at another location.

We then sorted organizations by the degree to which faith influenced them, according to the scale we had developed. Those results are shown in table 4.4. Approximately 41 percent of the nonprofit providers are faith based. Conversely, 80 percent of the for-profits are faith based (three are MFB and one is SFB). To date, for-profit faith-based providers have not been identified or systematically examined in the Charitable Choice literature, and the phenomenon raises a number of intriguing questions. Throughout the remainder of our analysis, we highlight the differences we found between traditional nonprofit FBOs and these for-profit FBOs. We found that SFB organizations are, on average, much smaller and newer than the NFB or the MFB organizations in our pool.

Findings

Although some of our findings were statistically significant, most
were not, and that is not surprising given the small number of cases
in each faith category. Provider categories are further broken down
in some of the comparisons that follow, compounding the problem. However, even in the absence of statistical significance, the
patterns found in the data and the direction of the relationships
between variables shed considerable light on the dynamics of faith-
based providers and provide a basis for further research.

The data reveal clear differences between the operations of SFB
and MFB organizations. All the SFB organizations used prayer to
guide organizational decisions, whereas only a third of the MFBs
did so (see table 4.5 for details).

Also, almost half the SFB organizations restrict staff and volunteer positions to those who share the same religious beliefs, and a
number use religious criteria to make staff assignments; none of
the MFBs does either. The MFB nonprofits were generally similar
to their for-profit counterparts, although they were somewhat less
likely to be religiously affiliated and somewhat more likely to use
religion or faith in their services and to display visible religiosity.

Table 4.5. Affirmative Responses to Faith-Influence Questions (percent)

	Moderately Faith-Based		Strongly Faith-Based	
Screening Question	NPO	FPO	NPO	FPO
Support to religious organizations	33	33	50	0
Religious affiliation	33	67	83	0
Staff and volunteers share faith	0	0	50	0
Religion or faith a part of services	67	33	50	100
Prayer, etc., guides decisions	33	33	100	100
Religious criteria used to assign staff	0	0	33	100
Visible religiousness	100	67	83	100
Implicit religiousness	33	33	33	100
Number	3	3	6	1

Note: NPO = nonprofit organization
FPO = for-profit organization
Source: Indiana IMPACT Provider Survey.

Size

We then looked at what the data could tell us about provider revenues, IMPACT contract income, and employee information. As table 4.6 shows, most SFB organizations were small, reporting annual revenue of $500,000 or less; 40 percent reported annual revenue of $100,000 or less. Conversely, all the MFB providers reported annual revenue over $500,000, and more than 70 percent of NFBs had revenue over $1 million. SFB providers also had the smallest IMPACT contracts, averaging $191,575. The IMPACT contracts for MFB providers were on average 12 percent larger, and those for NFB providers were on average 39 percent larger than those of the SFBs. In addition, SFBs were considerably more financially dependent on their IMPACT contracts, with contracts providing, on average, 75 percent of these providers' revenues. This was in contrast to MFB providers, which on average derived 38 percent of their revenues from IMPACT contracts; and to NFB providers, which received 24 percent of their income from such contracts.

When we looked into the reasons for the differences between nonprofit and for-profit faith-based providers, we found that the for-profit SFB providers tended to be small and to have correspondingly

Table 4.6. Revenue, IMPACT Contract, and Employees

Measure	Non-Faith-Based	Moderately Faith-Based	Strongly Faith-Based
Annual revenue			
$0–$100,000	0%	0%	40%
$100,001–$500,000	18%	0%	20%
$500,001–$1,000,000	12%	50%	20%
Over $1,000,000	71%	50%	20%
Average size of IMPACT contracts in 2002	$266,788	$215,474	$191,575
Average percent of annual revenue from IMPACT contract	24%	38%	75%
Average number of full-time-equivalent employees providing IMPACT services	5	4	2
Average number of total full-time employees	49	149	2

Source: Indiana IMPACT Provider Survey.

small IMPACT contracts—contracts that, despite their smaller size, provided 100 percent of the organization's income. In the MFB category, we also found the for-profit providers to be much more dependent on their IMPACT contracts. These contracts provided on average 75 percent of the total income of these organizations, compared with 13 percent of the income of their nonprofit counterparts.

There were also substantial variations between the average number of full-time employees of the organizations and the average number of full-time equivalent employees providing IMPACT services. These figures are another indication of organizational size and capacity. SFB organizations were the smallest by far when measured by number of employees, including both overall employment figures and the number of persons employed to provide IMPACT services. MFB organizations had the largest average number of employees, due to the presence in the pool of several large nonprofit providers. However, MFB and NFB organizations reported approximately the same number of employees working in their IMPACT programs.

CONSEQUENCES OF GOVERNMENT FUNDING

We asked a number of questions about the perceived consequences to the organization of their acceptance of government funding. The responses to these questions did not fall into any discernable pattern or demonstrate any significant differences between the nonprofit and for-profit faith-based providers (see table 4.7).

Most FBOs did not report having to change their religious practices, nor did they report even having been questioned about them. Sixty-seven percent of MFB and 83 percent of SFB providers did respond affirmatively to the question whether they had experienced changes as a consequence of involvement with the IMPACT program. These consequences are reported as being almost entirely positive, as the following quotations indicate:

- "Has given congregation reason to get off the pews and serve the community."
- "Clients have become members, members have become staff."
- "A chance to minister to the students."
- "People are attracted because of the community outreach."
- "Fit with our programs."

**Table 4.7. Affirmative Responses to Organization and Client
Questions (percent)**

Question	Moderately Faith-Based	Strongly Faith-Based
Any religious practices you feel you have had to curtail or eliminate because you receive government funds	0	14
Government officials questioned religious-based practices or asked you to change any of them	0	0
Received any criticism or pressure or lawsuits because of any of your religious-based practices	0	14
Consequences for your congregation because of your involvement with IMPACT	67	83
Had any issues with clients related to your religious-based practices	0	29
IMPACT clients attended congregational activities or services, or joined the congregation	33	43
Religion, including expressions of faith or personal testimony, a part of the IMPACT service	25	43

Source: Indiana IMPACT Provider Survey.

The only slightly negative comment was "Scheduling the use of facilities."

When asked to report any issues or objections clients had raised about religiously based practices, one SFB provider said that one client was Muslim and other students' expressions of faith had made her uncomfortable, but that she had stayed with the program. Another SFB said that some clients left because they did not want to be in a church. SFB providers were somewhat more likely than MFB providers to have their clients participate in congregational activities and to use religion in their IMPACT services. When asked to elaborate on how religion is part of their IMPACT services, providers responded with:

- "Clients initiate conversation."
- "Life skills, character issues, they share their faith if clients bring it up. Client is the most important person."
- "It is part of mentoring and 'body by choice' (nutrition and weight management, spiritual discussion)."
- "We expose, we do not impose, and do meditation with Twenty-Third Psalm."

HOLISTIC SERVICES

As we have noted, some proponents of Charitable Choice claim that religious social service organizations employ more holistic service delivery methods than their secular counterparts. To determine the degree to which Indiana's IMPACT providers were holistic, we evaluated the responses to several survey questions included to assess that dimension. Providers were handed a list of thirty-eight possible specific services that they could have provided under their IMPACT contract. We classified twenty-three of these as directly job related and fifteen as holistic in nature. Job-related services included job training; job readiness; job search, development, and placement; and education services. Holistically oriented services addressed other aspects of client's lives and included stress management, mental health treatment, and the like. We also asked whether the organization provided services to IMPACT clients other than those that were required under the contract, whether any services provided were nonreimbursed, whether the organization promoted goals for clients other than securing employment, and whether the program promoted values. This gave us a total of eighteen possible holistic elements in a provider's program. After compiling those results, the data (shown in table 4.8) indicated that holistic service delivery is characteristic of both NFB and faith-based providers. In some cases, ancillary services indicative of a holistic service approach were more frequently provided by one type of provider than another; in other cases, such services were more equally distributed.

In order not to draw unwarranted inferences from this information, it was important to account for the fact that the providers differed in the number of IMPACT services that they had contracted to deliver. The adjusted data are shown in table 4.9.

Table 4.9 shows that the mean numbers of both job-related and "extra" services (the delivery of such extras being a proxy for holistic service delivery) were similar for NFB and MFB providers. For SFB providers, however, though the mean number of holistically oriented services was similar to the other types of providers, the mean number of job-related services was notably smaller. This suggests that SFB providers put relatively more emphasis on holistically oriented services. That is, they did not provide more

Table 4.8. Percentage of Organizations Providing Holistic Services in Program (percent)

Holistic Element Included	Non-Faith-Based	Moderately Faith-Based	Strongly Faith-Based
Anger management	71	50	71
Budgeting / money management	71	83	43
Social skills	65	67	71
Self-image	71	83	71
Stress management	71	67	67
Drug treatment	35	17	33
Alcohol treatment	35	17	33
Mental health treatment	29	17	17
Case management	77	83	43
Teen pregnancy prevention	6	17	17
Small business assistance	6	0	0
Homeownership assistance	18	17	0
Mediate conflicts between employers/clients	29	33	17
Parenting	35	67	67
Provides services not specified in contract	6	17	29
Provided nonreimbursed services	41	50	86
Sought other goals for clients	88	100	86
Promotes values	82	100	86

Source: Indiana IMPACT Provider Survey.

holistically oriented services but chose to offer fewer job-related services. The MFB and NFB providers, conversely, provided a greater percentage of job-related services. This pattern differs somewhat from the pattern found by Monsma (2005); in his study, both his faith-based/segmented and faith-based/integrated providers (corresponding to our MFB and SFB providers, respectively) showed the same pattern as the SFB providers in our sample.

Table 4.9. Mean Number of Job-Related and Holistically Oriented Services Provided

Type of Service Provided	Non-Faith-Based	Moderately Faith-Based	Strongly Faith-Based
Job-related services	13.2	15.5	8.3
Holistic services	9.2	9.3	8.3
Total number of services	22.3	24.8	16.6

Source: Indiana IMPACT Provider Survey.

Finally, when the providers in our study were asked whether they offered additional services along with those required under the terms of their IMPACT contracts, SFB providers gave the highest percentage of affirmative answers (29 percent) and NFB providers gave the lowest (6 percent). In addition, 86 percent of the SFB providers said they were not reimbursed for these services, compared with 50 and 41 percent of MFB and NFB providers, respectively. We should also note that, upon further examination, the nature of such extra services as were provided appeared to be quite similar across provider types.

COMMUNITY NETWORKS

To determine how connected to their communities the providers in each category were, we asked respondents to specify the type and number of organizations with which they routinely interacted in the process of delivering IMPACT services: nonprofits, for-profits, government organizations, religious bodies, religious organizations or FBOs, and others. In addition, we asked them to indicate the type of interaction with each—specifically, whether the interactions involved the giving or receipt of funding or other resources; whether they included collaboration for the purpose of service provision; whether the interaction involved policy or regulatory compliance; whether it involved serving together on coalitions, committees, or task forces; or whether they involved a subcontracting relationship.

Overall, 83 percent of the MFB providers interviewed reported some formal affiliations with other organizations (see table 4.10). Though fewer providers in the other two categories identified such associations, 77 percent of NFB and 57 percent of SFB providers reported formal affiliation with other civic or umbrella organizations. For-profit providers in each faith category were less likely to report such formal affiliations than were the nonprofit providers. A noteworthy finding was that almost all the nonprofit SFB organizations reported that their contracting with IMPACT had led them to make other community connections, but only about a third of NFB and MFB providers reported similar results. These increased community involvements included increased interactions with other providers, new organizational memberships, participation in community events such as job fairs, and increased interactions with local government welfare offices.

Table 4.10. Networks and Effects of IMPACT Participation

Link	Non-Faith-Based			Moderately Faith-Based		Strongly Faith-Based	
	NPO	FPO	GOV	NPO	FPO	NPO	FPO
Organization formally affiliated with other organization(s) (percent)	69	0	33	100	67	67	0
Contracting with IMPACT led to other community involvements (percent)	38	0	33	33	33	80	0
Relations with other organizations changed due to IMPACT contract (percent)	40	100	33	33	0	60	0
Average number of links to other organizations (excludes competition)	7.2	6.0	12.0	12.0	6.3	8.0	3.0

Note: NPO = nonprofit organization
FPO = for-profit organization
GOV = government agency
Source: Indiana IMPACT Provider Survey.

In addition, two-thirds of the nonprofit SFB organizations reported that their relations with other organizations had changed as a result of contracting with IMPACT, a far higher percentage than we found for the nonprofits in the MFB or NFB categories. Among the for-profit providers, none in the MFB or SFB categories reported relationship changes. In response to questions about the nature of the changes in interaction with other groups or organizations as a result of contracting with IMPACT, responses were primarily positive; they included reports of strengthened ties with local welfare offices, increased opportunities for partnerships, increased opportunities for community involvement, development of a stronger network of organizations, enhanced visibility and credibility in the community, increases in dialogue and collaboration leading to the identification of new resources and ideas, and an increased awareness of community needs.

The findings also suggest that there is considerable variation in the size of the networks in which these different providers participated. Government and nonprofit MFB providers had the highest number of linkages to other organizations (an average of 12.0). That was followed by nonprofit NFB and SFB providers, which reported approximately the same average number of links (7.2 and 8.0). In each faith category, the for-profit providers were least connected to others in their communities. Before placing too much emphasis on this finding, however, we must note that this sample contained only one for-profit NFB and one for-profit SFB provider.

When we looked into the reasons that new linkages were being established, we found that most were the result of efforts to collaborate on service provision. This held true across provider types and faith categories. Two other notable findings were that government providers subcontracted more frequently than others, and that nonprofit MFB providers were more involved in collaborations on funding and resources. Providers in the other categories (including SFB providers) were unlikely to report linkages focused on the sharing of information about funding or resources.

USE OF VOLUNTEERS

We asked providers whether they used volunteers either in their general organizational operations or in their IMPACT programs. The majority of organizations in all three faith categories did use volunteers; 100 percent of the government and nonprofit MFB providers did so, as did approximately 67 percent of the remaining types of providers (including nonprofit SFB providers). Two exceptions were the one for-profit NFB provider and the one for-profit SFB provider, neither of which utilized the services of volunteers. Both government and nonprofit providers used volunteers in their IMPACT programs, including 100 percent of the government agencies, 56 percent of the secular nonprofits, 67 percent of the MFB nonprofits, and 75 percent of the SFB nonprofits. None of the for-profit providers used volunteers in their IMPACT program.

GEOGRAPHICAL REACH

We asked providers to identify their geographic service area by estimating the percentages of the clients they served who came from their immediate neighborhood (within a one-mile radius), from within a five-mile radius, and from more than five miles away.

Among the three categories, nonprofit SFB providers reported the highest percentages of clients from their immediate neighborhood (see table 4.11). Nearly one-third (28 percent) of nonprofit SFB clients come from within one mile of these organizations, compared with 12 to 15 percent of NFB clients and only 3 percent of nonprofit MFB clients. No clients of for-profit faith-based providers came from their neighborhoods, although we must note that there is a fair degree of missing data for the for-profit MFB providers. The majority of providers reported that most of their clients came from within a one- to five-mile radius. Nonprofit SFB clients were the least likely to come from more than five miles away (11 percent).

Conclusions

As outlined above, proponents of Charitable Choice tend to characterize FBOs as more holistic, more connected to and embedded in their communities, and better able to make effective use of volunteers than secular providers. The results of our interviews with our sample of Indiana providers suggest some necessary correctives to those rather broad and sweeping assertions, and they also contribute added information to the growing accumulation of scholarly knowledge about the operations of faith-based service providers.

Table 4.11. Geographic Service Area: Average Percent of Clients Served by Geographic Area (percent)

Geographic Area	Non-Faith-Based			Moderately Faith-Based		Strongly Faith-Based	
	NPO	FPO	GOV	NPO	FPO	NPO	FPO
Neighborhood (within 1 mile)	12	15	12	3	0	28	0
Organization's area of the city (within 1 to 5 miles)	52	45	42	78	33	44	100
Outside organization's area of the city (more than 5 miles away)	28	40	30	18	25	11	0

Note: NPO = nonprofit organization
FPO = for-profit organization
GOV = government agency
Source: Indiana IMPACT Provider Survey.

Those findings also raise a number of issues for public administrators and policymakers.

Our findings are decidedly mixed. In our sample, SFB providers were small, and they had relatively smaller IMPACT contracts; they were also much more dependent upon the income from those contracts. Religious symbolism and observance was a more pronounced element of the programming offered by SFB providers, which clearly felt comfortable using religion as an explicit part of their service delivery. As a result, they reported more clients who participated in religious activity, but they also reported more negative reactions to religious elements of programming from their clients. We found only a slight relationship between faith influence and a more holistic approach to service provision, and then only for SFB providers. SFB providers supplied fewer job-related services than MFB or NFB providers, but they were also more likely to provide non-IMPACT services for which they were not reimbursed. When we examined their community networks, we found that SFB organizations were somewhat less connected than MFB organizations. Given their small size, however, the average number of links that SFB providers did report is noteworthy. We also found that involvement with IMPACT led SFBs to increase their community involvements (thereby enlarging their networks) and change their relationships with other organizations. They were less likely to use volunteers, but when they did use them, they were more likely to use them to provide IMPACT services. (This may be one way they compensate for their smaller staff size.) Finally, SFB providers seemed to focus their service delivery more on their immediate neighborhood. The SFB providers' tighter service delivery areas may be intentional or simply a reflection of their smaller size and the likelihood that, as a result of that smaller size, they are less visible outside their immediate neighborhoods.

When we examined MFB nonprofit and for-profit providers, a number of differences emerged. The MFB for-profit providers were more dependent upon their IMPACT contracts for revenue. They were less likely to be formally affiliated with or otherwise linked to other organizations, and their relations with other organizations did not change as a result of receiving an IMPACT contract. Finally, they were less likely to use volunteers overall, and none of them reported using volunteers to provide IMPACT services.

These results are limited to job training and placement services, and additional research is needed to determine whether studies of other types of social service providers will yield similar data. Service area, population diversity, and other local characteristics may influence the desire and ability of FBOs to participate in government programs or use religion in service delivery. In addition, our small sample size limits our ability to draw statistical comparisons; it would be helpful to see if research on larger provider samples substantiates our results. Finally, work should proceed on how best to measure the role and impact of faith in social service organizations. We asked agency and program administrators a series of questions about organizational structure and process, but it would be helpful to have detailed interviews with service staff and on-site observations of service delivery to verify and quantify the role faith plays in service delivery and organizational operations, and to craft and refine more precise empirical measures.

Even these limited data, however, suggest several concerns for policymakers and public managers. Church–state issues have been among the most contentious areas of the policy debate surrounding Charitable Choice and the president's Faith-Based Initiative. Major concerns have included the potential for proselytizing vulnerable populations, for awarding state contracts based on criteria other than capacity (Kennedy 2003), and whether state governments have the resources and ability to monitor for constitutional compliance. Our findings suggest that at least some of these concerns may be justified. Providers reported oversight on fiscal and program matters, but not on religious content of the services being provided. In addition, some reported using religion quite explicitly in their IMPACT services and clearly did not feel a need to modify those practices. As we note in chapter 7, public managers have an obligation to ensure constitutional compliance by the providers with whom they contract. Discharge of that duty may require added training for providers and public managers alike.

It is also unclear whether some of the smaller, less-connected, and less-experienced FBOs would have received contracts if they had not received substantial technical assistance from the state through the FaithWorks program (Farnsley 2001). If the policy goal is to encourage FBOs to build capacity and thus enrich the pool of providers from which government agencies choose their partners, it would seem prudent to examine the cost-effectiveness of these extensive technical assistance programs. For example, our results suggest the SFB providers need the partnership with and training from government to enhance their networks and (presumably) to improve their service delivery. Any fiscal evaluation of the Faith-Based Initiative must consider the added cost to government agencies of providing that training. Cost/benefit analysis should be used to address this issue.

SFB organizations that rely upon volunteers to deliver services present a specific management challenge, depending upon the degree of professionalism that the contracting agency expects and has bargained for. The use of volunteers may allow an FBO to provide more caring services, or services that can be delivered for less money, but costs associated with higher turnover and deficits in professional training also often accompany a program delivered by volunteers.

Finally, we identified a number of for-profit faith-based providers in the course of this study that seem to operate differently from their nonprofit counterparts in several potentially important respects. The for-profits' heavier reliance on IMPACT funding may make them more vulnerable to future changes in the program or contract priorities. In addition, their smaller networks may limit their ability to form partnerships with other organizations in the service delivery system, and evidently their government contracts did not lead them to increase their relations with other organizations (possibly improving their service delivery). Their lack of volunteer use eliminates one of the benefits hypothesized for faith-based service delivery (although, as noted above, volunteer use is not without its costs). In terms of government contracting, therefore, for-profit organizations may bring different advantages and disadvantages to the table and funding agencies need to be aware of these differences to determine the most appropriate contract arrangements. It would be interesting to know why these organizations have chosen to operate as for-profit corporations—whether they began as traditional for-profits without a faith orientation that saw a business opportunity in Charitable Choice and moved to capitalize on it—or whether they are a genuinely new phenomenon on the social service landscape. This would certainly seem to be an area where further research is warranted.

New program approaches promise new ways of understanding service delivery and meeting the needs of clients. They also may require flexible management responses. Our research suggests that, in this respect, at least, Charitable Choice is no different. Further study will be needed to evaluate these new developments and assess the degree to which they are able to improve outcomes for both providers and clients. If we look at these findings in the context of the claims made by both supporters and opponents of faith-based initiatives, we can summarize them as follows:

- More strongly faith-based organizations were small and heavily dependent on government funding, which could lead one to question their capacity, stability, and contribution to the delivery system.
- The claim that FBOs provide more holistic services was not supported; the differences were, at best, marginal.
- The claim that Charitable Choice and its progeny would lead to widespread "load shedding" by government (i.e., an effort to reduce expenditures by inducing voluntary organizations to provide some services without charge) was only moderately supported, and occurred mostly with SFB organizations.
- Though there was some evidence of "mission creep," as feared by some religious critics, the changes that did occur were viewed as mostly positive by the organizations involved.
- There was some evidence supporting the contention that FBOs will make more use of volunteers.
- There was some evidence supporting the contention that SFB organizations were more "embedded" in their neighborhoods. They were, however, less connected to other providers; and government funding, in fact, increased their connection to others.
- Concerns about constitutional violations were supported by evidence of inadequate government monitoring and possibly inappropriate injection of religious elements in services by some FBOs.
- There is evidence that for-profit faith-based providers have entered the delivery system and that these providers display fewer of the "beneficial" characteristics of their nonprofit faith-based counterparts.

Chapter 5

The Management of

Faith-Based Service Providers

$\mathcal{A}$s we have seen, Charitable Choice legislation was an invitation to religious organizations—especially smaller, grassroots organizations—to work with government by contracting with state agencies to deliver social services to the poor. The invitation was expressly intended to attract participation by faith-based organizations (FBOs) that had not previously worked with government. Proponents saw these organizations as an "untapped resource," while opponents pointed to the transaction costs associated with such contracts and warned that small nonprofit organizations would not have the management depth to comply with government reporting requirements or to maintain state-mandated fiscal controls. This, of course, raised preliminary questions: What *are* the management capacities of FBOs? What are the management practices of religious service providers, and do the capacities of congregations and faith-based 501(c)(3) affiliates differ? A number of nonprofit scholars have investigated these issues, and many of their findings have been summarized in subsequent publications, primarily a special issue of *Nonprofit and Voluntary Sector Quarterly* (Milofsky and Cnaan 1997) and a largely theoretical book of readings by Demerath and his colleagues (1998). Articles aimed at practitioners have also appeared (Brinckerhoff 1999; Queen 2000).

Questions Asked: What Capacities Are Needed?

Obviously, the management capacities of FBOs are critical to the success of faith-based initiatives. Determining what those capacities are, however, is not simple. There is a robust literature on non-profit management; are the observations and conclusions of that literature equally applicable to FBOs? Are there assets or liabilities unique to such organizations? How able will FBOs be to cope with the accountability and reporting requirements that accompany government contracts? Will they have to shift resources from service provision to compliance, or do they have sufficient management skills and resources to avoid that problem? Will they have the resources and management skills to cope with cash flow issues in states like Indiana, which pay only upon receiving documentation of successful outcomes? And how well will FBO managers cope with the "moving targets" of state contract priorities and funding availability? These are the issues we wanted to explore with our sample of provider organizations.

Methodology

Although several management issues have been identified, the literature on the management of faith-based service providers is quite limited. We concluded that an exploratory approach to the measurement of management capacity was most appropriate for our research.

Identifying Management Challenges

The literature reminds us that FBOs can provide social services through a wide variety of organizational forms (Stone and Wood 1997; Cnaan, Wineburg, and Boddie 1999). These include congregational programs (in-house or outreach services), participation in coalitions and interfaith organizations, paradenominational organizations, religiously affiliated independent local agencies, religiously affiliated franchises, and more secularized affiliated organizations. Each of these organizational forms is different, and each is likely to face distinctive management challenges.

Religious versus Secular Authority
One prominent theme in the literature flows from the characterization of denominations as dual structures by Chaves (1993). Chaves described the existence and consequences of parallel religious

authority structures and agency structures. The latter are responsible for tasks which, while formally attached to the denomination, require additional activity beyond worship (e.g., producing educational material). Harris also discusses this distinction (1998, 183–85). As she notes,

> Ministers are seen by themselves and lay people as having an authority that is different in quality and derivation from that attributed to secular organization roles. In terms of Christian theological language, their authority is rooted in divine inspiration. Using Weberian terminology (1964), ministers acting in their congregational context carry "charismatic" or "traditional" authority, or some combination of the two.

However, congregations also need to respond to their external organizational environments. Consequently, Harris concludes, "Congregations can be seen, then, as having two different systems of authority; the traditional or charismatic one which attaches to ministers of religion in their congregational context, and the rational-legal one which is more familiar in secular voluntary organizations" (Harris 1998, 184).

This same duality has been identified in faith-based service providers. For example, in a study of 105 religiously based commercial ventures, La Barbera (1991) identified conflicts arising as a result of the organization's need to generate revenue and to engage in economic development activities in relation to the religious mission and "spiritual development" of the organization. Cnaan, Wineburg, and Boddie have also addressed the organizational implications of faith-based social service provision (1999, 303–4) and the complexity of dual authority systems. Providers may thus be subject to both religious and secular authority (e.g., state regulations), and these authorities may often be in conflict. Jeavons (1994, xvii) outlines a number of quite basic issues that FBOs may face in attempting to meet such a dual mission of witness and service: (1) creating and sustaining a religious organizational culture and basic principles of human resource management for staff and volunteers; (2) ensuring that resource development and fundraising remain consistent with their religious witness and values; (3) determining the appropriate roles and activities of boards and executives; and (4) careful, formal organizational planning that recognizes—and takes advantage of—the distinctive aspects of religious organizations.

Managing Growth

A second theme in the literature has revolved around issues that emerge as service delivery moves from congregationally based programs to larger, freestanding service organizations. Stone and Wood (1997) have outlined the problems that may arise when organizations that began with simple structures, uncomplicated networks, and the dominance of a founder's religious vision expand and grow. The challenges include an increasing need for internal coordination, an ability to interact with larger numbers of external actors, and the increased salience of competing standards of legitimacy. Nitterhouse (1997) discovered financial management, information, and control system problems in a small sample of faith-based providers as organizations moved from informal systems to 501(c)(3) status. Home congregations were often not able to help with this transition, due to their own limited capacities. The resulting deficiencies had the potential of exacerbating problems, and they especially complicated the effort to convince funders that the provider remained viable and capable of performing.

General Management Problems

FBOs must cope not only with these specialized issues but also with the general management challenges common to all organizations. Jeavons's scholarship is particularly illuminating; he used case studies of seven FBOs to discuss the principal concerns of management in Christian service organizations. He described "ten points of focus" requiring attention by those responsible for the leadership, management, and governance of Christian service organizations (Jeavons 1994, 211–18). He identified these as the need to focus on vocation; witness as well as service; means as well as ends; servanthood; stewardship; engagement in ministry; and caring for, creating, and sustaining a Christian organizational culture, integrity, and leadership. Many of these management tasks—means and ends, stewardship, maintenance of an organizational culture—are challenges experienced in all service organizations, whether faith based or secular.

Finally, several studies have looked in more detail at a variety of specific management challenges. La Barbera (1991) identified a number of staff difficulties experienced by religiously based commercial ventures. These included the interrelated problems of attracting skilled staff, the inability to pay competitive salaries, overwork and burnout, high turnover, and inadequate staff skills and training. Poole and others (2002) examined fifteen government-funded community-based organizations (CBOs) involved in welfare reform in Texas, of which seven were FBOs. They evaluated organizational capacity in terms of goals, management, technology, funding, and community involvement. Though most CBOs had skilled managers, a number of the small FBOs lacked experience in contract management. In addition, the smaller organizations (FBO and secular alike) had the least sophisticated management control systems. There was great variation in the degree to which providers were integrated into community structures, and most CBO managers did not have expertise in community development. Finally, in a study of community service organizations, Kearns, Park, and Yankoski (2005) found few differences between secular and faith-based providers in terms of self-reported capacity to deliver services, organizational design, and administration, though FBOs reported a lower capacity to use objective data and analysis in decision making.

Our goal was to advance this discussion by exploring the degree to which a provider's faith orientation affects organizational management. To measure management challenges, we drew upon the organizational theory literature to assess the factors that had been identified as important to mission and governance, internal operations, and external relations. Our analysis focused on the following issues: (1) how management challenges and capacity should be measured; (2) the degree to which the management challenges of faith-based providers and non-faith-based (NFB) providers differed; and (3) how management challenges related to other organizational factors, such as age, size, and contracting experience.

Background on the Indiana Experience

The providers in our sample were located in Indiana, and the composition of this sample was a product of Indiana's experience with implementation of Charitable Choice; it is thus useful to preface our empirical analysis with a brief overview of that experience.

In 1999, Indiana began an aggressive effort to reach out to FBOs, and it instituted an awareness and technical assistance program called FaithWorks. It awarded a contract to a for-profit consultant and sponsored workshops around the state to which religious organizations were invited. (Nonreligious providers were not specifically targeted but were welcome to attend, and many did.) In 2000, approximately 75 of the over 400 organizations that had attended these workshops applied for state contracts. The result was that the number of faith-based providers in the Indiana Manpower Placement and Comprehensive Training (IMPACT) program tripled between 2000 and 2001—from 3 providers to 9. Even that number subsequently dropped. In contract year 2002, it was reduced to 5, and by contract year 2003, it was back to 3. We explored the reasons for the attrition, and found that it was largely the result of decreased state funding and corresponding shifts in contracting priorities. By 2003, the faith-based and secular providers that had continued contracting with the IMPACT program reported reduced contract size and changes in program emphases. Those that were no longer contracting with IMPACT reported a variety of reasons for dropping out: decreased funding levels, rejection of their bids, or simply an organizational decision that the burdens of doing business with the state outweighed the benefits. Many of the providers that were no longer involved reported negative consequences flowing from the nonrenewal of their contracts; those negative consequences included the termination of programs, reduction of services, and staff layoffs. It is not possible to assess what percentage of the organizations experiencing these difficulties failed to be renewed because they lacked the management depth and resources to cope with the demands of a government contracting regime, but the likelihood that such deficits were implicated underlines the need for better understanding of the challenges and pitfalls of Charitable Choice's invitation to FBOs.

Data: Management Challenges Measured

A number of factors are commonly used to assess organizational capacity (e.g., see Poole et al. 2002). In the survey we administered, we asked about a variety of these factors. We asked about the organization's use of technology, its written policies, how it handled program evaluation and reporting, its recruitment and training mechanisms, and questions intended to gauge its financial health. In addition, for this exploratory study, we added an open-ended question we felt would assist us in assessing capacity, in which we asked managers to identify what they believed to be significant organizational challenges. That is, we asked managers to identify areas where, in their opinion, their organization lacked sufficient capacity to address important issues affecting program delivery and effectiveness. In addition to that open-ended inquiry, we asked respondents specifically about thirty-one factors that might pose organizational problems. We combined these into three indices of management challenges as follows:

- Mission and governance (five questions): clearly defining our mission, achieving our mission, recruiting/keeping effective board, smoothly functioning board, managing board/staff relations.
- External relations (ten questions): obtaining adequate information, identifying and targeting results, strategic planning process, implementing plans, delivering high-quality services, meeting the needs of current clients, attracting new clients, enhancing visibility and reputation, developing/maintaining good relations with other organizations, measuring program outcomes.
- Internal operations (sixteen questions): recruiting/keeping qualified administrators, recruiting/keeping qualified staff, recruiting/keeping qualified and reliable volunteers, managing human resources, managing programs, communicating internally, developing and using teamwork, developing/sustaining good working relationship in the organization, dealing with disputes in the organization, reorganizing structure if needed, anticipating financial needs, obtaining funding or other financial resources, financial management and accounting, managing the facilities/space, using information technology effectively, using technology for service provision.

Several other factors with the potential to affect management practices or capacity were also measured. These included organization size (as measured by number of full-time employees) and age, the number of years the organization had contracted with

IMPACT, the length of the executive director's tenure, and whether or not the organization had received state technical assistance.

Findings: Relationships among Faith, Capacity, and Other Factors

The data disclosed a great deal of diversity among providers. Descriptive statistics for the variables used in this analysis are shown in table 5.1. For each of our management indices, possible scores ranged from zero to the maximum. The means show the average number of challenges of each type that the organizations in the data set had. For example, the average number of mission and governance challenges our organizations had was 0.93. Because each organization in the data set could have had from 0 to 5 mission and governance challenges, the low mean shows that, on the whole, these organizations had relatively few of these types of challenges. Among the other variables, the faith-based index ranged from 0 to 7 (with a mean of almost 2), organizational age ranged from 2 to 100 years (with a mean of 33), director tenure ranged from less than 1 to 37 years (with a mean of 11.8), and the number of years contracting with IMPACT ranged from 1 to 12 (with a mean of 5).

Most of our findings were not statistically significant. Again, that is not surprising, given the small number of providers studied and the fact that even this small sample is further broken down into organizational subsets in some analyses. Despite the lack of statistical significance, analysis of the data reveals interesting patterns of correlations, which arguably illuminate the relationship between faith and organizational capacity and open avenues for further analysis. (Table A.1 in appendix A shows the correlations between the variables.)

Management Challenges versus Organizational Characteristics

The large correlations among the management challenges, especially internal and external challenges (0.717), indicated that management can be weak or strong on a number of dimensions simultaneously. For example, organizations that had more internal

Table 5.1. Descriptive Statistics of Management Challenge Indices and Key Variables

Statistic	Mission and Governance	External Relations	Internal Operations	Faith-Based Index (0–8)	Size (log)	Age	Received Technical Assistance	Director Tenure	Number of Years Contracting with IMPACT
Mean	0.93	4.14	5.45	1.93	1	33	0.69	11.75	5.03
Median	0	4	5	0	0.85	23	1	6.5	5
Standard deviation	1.28	2.89	4.15	2.43	0.77	30	.47	10.46	3.35
Minimum	0	0	0	0	0	2	0	0.33	1
Maximum	5	10	16	7	2.93	100	1	37	12

Source: Indiana IMPACT Provider Survey.

challenges would also be quite likely to have had more external challenges (and vice versa). The correlation between the internal management challenges and the mission and governance challenges is also positive, although smaller (0.518). This means that those organizations with more internal management challenges were also likely to have mission and governance challenges (although the likelihood of having these two types of challenges is not quite as strong as the likelihood of having both internal and external management challenges). The relationship between external management challenges and mission and governance challenges is essentially the same as the one between internal management challenges and mission and governance challenges. Larger organizations were more considerably likely to be older and less likely to be faith based. Older organizations were more likely to have had the same executive director longer and more likely to have contracted for a longer period of time with IMPACT; they were less likely to be faith based. Older organizations were also more likely to report lower numbers of mission and governance challenges.

Overall, organizations indicated slightly fewer challenges with respect to mission and governance if they had contracted with IMPACT for a longer period of time and if their director had longer tenure. There were relatively small correlations for technical assistance, number of years contracting with IMPACT, and director tenure, and we concluded that these variables were not strongly related to management challenges. We thus focused the remainder of the analysis on the effects of age, size, and faith orientation.

We examined the management indices in detail, using the following logic: We first determined the percentage of providers by degree of faith orientation (not faith-based, NFB; moderately faith-based, MFB; or strongly faith-based, SFB) that had identified specific management challenges (see appendix A, table A.2). To discover where faith differences might be related to those management challenges, we identified challenges where we found a substantial percentage difference (defined as 19 percent or more in the fifth column of the table) between SFB and NFB organizations. We then computed a correlation between the faith-based scale and the management challenges. We used these and partial correlations to examine the extent to which age or size appeared to be related to the management challenges. For example, if a partial correlation between faith influence and a management challenge, controlling for size, is much smaller than the original faith influence–management challenge correlation, we concluded that size is likely a factor in that particular management challenge. To further analyze that likelihood, we then computed the partial correlation between size and the management challenge, this time controlling for faith influence. (These results are shown in table A.3 in appendix A.) That calculation allowed us to determine the direction of the size–management challenge relationship. In other words, if there is a size relationship, is it larger or smaller organizations that experience more management challenges? We then repeated this procedure for age as a potentially influencing variable. Appendix A provides more details on these calculations.

This process allowed us to identify several challenges that were positively related to faith influence and for which correlations did not change when we controlled for age or size. More SFB providers indicated greater challenges with the strategic planning process and with the management of facilities and space. After controlling for age, the correlation was even higher in both cases; and after controlling for size, the correlation was higher for facilities management. Regardless of the age or size of the organization, SFB organizations appear likely to have problems with strategic planning and facilities management.

There are, conversely, several areas where the challenges appeared to be higher for less faith-based organizations. Those included "achieving our mission," "communicating internally," "developing and sustaining good working relationships," "anticipating financial needs," "obtaining funding," and "using technology for service provision." These areas were reported to be more problematic for less faith-based organizations, and they remained so even after we controlled for age and size. In addition, the item asking about recruiting and retaining qualified administrators, though not meeting the 19 percent difference threshold we had established between NFB and SFB criteria, was reportedly more of a problem for NFB organizations.

There were several areas where FBOs indicated they had more challenges but where partial correlations decrease after controlling for age or size. These included "recruiting/keeping effective board members," "managing board/staff relations," "delivering high-quality services," "attracting new clients," and "using information technology effectively." When we explored the relationship between these challenges, faith influence, age, and size, the original faith influence–management challenge correlations dropped, and they did so when either age or size was controlled. (The size of those correlations can be seen in table A.3 in appendix A.)

The partial correlations for "recruiting/keeping effective board" and "managing board/staff relations" dropped when we controlled for age, indicating that age as well as faith influence were related to these management challenges. However, the partial correlation of the faith influence with management challenge does not disappear completely, an indication that faith influence is still related to the management challenges. To determine the direction of the age effect, we then performed partial correlations of these management challenges and age, controlling for faith orientation. We found a negative correlation with age in both cases, which implies that younger organizations encounter greater challenges recruiting board members and managing their board and staff relations. This is in addition to the difficulties in these areas that more SFB organizations experience.

The positive correlation of faith and challenges with delivering high-quality services and attracting new clients both dropped when we controlled for the size of the organization. Again, the partial correlation for delivering high-quality services and faith influence did not disappear, indicating that this challenge is still related to faith influence. The partial correlation for attracting new clients and faith influence, however, drops, and we can conclude that there is no independent faith orientation influence on this particular management challenge. There are strong negative partial correlations for both of these challenges and size, controlling for faith, which would imply that smaller organizations experience more of these challenges, after controlling for faith influence.

There were several other noteworthy findings. The negative correlation between faith influence and the challenges of managing programs and using information technology effectively indicated that more SFB providers had fewer problems in these regards. These correlations decrease when we control for age and size, respectively, indicating that these are also relevant variables. In fact, the correlation between using information technology effectively and faith drops when controlling for size, indicating that faith influence is not independently related to this management challenge. The partial correlation between program management and age, controlling for faith, is positive, indicating that older organizations have somewhat more problems with program management. The partial correlation between effective technology use and size, controlling for faith, is also positive, indicating that larger organizations experienced challenges in the effective use of technology more often than smaller organizations did.

FOR-PROFIT PROVIDERS

Because we had four faith-based for-profit providers in our sample, we had the opportunity to examine how the management challenges they faced compared with those faced by the nonprofit faith-based providers. We were also able to compare the management challenges of government contractors with those of the private NFB providers. These comparisons are displayed in table 5.2.

Our data showed that, among the NFB providers, the nonprofits reported a wide variety of management challenges. The one NFB for-profit provider indicated only a few management challenges, none of which involved organizational mission and governance. The three government providers, however, indicated difficulties in achieving their missions. They also reported numerous problems with external relations, in most cases in higher numbers than the nonprofits. In fact, all of them reported problems with implementing plans, delivering high-quality services, and meeting the needs of current clients. In addition, they reported a range of problems with internal relations, and all of them reported problems in anticipating financial needs.

In the moderately faith-based category, we had the same number of nonprofits and for-profits. This category, therefore, provided us with the best opportunity to make non- and for-profit comparisons. Neither group reported widespread problems with mission and governance. They were also similar in the degree to which they reported a variety of problems with external relations. They differed, however, in the degree to which they experienced internal problems. In most cases, the for-profits reported fewer internal challenges than the nonprofits.

In the SFB category, we had only one for-profit organization, and that organization reported no management challenges (even

Table 5.2. Faith Influence, Organizational Auspice, and Management Challenges (percent)

Management Challenge	NFB			MFB		SFB	
	NPO (13)	FPO (1)	GOV (3)	NPO (3)	FPO (3)	NPO (5)	FPO (1)
Mission and governance							
Clearly defining our mission	15	0	0	0	0	20	0
Achieving our mission	31	0	67	0	33	20	0
Recruiting/keeping effective board	23	0	0	0	0	60	0
Smoothly functioning board	15	0	0	0	0	20	0
Managing board–staff relations	31	0	0	0	0	60	0
External relations							
Obtaining adequate information	54	100	67	0	33	60	0
Identifying and targeting results	46	0	67	33	33	40	0
Strategic planning process	38	0	67	33	33	80	0
Implementing plans	23	100	100	33	33	40	0
Delivering high-quality services	8	0	100	0	33	60	0
Meeting the needs of current clients	46	0	100	33	33	80	0
Attracting new clients	54	0	67	33	67	100	0
Enhancing visibility and reputation	77	0	33	0	0	80	0
Developing/maintaining good relations with other organizations	31	0	33	0	0	20	0
Measuring program outcomes	46	0	0	33	33	20	0
Internal operations							
Recruiting/keeping qualified administrators	15	0	0	0	0	0	0
Recruiting/keeping qualified staff	38	0	33	0	0	60	0
Recruiting/keeping qualified and reliable volunteers	31	0	33	67	0	40	0
Managing human resources	31	0	67	0	0	40	0
Managing our programs	31	0	67	0	33	20	0

Table 5.2. continued.

Management Challenge	NFB			MFB		SFB	
	NPO (13)	FPO (1)	GOV (3)	NPO (3)	FPO (3)	NPO (5)	FPO (1)
Communicating internally	62	0	33	67	0	20	0
Developing and using teamwork	54	0	0	0	0	40	0
Developing/sustaining good working relationships in the organization	54	0	33	33	0	20	0
Dealing with disputes in the organization	31	0	0	0	0	40	0
Reorganizing structure if needed	38	0	33	33	0	60	0
Anticipating financial needs	54	0	100	33	33	40	0
Obtaining funding or other financial resources	92	100	67	67	33	80	0
Financial management and accounting	31	0	67	0	0	40	0
Managing the facilities/ space	23	0	33	33	0	60	0
Using information technology effectively	46	100	67	33	33	40	0
Using technology for service provision	54	100	33	0	33	20	0

Note: NFB = non-faith-based
MFB = moderately faith-based
SFB = strongly faith-based
NPO = nonprofit organization
FPO = for-profit organization
GOV = government agency
Source: Indiana IMPACT Provider Survey.

after a series of prompts and probes during the interview). SFB nonprofits, however, in many cases reported the highest levels of management challenges of any group. Eighty percent of them reported problems with strategic planning, meeting the needs of current clients, enhancing visibility and reputation, and obtaining funding; and all of them reported problems with attracting new clients. It must be remembered, however, that they were also the smallest and youngest organizations.

Conclusions

Our data clearly indicate that there is a relationship between management challenges and the faith dimension of organizations. The causes of those management challenges, however, were not limited to the effects of faith—we found significant relationships between management challenges and organizational age and size.

Our research suggests that FBOs demonstrate both management strengths and weaknesses. More SFB providers indicated greater challenges in the areas of governance and external relations. The former includes recruiting and retaining effective board members and managing the relationship between the board and staff. The latter category includes strategic planning and the delivery of high-quality services. FBOs also had more challenges with internal operations like facilities management. A number of these challenges were also related to age or size.

These governance challenges may be a reflection of a dual authority structure; for example, religious leadership may have difficulties recruiting and working with nonreligious board members. Staff may experience similar difficulties. The literature suggests that newly established or growing FBOs might encounter issues with external actors and competing standards; if so, that might account for the difficulties our FBOs had with strategic planning and facilities management. The strategic planning process may be more of a challenge for FBOs because they may not be as familiar as other nonprofits with the process, especially the assessment and evaluation of complex external environments. Managing their facilities may pose more of a challenge because faith-based groups may face competing demands for their facilities from their congregations or from other community programs.

Conversely, more SFB providers reported fewer challenges with mission focus and accomplishment; and they also reported fewer challenges with a number of internal processes, including internal communication, internal working relationships, anticipating financial needs, obtaining funding, using technology for service provision, recruiting and retaining qualified administrators, and managing programs. None of these challenges was related to size, and only the last was related to age.

The finding that FBOs have fewer internal problems may indicate that, while it may be problematic for governance, a dual authority structure does not seem to be creating internal stresses and strains. More specifically, achieving their mission may be less of a challenge for FBOs because they usually have a well-articulated and focused mission related to their faith. Communicating internally and developing and sustaining good working relationships may be less of a challenge because their employees and volunteers are likely to share the same faith and religious culture; shared backgrounds and worldviews would certainly facilitate communication. Similarly, obtaining funding and anticipating financial needs may be less of a challenge for FBOs because they can often draw on the support of a congregation or other affiliated religious institution or community.

Our comparison of non- and for-profit providers indicates that the for-profits reported fewer management challenges than the nonprofits in every faith orientation category. Because there was only one for-profit in the NFB and SFB category, the only meaningful comparison of faith-based nonprofits and for-profits was among providers in the moderately faith-based category. In that category, nonprofits and for-profits were similar with regard to governance, mission, and external relations. For-profits, however, indicated fewer problems with internal operations. We might speculate that in for-profit organizations, the focus upon the bottom line should lead to more explicit lines of authority and greater clarity of mission, both of which would be reflected in the internal management of the organization. Our small numbers and lack of explicit data make these results, and our interpretation of them, speculative. This would seem, however, to be a fruitful area for future research, adding an additional dimension of variation for assessing the performance of faith-based service providers.

Indeed, each of these findings suggests a number of additional questions requiring further study. If other research identifies differences in nonprofit and for-profit internal operations, what might cause these and what might the consequences be for the providers, their clients, and their funders? Is provider efficiency, effectiveness, or survival enhanced or attenuated? Are client outcomes better or worse? The answers to these and related questions will be important for government funders, which are ultimately responsible for the operations and consequences of publicly funded service delivery systems.

To sum up: our investigation of these issues suggests that public managers cannot rely upon the existence of a "faith component" to indicate whether a potential provider will be well or poorly managed. Overall, with respect to organizational management, religious providers are neither better nor worse than secular ones; however, they are likely to be different. Strongly religious providers as a category display a more consistent focus upon their organizational mission; at the same time, our findings suggest that SFB organizations (especially smaller and newer ones) are the providers most likely to experience management problems in governance and external relations.

Chapter 6

Measuring Effectiveness

*A*MONG ALL THE ASSUMPTIONS AND CLAIMS
MADE BY PROPONENTS OF CHARITABLE
Choice laws and President George W. Bush's Faith-Based Initiative,
the most insistent—and arguably the most important—was the repeated assertion that faith-based organizations (FBOs) were "more
effective" than secular providers. Members of Congress routinely
intoned that "everyone knows" religious organizations achieve better results. The president frequently alluded to the importance of
what he called "the faith factor," and on more than one occasion he
insisted that "faith works."

There was an essential incoherence to many of these claims that
bothered many scholars; if "faith" is indeed the essential element in
effective service delivery, Charitable Choice efforts will meet with
an insurmountable constitutional barrier. As we have noted several
times in previous chapters, the First Amendment does not prevent
government from purchasing secular services from religious vendors, but it most definitely does forbid the exchange of tax dollars
for religious goods and services. If FBOs produce better results because their own faith or mission somehow enhances their ability
to provide effective services, there is no constitutional barrier to
partnerships between these organizations and government agencies—but there is also no reason to believe that this is the case, and
there was none in 1996 when Section 104 of the Personal Responsibility and Work Opportunity Reconciliation Act of 1996 was first
enacted.

The claim that FBOs achieve better results for clients raises a
number of definitional issues, not least the question with which
we started our study: What do we mean by "faith-based"? Are all
religiously affiliated organizations more effective? If not, how do
we know which ones? Are FBOs more effective at certain social

services than others? What is the evidence upon which claims of greater efficacy are based? What are the organizational dimensions that will characterize effective FBOs, and differentiate them from others? And for that matter, what do we mean by "effective"?

Questions Asked: Seeking Outcomes

There were absolutely no empirical, quantitative data comparing outcomes of faith-based and secular social services providers when we began our study; and to the best of our knowledge, there are still no such data. Researchers have continued to do qualitative evaluations instead, and the reasons are quite clear: The methodological challenges—and the incredible difficulty of obtaining usable data—are formidable, as we have previously recounted. Our challenge was to limit the question sufficiently to allow us to produce reliable results.

We began with a deceptively simple question: Do faith-based job training and placement providers do a better job than secular job training and placement providers? We defined "better job" only by objective, measurable criteria, that is, placement rates, and wages and benefits paid. And we limited that inquiry to the organizations providing those services as part of the Indiana Manpower Placement and Comprehensive Training (IMPACT) program. That we chose to work with so narrow a sample, coming from one state and one type of social service, meant that our findings would not necessarily be generalizable; but it also meant that we should be able to produce statistical analyses that would be both meaningful and credible. It would, in short, be a beginning. And it would provide something that had thus far been lacking in a debate over effectiveness that was being conducted entirely through warring recitations of anecdotes: actual data.

Methodology

Perhaps our most significant finding was our first: There is very little research about effectiveness of social services—not just analyses of services provided by religious organizations but also analyses of services delivered by any providers. When we began a literature review looking for studies of faith-based provision, we found that Chaves and Tsitsos (2001) had investigated the question of what social services religious organizations provide and how they do it. Kramer and others (2002) had asked similar questions, but they limited their inquiry to the provision of employment-related services. Monsma and Mounts (2002) have examined how faith-based welfare-to-work programs differ from their secular counterparts, in terms of both funding from government and the services offered. We found little or no published literature examining differences in outcomes for clients who receive social services from faith-based versus secular providers. What was more surprising, however, was that we found comparatively little information about the consequences of providers' different organizational attributes for social welfare outcomes, in spite of the fact that there is a large literature on their differences in other dimensions (Heinrich 2000).

Looking at this deficit of information in the context of nonprofit versus for-profit providers, Salamon (1993) and Weisbrod (1989) have suggested that the lack of empirical research is due mainly to problems associated with measuring outcomes, particularly those of social welfare programs, where quality is not easily quantified and multiple objectives and constituencies frequently exist. These arguments are equally valid in examinations of differences between faith-based and secular providers of services. Job training programs arguably have the most easily quantifiable outcomes, with comparatively well-defined objectives. Unlike social services more generally, there also is a considerable literature on evaluations of the efficacy of job training programs (Bloom et al. 1997; Heckman, Lalonde, and Smith 1999; Orr et al. 1996). Consequently, a comparison of job training programs provided by faith-based and secular providers of social services seemed a logical place to start.

RESEARCH DESIGN

The credibility of any research conclusions depends upon the appropriateness and adequacy of the methodology employed by the researchers. Because the "real world" seldom offers ideal conditions for empirical research, decisions about research design often must be made to accommodate imperfect realities, and those decisions must be explained and justified, in order to allow others to assess the usefulness of the information.

In our case, the ideal study design would have begun with the random assignment of individuals into the available training programs, and it would have continued with observation of their outcomes over an extended period of time after they completed training and were placed (if they were) in employment. Unfortunately, the data available to us were observational and consisted only of information on those individuals who received job training from faith-based and secular programs over a period of two and a half years. Clients were assigned to faith-based and secular job training providers by caseworkers. Their initial assignments to those caseworkers were made in a systematic fashion, and they were based on the order in which they arrived at the welfare office. If we had concluded that the caseworkers were proceeding to assign individual clients randomly to participating faith-based and secular programs, we still could have justified the employment of statistical methods appropriate for randomized designs. That is, the causal effect of job training at a faith-based provider, as compared with training at a secular provider, could have been obtained by a regression analysis to determine the impact on labor market outcomes (dependent variables such as wages and hours worked) of a variety of factors; that is, we could have determined whether training was provided by a faith-based or secular provider (our independent variable of interest), while controlling for client characteristics such as gender and education.

However, even though client assignment to a caseworker could reasonably be considered quasi-random, it is more plausible to believe that individual caseworkers would possess systematic preferences for particular providers, faith based or secular, based upon their own religious or professional convictions, their prior experience with particular providers, or other predispositions. If that is indeed the case, standard regression methods will provide biased estimates of the causal effects of the type of job training provider on labor market outcomes. To avoid that potential bias, we used an instrumental variables regression approach to estimate the causal impact of type of job training provider. This is a two-stage regression analysis, where the influence of caseworker assignment is removed from the final stage. (See tables A.4 and A.5 in appendix A for further information.)

Employment Outcome Data

The dataset we used was compiled from three sources: financial management report, extracts from the Indiana Client Eligibility System (ICES), and monthly job placement reports submitted by the counties, recorded in fiscal years (October 1–September 30) 2000 and 2001, and October 1 through December 31, 2002. We used financial management reports to identify the provider of the job training services. The ICES contains basic demographic information for clients: sex, age, race, and education levels, and the identity of the caseworker. We used monthly job placement reports to identify the clients who were placed into jobs; those reports also contained information on the client's wage rate, the number of hours worked, and whether the client received health insurance benefits. The data set contained employment data for twenty-six of our thirty providers. (It is not clear why the Family and Social Services Administration did not have the data for the other four providers. During our personal interviews conducted with these omitted providers, they all reported that they expected to fulfill significant portions of their contracts, indicating that they had active programs. These four providers had been in business for over twenty years, and only one was small. In addition, two of these providers were faith based and two were secular.) The analysis we conducted includes only the twenty-six providers for which we have employment data.

Providers of job training services were categorized as faith based or secular in the same way we had categorized them for purposes of organizational analysis. We used surveys completed by the providers to measure eight dimensions related to the influence of faith in the organization (Bielefeld, Littlepage, and Thelin 2002). In this analysis, providers of job training services were categorized as faith based or secular in the same way we had categorized them for purposes of organizational analysis in chapters 4 and 5. Zero indicates not faith based and eight indicates most strongly faith based. Table 4.3 lists the eight dimensions we used to compute the degree to which faith influenced an organization. Organizations scoring positively on one or more dimensions were classified as faith based in this study, and their value on an 8-point scale was used to designate the degree to which faith influenced the organization. We considered only individuals receiving services in Marion and Lake counties because these were both urban counties and contained the vast majority of all Indiana clients. After appropriate cleaning of the raw data files, including manual verification of certain data elements on a case-by-case basis, the sample suitable for analysis contained 5,683 observations.

The first measure of outcome is a binary (0, 1) variable for whether or not the client was placed in a job after completing training. Conditional on being placed, the outcomes are a binary variable for full-time versus part-time work status, the hourly wage rate, and a binary variable for whether the client was covered by health insurance at the job. We defined full-time employment as working at least thirty-five hours per week. However, to check the robustness of our results, we also estimated models in which full-time employment status was defined by at least forty hours of work per week.

The main independent variable of interest was a variable for the degree of faith orientation of the job training provider to which the client was assigned by the caseworker. A number of dummy variables were also included as controls. For these, a reference, or omitted category, must be specified. The variables and their included and omitted categories included a dummy variable for whether they lived in Marion County (as opposed to Lake County), a dummy variable for whether they were female (as opposed to male), a dummy variable for whether they were white (as opposed to nonwhite), and two dummy variables indicating whether the client had a high school diploma and whether the client had any additional education beyond high school (as opposed to having less than a high school education). In addition, to control for macroeconomic trends, we included two dummy variables for fiscal years 2001 and 2002 (as opposed to fiscal year 2000).

We identified the caseworker via the assignment of a scrambled identifier. Each caseworker with a sufficient number of clients was assigned a dummy variable. These are our instrumental variables; that is, we expected caseworkers to have differing propensities to assign clients to faith-based versus secular job training providers based on their own predispositions, but we assumed the caseworkers were unlikely to directly affect the labor market outcomes of clients after training. We recognize that these instruments are a "black box" and provide little insight into the assignment process, but they are potentially valid instruments for obtaining estimates of the causal effects of job training by secular versus faith-based providers.

The period during which we collected our sample coincided with an initiative by the state's Family and Social Services Administration to encourage religious social service providers to contract with the state to provide job training and other social services to welfare clients. As a result of the state's efforts and the FaithWorks program (described in chapter 3), a number of new providers were added to the existing set of job training providers available to welfare clients. In our data set, we identified five faith-based providers that were either less than five years old and/or had contracted with IMPACT for two years or less. Because these providers were relatively young and new to the welfare landscape, differences between their capacities, capabilities, and resources compared with those of existing religious providers had the potential to contaminate the estimated effect of religious providers. To ensure that such contamination did not affect our results, we also conducted our analysis without them; in that analysis, the sample size was 4,910. (Characteristics of both samples are reported in table A.4 in appendix A.)

Findings: Employment Outcomes

In the sample including all faith-based providers, as shown in table A.4, 40 percent of clients who engaged in job training were successfully placed in jobs after training. Of those who were placed, 44.5 percent worked full time when full time is defined as at least thirty-five hours per week (that fell to 35.4 percent if full-time status is defined as working at least forty hours per week). They earned an average of $6.88 per hour. Approximately 6 percent of these individuals were covered by employer health insurance plans. These characteristics did not change substantially when the new faith-based providers were removed from the sample. The individuals in these samples were disproportionately female (77 percent) and nonwhite (20 percent white). Though a little over half the clients had high school diplomas, only about 7 percent reported any additional education.

Appendix A describes the procedure we used to arrive at the final regression results. These final results are shown in tables 6.1 and 6.2. As table 6.1 shows, there was no significant difference in placement rates between faith-based and secular providers of job training services. Women, minorities, and those with a high school education or more are significantly more likely to be placed into jobs. Clients were less likely to be placed in fiscal year 2002, reflecting the macroeconomic downturn. Among those who were placed, clients who received their training at more strongly faith-based providers were significantly less likely to work full time, and regardless of whether full-time work is defined as working thirty-five or forty hours, clients of faith-based providers were, on average, less likely to be employed full time. For full-time defined as thirty-five hours, clients of faith-based providers were 7 percentage points less likely to be employed full time for each 1 point increase in their provider's faith-influence scale value. When full-time employment is defined as forty hours, the percentage point decrease in the likelihood of full-time work was 6.1 for each 1 point increase in provider faith orientation. Clients who lived in Marion County and clients who were relatively more educated were significantly more likely to work full time, while women were significantly less likely to work full time. Wage rates were not significantly different for clients who received training from faith-based providers compared with those who received training from secular providers. Workers who lived in Marion County earned more than $1 per hour more, on average, than those who lived in Lake County. Relatively educated clients and white clients earned significantly higher wages than the average, and women earned significantly lower wages. With respect to the probability of having health insurance through the job, as with the probability of full-time work, we found that clients of faith-based providers were significantly less likely to be offered health insurance coverage than were clients of secular providers. The decreased likelihood in this case was 2.1 percentage points for each 1 point increase in provider faith orientation. Those living in Marion County as well as the relatively more educated were, once again, more likely to have health insurance. The causal effects of provider type on labor market outcomes for the sample in which new faith-based providers are excluded are qualitatively identical to those in which they are included (see table 6.2).

Table 6.1. Instrumental Variable Regressions of Labor Market Outcomes—All Faith-Based Providers

Characteristic	Placed	Full time (35 hours)	Full time (40 hours)	Wage	Insurance
Provider faith	–0.024	–0.070**	–0.061**	0.112	–0.021*
degree	(0.019)	(0.024)	(0.023)	(0.089)	(0.011)
Marion County	0.013	0.140**	0.092**	1.011**	0.040**
	(0.021)	(0.029)	(0.028)	(0.107)	(0.014)
Female	0.182**	–0.076**	–0.073*	–0.610**	–0.008
	(0.016)	(0.031)	(0.030)	(0.114)	(0.015)
White	—	–0.022	0.018	0.249*	–0.022
	–0.081**				
	(0.019)	(0.030)	(0.029)	(0.112)	(0.014)
High school	0.069**	0.091**	0.078**	0.518**	0.018
diploma	(0.014)	(0.024)	(0.023)	(0.088)	(0.011)
More than	0.095**	0.117**	0.090*	0.953**	0.064**
high school	(0.027)	(0.043)	(0.041)	(0.159)	(0.020)
Fiscal year 2001	0.012	0.017	–0.004	0.115	0.011
	(0.014)	(0.022)	(0.022)	(0.084)	(0.011)
Fiscal year 2002	–0.080*	0.137*	0.130*	0.020	0.028
	(0.042)	(0.064)	(0.062)	(0.240)	(0.030)
R^2	0.035	0.045	0.031	0.088	0.018

Note: Robust standard errors are in parentheses.

* Statistically significant at the 5 percent level.

** Statistically significant at the 1 percent level.

Source: Data from Indiana Family and Social Service Administration.

Clients of more strongly faith-based job training providers, as compared with those of secular providers, were equally likely to be placed into jobs and, among those with jobs, likely to earn similar wages. But they were less likely to work full time and have health insurance. Moreover, the magnitudes of these full-time work and insurance effects are similar and, in the case of working full time at thirty-five hours, are greater. In this case, the decreased likelihood of full-time employment was 16.8 percentage points for each 1 point increase in faith orientation. The analysis of this sample, therefore, suggests that differences we found between faith-based and secular providers were not driven by the inclusion of new and possibly inexperienced faith-based providers.

Table 6.2. Instrumental Variable Regressions of Labor Market Outcomes—Excludes New Faith-Based Providers

Characteristic	Placed	Full time (35 hours)	Full time (40 hours)	Wage	Insurance
Provider faith	−0.026	−0.168**	−0.059**	−0.039	−0.024*
degree	(0.019)	(0.024)	(0.024)	(0.091)	(0.012)
Marion County	−0.007	0.156**	0.114**	0.998**	0.048**
	(0.018)	(0.026)	(0.025)	(0.096)	(0.012)
Female	0.173**	−0.102**	−0.098**	−0.576**	−0.007
	(0.017)	(0.032)	(0.031)	(0.120)	(0.015)
White	—	0.022	0.015	0.252*	−0.017
	−0.077**				
	(0.017)	(0.030)	(0.029)	(0.111)	(0.014)
High school	0.055**	0.084**	0.076**	0.544**	0.015
diploma	(0.015)	(0.024)	(0.023)	(0.090)	(0.011)
More than	0.076**	0.108*	0.088*	0.950**	0.046*
high school	(0.029)	(0.046)	(0.044)	(0.172)	(0.022)
Fiscal year 2001	0.015	0.020	−0.007	0.110	0.023*
	(0.016)	(0.025)	(0.024)	(0.092)	(0.012)
Fiscal year 2002	−0.062	0.112	0.098	−0.073	0.030
	(0.047)	(0.075)	(0.073)	(0.282)	(0.036)
R^2	0.030	0.048	0.036	0.098	0.020

Note: Robust standard errors are in parentheses.

* Statistically significant at the 5 percent level.

** Statistically significant at the 1 percent level.

Source: Data from Indiana Family and Social Service Administration.

Conclusions

In this study, we attempted to determine whether the measurable, labor market outcomes of job training programs differed depending upon whether the provider was faith based or secular. We controlled, to the extent possible, for the possibilities of caseworker selection and assignment bias, and we controlled for size, age, and contracting experience. We found that faith-based and secular providers placed clients into jobs at essentially the same rates, and that those jobs paid similar hourly wages. However, we also found that clients who received their training and placement from more strongly faith-based providers were substantially less likely to be placed into full-time jobs, and substantially less likely to be employed in positions providing health insurance coverage.

The reasons for these results are not clear, and it is not possible to determine those reasons definitively from our data. One hypothesis that might explain the discrepancy is a qualitative difference in the networks of secular and faith-based providers, differences that could allow secular providers better access to high-quality job opportunities. More work is clearly needed to more fully explain these results.

As we noted above, we made an extra effort to ensure that our results were not biased by running analyses on two samples of data, one of which excluded those faith-based organizations that had received government funding only recently (most likely as a result of a recruitment initiative targeted at such organizations). We obtained quite similar results for the two samples, demonstrating that differences between these "new" faith-based providers and older, more established ones were not the source of the differences in outcomes. In other words, there was no evidence that the new FBOs were substantially different (better or worse) than the older, more established FBOs.

Our findings, although robust within the samples of data we have used, should be treated with some caution for two reasons. First, in spite of our careful statistical treatment of self-selection, our study does not have the same validity as a totally randomized experimental study would have. Second, our data are from two counties in Indiana, and so obvious questions of external validity can be raised. We examined only one type of social service—job training and placement—raising the question whether similar results would be obtained from quantitative analyses of other services.

Nevertheless, we believe that these results are accurate within the parameters of our study and are highly likely to have external validity in similar environments. This raises obvious policy questions: If there is no evidence of superior outcomes by faith-based providers, should we be diverting our limited public resources to programs recruiting and training such providers? Or should faith-based initiatives concentrate on ensuring equal access to government programs for all providers—religious or secular—that can demonstrate that they already possess the capacity to produce positive results? Would policymakers not be better advised to fund general social service program evaluation efforts, so that public managers will know what works and what does not and will be able to spend public dollars more wisely?

Finally, we would strongly urge others to do quantitative analyses of outcomes and effectiveness. Qualitative evaluations and case studies are immensely helpful, and they provide insights that numbers cannot provide. But qualitative evaluations can also lend themselves to more nuanced and subjective interpretation. When dramatic policy changes are being justified by assertions that A is more valuable than B, it behooves scholars and lawmakers to thoroughly test those assertions—and to do so using the most objective tools available. Though the methodological challenges and especially the difficulties in accessing reliable data are formidable, as we noted above, and the costs of conducting quantitative research are extremely high, we argue that the problems created and costs incurred by policies not grounded in measurable, objective, and quantifiable information are far higher.

Chapter 7

Constitutional Concerns

*T*HE LEGAL DEBATES AROUND CHARITABLE CHOICE LEGISLATION AND THE PRESIDENT'S Faith-Based Initiative occur within a legal system in which the role of the state and the scope of state power are central constitutional concerns. Public policies in the United States are constrained by foundational, normative assumptions about individual rights and the authority of government. Primary among those assumptions is the belief that rights are negative; that is, unlike most other Western democratic countries, the American legal system does not constitutionalize so-called affirmative rights. Any right of citizens to health care, adequate housing, education, or social welfare is a creation of a statute, subject to revision by a simple act of Congress. Such affirmative entitlements are not part of the fundamental law of this country. Instead, rights are understood in the classic Enlightenment construct, as limitations on the reach of the state. As Ronald Cass has reminded us, those who crafted our constitutional framework "saw constraining discretionary power of government officials—the central focus of the rule of law—as essential to the society they hoped to create" (Cass 2001, xii).

It is instructive to recall that the early arguments between the Federalists and Anti-Federalists over the necessity of a Bill of Rights had nothing to do with the importance of individual rights, so understood. That was a matter upon which both sides agreed. The Federalists believed that, because the government they had created had only the powers specifically delegated to it by the Constitution, it lacked the power to infringe upon the "inalienable" rights of its citizens. (Federalists like Alexander Hamilton also argued that an enumeration of rights would be dangerous, because any right not included might be deemed to be unprotected.) The Anti-Federalists believed that it was in the nature of governments to acquire powers not originally contemplated; they therefore felt it prudent to spell out specific limitations on the jurisdiction of the state. The Anti-Federalist argument prevailed, and the Bill of Rights that was eventually ratified was conceived of as a libertarian "brake" on the power of popular majorities to direct state action in ways that would infringe on the inalienable rights of the minority. This focus upon the proper role of a limited state frames all American constitutional discourse.

Although the scope and effect of the First Amendment's religion clauses have always been a subject of debate (especially since passage of the Fourteenth Amendment and the application of those clauses to the states), many historians and legal scholars argue that they were a primary example of the Founders' emphasis upon limiting the jurisdiction of the state. In this view, the original purpose of the religion clauses was to remove matters of religious belief and practice from the cognizance of the state (Muñoz 2003). Whatever the Founders' intent, the Supreme Court's First Amendment jurisprudence over the years has vacillated between so-called strict separation and contemporary accommodationism. Each shift of interpretation has been met with satisfaction by some factions and denunciation by others. To characterize these highly politicized interpretations of the religion clauses as "contested" is a distinct understatement; partisans view each case not just as a resolution of the matter at hand but as a harbinger of decisions to come. When faith-based initiatives are introduced into this highly charged context, extravagant claims—pro and con—are only to be expected.

Though much of the political discourse has focused on the First Amendment, it is important to recognize that there are other constitutional issues raised by Charitable Choice and the President's Faith-Based Initiative. There are, first of all, the general "state action" issues that arise in privatization/contracting situations generally. There are significant equal protection concerns. There are separation of powers issues raised by the manner in which the Faith-Based Initiative has been implemented, and federalism concerns involving the operation and effect of state constitutional provisions prohibiting the transfer of public funds to religious organizations. In the following pages, the general, normative contours of these issues are considered.[1]

Privatization and State Action

Charitable Choice provisions are yet another manifestation of a trend to outsourcing that has significantly altered the way government agencies in the United States do business. Over the past quarter century, there has been a vast increase in the use of private for-profit and nonprofit providers to deliver government services pursuant to contractual agreements. Though government has always purchased goods and services in the market, the practice has grown significantly (Guislain 1997) and has extended into social services where contractors are more likely to be nonprofit agencies with social missions than business organizations seeking profits, and where it presents issues quite different from agreements to purchase computers or to pave city streets (Smith and Lipsky 1993).

Thus, more and more services are provided and paid for by government but delivered by contractors, and that delivery mechanism creates new—and thorny—constitutional issues. If, as has been suggested, these partnerships with businesses and nonprofit organizations are creating a new definition of government (Kennedy 2001), what are the constitutional implications of that change? Does the substitution of an independent contractor for an employee equate to a reduction in the scope of government, as proponents believe? Or, as Donald Kettl has suggested (1993), does the substitution operate instead to shift the locus but not the scope of government activity and thereby blur the boundaries between public and private, making it ever more difficult to decide where "public" stops and "private" begins? If we are altering traditional definitions of public and private by virtue of these new relationships, what is the effect of that alteration on a constitutional system that depends upon the distinction as a fundamental safeguard of private rights?

In one of the earliest and most important investigations of social service contracting, Stephen Rathgeb Smith and Michael Lipsky contended that workers in nonprofit agencies executing government contracts must be considered agents of government (Smith and Lipsky 1993), and they expressed concern that political accountability has been compromised by the lack of transparency that is an inevitable component of such arrangements. As they noted, from the point of view of welfare state clients, advocacy groups, and the general public, the state has virtually disappeared, making it extremely difficult to assess legal or political responsibility or ensure accountability. That difficulty is compounded when government services are provided by pervasively sectarian faith-based organizations (FBOs). We rely upon our understanding of the state action doctrine fashioned by the courts to know when we may ask those courts to restrain government agencies. If we do not have comprehensible rules defining the actions we may legally attribute to the state, the efficacy of constitutional litigation is compromised, and an important constitutional constraint on state power is lost.

"State action" was first defined by the Supreme Court in 1883, in the *Civil Rights Cases* (1883). Passage of the Fourteenth Amendment had prohibited states from denying, to persons otherwise entitled to them, the "privileges and immunities" of citizenship. Addressing the scope of that prohibition, the Court stated:

> The Fourteenth Amendment expresses prohibitions (and consequently implies corresponding positive immunities), limiting State action only, including in such action, however, action by all State agencies, executive, legislative, and judicial, of whatever degree.
>
> . . .
>
> It is State action of a particular character that is prohibited. Individual invasion of individual rights is not the subject-matter of the amendment. It has a deeper and broader scope. It nullifies and makes void all State legislation, and State action of every kind, which impairs the privileges and immunities of citizens, or which injures them in life, liberty or property without due process of law, or which denies to any of them the equal protection of the laws. (*Civil Rights Cases*, 109 U.S. 3 [1883], 7)

As the Court recently restated the doctrine,

> "[E]mbedded within our Fourteenth Amendment jurisprudence is a dichotomy between state action, which is subject to strict scrutiny under the Amendment's Due Process Clause, and private conduct, against which the Amendment affords no shield, no matter how unfair that conduct may be. (*National Collegiate Athletic Association v. Tarkanian*, 488 U.S. 179, 191 [1988])

The Court has thus confirmed the distinction between invasions of rights that are constitutionally forbidden ("public" invasions) and those that are not ("private" invasions), and that distinction rests upon the identity of the actor. Consistent with the Founders' original conception of rights, the citizen's protection is against the public actor only. Discriminatory acts, or denials of due process, or restrictions on speech by private parties are constitutional; indeed, they are entirely legal unless prohibited by virtue of legislation like the Civil Rights Act of 1964 or the Americans with Disabilities Act.

The distinction between public and private acts loses clarity in a number of contexts (indeed, it has been referred to as a "conceptual truth"; Stone et al. 1991), and the Court has been obliged to develop a jurisprudence allowing certain private acts to be attributed to government. Recognizing that we need such rules—especially in outsourcing situations—and actually fashioning them, however, have proved to be very different matters. (As one commentator wryly noted, the Court's "sifting" and "weighing" in state action cases "differs from Justice Stewart's famous 'I know it when I see it' standard for judging obscenity mainly in the comparative precision of the latter " (Brest 1982, 1298). The incoherence of state action case law has been the subject of numerous articles by legal and public administration scholars, and the specifics of those analyses need not be repeated here; suffice it to say that the state of that jurisprudence does not allow easy prediction of what sorts of otherwise "private" actions will be attributed to government for purposes of constitutional liability.

Blum v. Yaretsky, decided by the Supreme Court in 1983, may serve as an example of the inadequacies of current state action doctrine. The case involved an alleged due process violation arising out of involuntary discharges and transfers of Medicaid patients in a nursing home. Justice William Rehnquist, writing for the Court, declined to find state action. He articulated the standard to be met in the following language:

> . . . a state normally can be held responsible for a private decision only when it has exercised coercive power or has provided such significant encouragement, either overt or covert, that the choice must in law be deemed to be that of the State. (*Blum v. Yaretsky*, 457 U.S. 991 [1983], 992)

Acknowledging that more than 90 percent (and perhaps as many as 99 percent) of the patients in the facility were being paid for by the government, and that the nursing home was subject to pervasive governmental regulation as a condition of receiving those government payments, the Rehnquist majority nevertheless held

> [t]hat programs undertaken by the State result in substantial funding of the activities of a private entity is no more persuasive than the fact of regulation of such an entity in demonstrating that the State is responsible for decisions made by the entity in the course of its business. (*Blum v. Yaretsky*, 1011)

In an acerbic dissent joined by Justice Thurgood Marshall, Justice William Brennan underscored the facile nature of this analysis:

> The Court's analysis in this case [proceeds] upon a premise that is factually unfounded. . . . A doctor who prescribes drugs for a patient on the basis of his independent medical judgment is not rendered a state actor merely because the State may reimburse the patient in different amounts depending upon which drug is prescribed. But the level of care decisions in this case, even when characterized as the "independent" decision of the nursing home, have far less to do with the exercise of independent professional judgment than they do with the *State's* desire to save money. . . . On the contrary, the two levels of long-term institutionalized care enshrined in the Medicaid scheme are legislative constructs, designed to serve governmental cost-containment policies. . . . In my view, an accurate and realistic appraisal of the procedures actually employed in the State of New York leaves no doubt that not only has the state established the treatment levels and utilization review in order to further its own fiscal goals, but that the State [has] set forth precisely the standards upon which the level-of-care decisions are to be made, and has delegated administration of the program to the nursing home operators, rather than assume the burden of administering the program itself. (*Blum v. Yaretsky*, 1014–19; emphasis in original)

Blum may be one of the more extreme examples, but numerous other cases reach similarly tortured results. This lack of clarity in the application of state action doctrine, and judicial reluctance to find state action where ordinary people would see it, is one reason for current disquiet over programs to contract out social services to FBOs. Members of minority religious faiths, in particular, are sensitive to the dangers of turning vulnerable client populations over to well-meaning ministries arguably unconstrained by the Fourteenth Amendment. Providers have worries of their own: If government agencies impose guidelines, and the providers following those regulations get sued (as in *Blum*), will the provider, rather than the government, be held liable? What about employment discrimination—will the legislative provision allowing FBOs to discriminate in hiring withstand constitutional muster? If not, what is the potential liability of contractors who have relied upon that provision?

Legal scholars continue to propose conceptual formulas to clarify state action jurisprudence and provide the sort of predictability that is currently lacking. But the only certainty is that the adoption of any of their approaches will not occur any time soon. Meanwhile, the situation facing public managers and contractors alike was summarized in one law review article as follows:

> It is a truism of every high school and college government class that the Bill of Rights applies only to the government, that there must be state action in order to find a constitutional infringement. But by "reinventing" government, we have created mutants and hybrids, neither public nor private, but some admixture of the two. The courts have encountered those mutations much as the blind men encountered the elephant: one finding a snake, one a wall, one a tree trunk. Unless the courts can come to grips with the whole animal, protean and evolving as it is, and fashion a coherent jurisprudence that will safeguard the distinction between public and private and thus protect constitutional liberties without engulfing truly private enterprises, we will find ourselves dealing with 19th century animals in a 21st century legal zoo. (Kennedy 2001, 223)

That Elusive Level Playing Field

There is an old story about two businessmen who take a quarrel to the village rabbi. He listens to the first man tell his side and says

"Yes, you are right." The second man then gives his version of the affair, and once again the rabbi says "You are right." At that point, an onlooker protests "They can't both be right!" to which the rabbi responds "Ah yes. You also are right." American public administrators charged with treating citizens equally are increasingly in the position of that rabbi, needing to acknowledge the legitimacy of competing claims on government that are seemingly both correct and yet are mutually exclusive.

The idea of equality is a bedrock element of the American legal and political systems; we strive for a meritocracy and affirm the obligation of government to treat similarly situated citizens equally. The "level playing field" is a favorite metaphor for politicians and public administrators alike. Whether a playing field is truly level, however, is often a matter of perspective. There is virtually unanimous agreement that equality is an ideal, but there is no comparable agreement on what equality means. Libertarians want equality of rights, or equality before the law. Egalitarians want equality of results in varying formulations. Free market advocates want equal access to markets. Americans speak often of "equality of opportunity," a term often defined as the opportunity to compete on—what else?—a level playing field.

In the United States, discussions of equality generally, although certainly not always, begin with discussion of the role of government and the meaning and application of the equal protection clause of the Fourteenth Amendment, passage of which, as Akhil Reed Amar has persuasively argued, profoundly changed the way in which America defines its constitutional principles, including principles of equality (Amar 1998). The Fourteenth Amendment prohibited states from denying to persons within their respective jurisdictions "the equal protection of the laws," but long after the equal protection clause was applied to the states, notions of equal protection continued to allow treatment that was "separate but equal." Not until *Brown v. Board of Education* in 1954 did the Supreme Court conclude that separate was inherently *un*equal.

The equality protected by the Fourteenth Amendment is narrower than equality as described by most political philosophers; it is limited to the right of similarly situated citizens to be treated equally by their government—that is, as discussed in the foregoing section, the right to equal protection depends first upon a determination that the state has acted. If that threshold question is answered in the affirmative, the Supreme Court will proceed to apply a highly technical template that it uses to determine whether there has been a violation of the Fourteenth Amendment.[2]

Equal protection jurisprudence has evolved without benefit of any overarching, generally accepted theory of equality, negative or positive. It should not come as a surprise, therefore, that political constituencies unschooled in the arcane language of legal analysis view much of it as unfair and decidedly unequal. Because the stability of a society depends in large measure upon the extent to which the members of that society feel that they are being treated justly, this popular resentment is no small matter. If the rules promulgated by the state are believed by large segments of the citizenry to differ substantially from their internalized notions of fair play and equal treatment, the consequences for legal legitimacy and voluntary compliance can be quite serious.

The disparity between popular understanding of equality and its legal or constitutional definition takes on added urgency as government becomes a more pervasive element of the everyday experiences of citizens. In a society where the operations of the state reach increasingly into areas that were previously entirely private, the way in which that state conducts its business, the ways in which it uses its power to shape law and provide for the common welfare, become critical elements in the formation of a society and the degree to which that society values or devalues particular notions of equality. It is impossible to understand the political passions aroused by Charitable Choice (or affirmative action, or any other government action that specifically recognizes difference in order to achieve equality) without first understanding the importance Americans attach to state neutrality.

Most Americans will agree, at least publicly, that our goal is the establishment of a society in which skin color, religion, gender, and the like are officially irrelevant and where the same neutral rules apply to everyone in equal measure. If one believes that it is profoundly immoral to disadvantage someone on the basis of race, religion, gender, sexual orientation, or other aspects of identity, it seems morally and intellectually inconsistent to award advantage on that same basis. Furthermore, programs that single out particular groups for protection or other special treatment raise the specter of misuse of government power: How do we ensure that such programs are based upon a desire to remedy demonstrable inequalities and not on considerations of political or other advantage? If government can "bend the rules" for one group, what is to keep it from advantaging others who are less deserving? How shall we define desert for such purposes?

Because official neutrality, like equality, is highly valued but rarely defined, it is often argued that application of "special rules" to certain groups actually furthers more general neutrality. Alan Brownstein (1999) has argued that Carl Esbeck and other influential proponents of Charitable Choice use "neutrality theory" in that way—to justify what is really a form of affirmative action for FBOs.

One of the major justifications of Charitable Choice and the President's Faith-Based Initiative has been the asserted necessity to address government bias against religious social service providers.[3] Proponents of greater involvement by grassroots religious providers in the complex network of governmental social supports argue that Section 104 of the Personal Responsibility and Work Opportunity Reconciliation Act of 1996 was necessary to level the playing field. They assert that confusion over the application of the First Amendment establishment of religion clause had caused government officials to disfavor religious bidders in some cases and to impose burdensome requirements on those with whom they did do business in others. To overcome the residual effects of that asserted bias, advocates of greater faith-based participation in welfare programs encouraged states to reach out to such organizations and to actively invite their participation. Some states, like Indiana, have responded aggressively, instituting extensive (and relatively expensive) programs designed to acquaint small religious providers with opportunities for government collaboration. Predictably, these efforts have raised many of the same questions as traditional affirmative action programs.

One of the thorniest of the level playing field issues involves bidder qualifications: Shall the same criteria be applied to FBOs as are applied to secular providers? In an article published in *Commentary*, Les Lenkowsky argued for the "elimination of arbitrary rules that allow, for example, the use of professional therapy but not pastoral counseling" (Lenkowsky 2001, 112). If an agency is putting together a request for proposals for counseling services and requires that responsive bidders employ licensed social workers or certified drug counselors, Lenkowsky clearly believes that the state has discriminated against religious providers offering unlicensed "pastoral counseling." A number of religious spokespersons disagree. Addressing the House Committee on Government Reform's Subcommittee on Criminal Justice, Drug Policy, and Human Resources during one hearing on faith-based social services, the Reverend Horace R. Smith, president and chief executive of Group Ministries in Baltimore, testified:

> In its present state, the proposed initiative seems to allow funds to be distributed to community and faith-based organizations basically because they meet the criteria that they are either community or faith based. The criteria for distribution of funds need to go beyond that narrow stipulation. There should be some form of standardization these organizations are held to. There's a danger that those we seek to service won't receive the level of help they actually need because there presently is not any standard of care within the faith-based community.

In a hearing on faith-based solutions before the Senate Committee on the Judiciary, John L. Avery of the Association for Addiction Professionals focused upon the same issue:

> [The National Association of Alcohol and Drug Abuse Counselors'] concern is not with who provides care, but rather by what clinical standards that care is provided. We are committed to the application of science-based best practices, perhaps as most succinctly stated in the National Institute of Drug Abuse (NIDA) publication, *Principles of Drug Addiction Treatment: A Research-Based Guide*. (U.S. Senate, Committee on the Judiciary 2001)

As with affirmative action, equal treatment is often in the eye of the beholder. If the state insists that a responsive bidder employ licensed social workers or credentialed drug therapists, is that discrimination against faith-based providers whose programs use pastors rather than social workers or trained counselors? Conversely, if the state relaxes certification requirements for religious bidders, has it created an unconstitutional preference benefiting religious providers? What is the difference between "equal treatment" and "special rights"? The provisions of Charitable Choice laws that allow religious providers to discriminate on the basis of religion in employment (discussed below) have been widely attacked, by secular and religious organizations alike, as a special accommodation unwarranted by public policy. Defenders of the provision argue, however, that a failure to recognize and accommodate the religious nature of faith-based providers would amount to a special burden on faith and would be discriminatory (Esbeck, Carlson-Theis, and Sider 2004).

The contested nature of equality in a system based upon limited government and negative rights makes the resolution of such issues very difficult. Tell religious organizations that they must meet the same standards as secular service providers and they will argue that such a position fails to take into account their essential nature and is discriminatory. Make special rules for such organizations and their secular competitors will protest that the playing field has been unfairly tilted. Where you stand, as the saying goes, depends upon where you sit.

Lost in these arguments about fair play and equal treatment are cautionary notes sounded by social science researchers, who warn that the consequences of competition between groups are often more polarizing than competition between individuals:

> Taking more for one's group seems to be more legitimate than taking more for oneself, even though one benefits in both cases. Implicit in the act of allocating to one's group is the justification that other people will benefit; there exists the possibility that taking more for one's group may reflect the individual's genuine concern with the welfare of fellow group members and not just greedy behavior. . . . The problem arises when one's opponent in the negotiation is also representing his/her group. (Diekman, Tenbrunsel, and Bazerman 1997, 196)

To the extent that policies intended to be inclusive inadvertently invite group conflict, those policies may have quite negative unintended consequences.

First Amendment Issues

In 1946, Justice Hugo Black summarized the meaning of the First Amendment's religion clauses in an eloquent paragraph that has been cited in numerous religious liberty cases:

> The Establishment Clause means at least this: Neither a state nor the Federal Government can set up a church. Neither can pass laws which aid one religion, aid all religions, or prefer one religion over another. Neither can force nor influence a person to go to or to remain away from church against his will or force him to profess a belief or disbelief in any religion. No person can be punished for entertaining or professing religious beliefs or disbeliefs, for church attendance or non-attendance. No tax in any amount, large or small, can be levied to support any religious activities or institutions, whatever they may be called, or whatever form they may adopt to teach or practice religion. (*Everson v. Board of Education*, 330 U.S. 1 [1946], 16)

The mere fact that tax dollars are paid to a religious organization is not equivalent to funding religion, and a contract with a government agencies does not, without more, turn the contractor into an arm of the state for constitutional purposes. Government may constitutionally purchase services, including social services, from sectarian sources or enter into other partnerships that involve the transfer of tax dollars to such entities so long as the funds support secular rather than religious activities. The difficulties arise when government contracts with "pervasively sectarian" organizations or with organizations that ignore applicable First Amendment constraints. "Pervasively sectarian" organizations are defined by the courts as those in which the religious elements are so fundamentally interwoven into every aspect of programming that it would be impossible to separate them for purposes of ensuring that support goes only to the permissible, secular activities. The phrase "pervasively sectarian" is not the functional equivalent of the "inherently religious" language that has been employed by the George W. Bush administration in describing what activities cannot constitutionally be funded by government; nor does the question of constitutionality end with the inquiry into whether an institution is pervasively sectarian. As Lupu and Tuttle have written,

The U.S. Supreme Court's current interpretation of the Establishment Clause bars government funding of a broader set of activities than that encompassed by the phrase "inherently religious activities." The Court's interpretation does prohibit direct government funding of activities that are "inherently religious, . . . such as religious worship, instruction or proselytization," but it also prohibits funding of any activity that has significant religious content, whether or not that activity is "inherently religious." (Lupu and Tuttle 2004, 73)

First Amendment issues implicated by faith-based outsourcing can be either administrative or substantive; that is, they can arise because of the way a program is administered or conducted or because the provisions of the law (or the nature of the program) are unconstitutional. One recurrent concern with implications for both equality and religious freedom is the potential for religious bias in the bid process. In testimony before the Senate Judiciary Committee, constitutional law professor Douglas Laycock noted that "choosing someone to deliver social services is more complex than picking the low bidder on a pencil contract. How do you keep thousands of federal, state, and local government employees from discriminating on religious grounds when they award grants and contracts?" (U.S. Senate, Committee on the Judiciary 2001).

The saliency of Laycock's concern was underscored by statements issued by Pat Robertson and others during the original debates over Section 104, warning the administration against contracts with the Nation of Islam or the Scientologists. Laycock endorsed a "reporting requirement" that would require "explanation" of any "obvious over-or-under representation" of religious providers. Whatever the merits of such a requirement, it would be yet another technical, bureaucratic task requiring at least some level of resource allocation. Whether such a mechanism would minimize claims of bias is arguable. As Richard Foltin of the American Jewish Committee noted well before the passage of Charitable Choice laws,

> It seems almost inevitable that, whatever claims may be made that contracts will be allocated on the basis of merit, in any given community the religious groups most likely to receive funds will be those associated with "mainstream" faiths. And, even if the contracts are allocated on a totally objective basis, there is likely to be sharp

distrust and suspicion that this is not the case. (American Jewish
Committee 1990, 3)

These warnings have proved prescient. Since 1996, a number of
cases have been brought alleging preference for religious organizations. In some cases, the preference was quite explicit; in *American
Jewish Congress v. Bernick* (Superior Court, State of California, City
of San Francisco, 2001), the challenge was to a California "solicita-
tion for proposals" that was by its terms limited to "faith-based organizations or their nonprofit affiliates"—the state had established
a religious "set aside" program. California responded to the lawsuit
by settling the case and discontinuing the program.

There are also First Amendment issues involved in contract
monitoring. The free exercise clause protects religious organizations against unwarranted intrusion, and the Supreme Court has
interpreted the establishment clause as prohibiting "entanglement" between government and sectarian organizations. What is
"unwarranted" and what degree of supervision amounts to "entanglement" are subject to interpretation. Even if audit and accountability measures are perfectly appropriate constitutionally, elected
officials have expressed concerns that, should state agencies find
FBO compliance inadequate, charges of bias will be leveled and
may well resonate politically. (To the extent that Charitable Choice
laws focus on inner city churches, race will inevitably become a
part of the political equation in such situations, a prospect that
concerns even strong supporters of vigorous outreach to religious
providers.) If government oversight is not to be viewed as racially
or religiously discriminatory, great care will need to be exercised to
eliminate unintended disparities in the monitoring process. Oversight methodology and criteria will need to be well conceived and
communicated to faith-based contractors before the fact and with
clarity. Our research suggests that few, if any, states currently meet
this standard.

State agencies are constitutionally required to ensure that government funds go only to support secular activities. Consistent with
that requirement (if somewhat underprotective of it), Charitable
Choice laws prohibit the use of tax dollars for proselytizing and
prohibit conditioning service delivery upon participation in religious activities. However, states have limited managerial resources

with which to monitor programmatic content for constitutional compliance. Middle managers hired to administer service contracts cannot be expected to recognize any but the most egregious First Amendment violations, and most have very limited time to devote to such issues. If a constitutional violation is alleged and proven, the state can be held liable, but because Charitable Choice laws do not define "religious organizations" or "proselytization," state contract officers do not get much in the way of guidance on these matters. The Welfare Information Network, a widely consulted Internet resource for government officials and others who deal with welfare issues, has noted that "dialogue and 'gut instinct' are guiding the implementation of the ban on proselytization when contracting with federal funds" (see http//:www.welfareinfo.org).

Inadequate monitoring resulting either from a lack of resources or a lack of sufficient constitutional competence has been highlighted by several lawsuits, some of which were described in chapter 3. In Arizona, early in 2005, a federal judge blocked the Bush administration from providing future funding to a mentoring group that injected religion into its programming. The evidence was that MentorKids USA used tax dollars to support worship and religious instruction; the program hired only Christians to work as mentors and required mentors to sign and adhere to a "Christian Statement of Faith" and code of conduct (*New York Times* 2005). In another case, a federal magistrate ruled unconstitutional a Montana faith-based rural health program based upon its "overt religiosity" and commingling of faith and health services (*Freedom from Religion Foundation v. Montana Office of Rural Health* [filed 10-26-2004, Ninth Circuit Court of Appeals]).

The challenge faced by state program managers is to ensure constitutional compliance by religious contractors but without undue interference with their operations—interference that might be deemed to be "entanglement," and thus a violation of those contractors' First Amendment rights. As the Reverend Robert Castanon of the United Methodist Church warned in testimony to the Senate Judiciary Committee hearing on faith-based solutions,

> As long as government attempts to separate what is religious from
> secular in entities like churches, synagogues, mosques, etc., it risks
> becoming excessively entangled with religion, thus advancing it or

hindering religion, both clear violations of the establishment clause.
(U.S. Senate, Committee on the Judiciary 2001)

Managing contracts and evaluating contractor performance
without intruding upon the constitutional prerogatives of the religious organization involved can be especially difficult when the
faith-based provider has chosen not to form a 501(c)(3) affiliate, because the monitoring and evaluation of fiscal performance
will require review of books and records, and program costs may
not have been segregated from other financial information. Even
if there is a separate entity, some inquiry into the finances of the
religious organization may be necessary if, for example, a church
or synagogue is entitled under the contract to reimbursement of
substantial in-kind support for the program. Analysis of the cost
of providing services may include the value of volunteer time, use
of church equipment and facilities, and similar accommodations.
Valuing those accommodations may require more review than the
FBO feels is constitutionally appropriate.

Finally, there is the requirement that public administrators provide secular alternatives for program participants who do not want
a faith-based provider. Even assuming that welfare recipients know
they have a right to a secular provider and are willing and able
to exercise that right—an assumption that may be unwarranted
(Kramer, De Vita, and Finegold 2005)—providing an alternative
can be a challenge in more rural states or rural areas of states. Alternative providers are often not available in such locations. Even in
urban areas, access to more than one or two providers is frequently
inconvenient or impractical for welfare clients who must depend
upon public transportation.

Ensuring that administrative processes conform to constitutional requirements may be a more complicated task than lawmakers recognize, but it is certainly possible. Much more difficult
issues arise when the social programs being funded are essentially
religious in nature. When government is directly contracting with
faith-based drug treatment providers, or engaging in religiously
infused prison counseling, there is an almost insurmountable constitutional barrier. The nature of the dilemma is illustrated by the
testimony of numerous advocates of religious interventions, including President Bush: They are very clear that they believe the

most effective way to help drug addicts or prisoners is through religious transformation—what the president calls "the power of faith" (Milbank 2001). A quotation from Jack Cowley, national director of operations for the InnerChange Prison Fellowship Ministry, is illustrative. According to Cowley, "We see crime as a result of sin and therefore we know that a relationship with Christ can heal people." Unlike social services like job training and placement, day care, or medical assistance—services that can be delivered in a constitutionally appropriate manner—many drug and prison programs are not merely faith based, they are faith *infused*. It is not accidental that so many prison programs are called "ministries."

Programs like InnerChange, Teen Challenge, and House of Hope are centered on religious belief. Acceptance of Jesus, and the importance of biblical precepts and morality, *are* the program. Prison Fellowship Ministries, one of the most prominent of the religious prison programs, describes itself as "Christ-based" and its vision as "That God's kingdom will be manifested as the redemptive grace and peace of Jesus Christ are experienced by those impacted by crime." The organization's web page argues that crime is fundamentally a moral and spiritual problem that requires a moral and spiritual solution, and goes on to state that "offenders do not simply need rehabilitation; they require regeneration of a sinful heart."

In 1990, one of the few evaluations of prison fellowship programs was conducted by Loyola College in Maryland for Prison Fellowship Ministries. The final report on Year One Prison Fellowship Program concluded that religious commitment variables are infrequently studied in criminal justice research and noted that the methods used to measure religious commitment have not been the most useful in analyzing the complexity of religious commitment. However, the study also emphasized that offenders who succeeded in such programs (i.e., those who had a lower rate of recidivism and committed less serious crimes than a control group) had undergone intensive Christian discipleship training (Gartner et al. 1990). Faith-based drug treatment programs are equally focused on spiritual transformation as a methodology. Sara E. Trollinger, testifying on behalf of House of Hope to the Subcommittee on Criminal Justice, Drug Policy, and Human Resources, said that "we know that you can't just treat behaviors but that you must address the soul."

Perhaps the best-known exemplar of faith-based drug treatment programs is Teen Challenge. Whatever the methodological inadequacies of the studies cited by the organization to demonstrate high rates of success, those studies all confirm the centrality of its religious content. The following information from Teen Challenge's website, citing an unnamed and presumably unpublished "University of Tennessee study," is illustrative:

> The main focus of Teen Challenge of Chattanooga, Inc., is that of being a spiritual growth center where biblical principles are taught. 80 percent of the respondents credited developing a personal relationship with Jesus Christ as a major influence in helping them to stay off drugs.

The results of a survey attributed to the National Institute of Drug Abuse are introduced as follows:

> The main premise of the study was to demonstrate that introduction of a religious component into the treatment of drug addicts is the one aspect which produces the large success rate.

A review of a study by Aaron Bicknese, also posted on the Teen Challenge website, contains the following passage:

> Responses to survey questions by Teen Challenge graduates confirm that a commitment to Jesus Christ provided them with the moral willpower needed to overcome a wide range of serious addictions. ... The study found that according to responses from graduates, the nature of the commitment to Jesus Christ was crucial; it was not enough to have a vague belief in a higher power, one must commit to the Christ of the Bible.

Successful or not, government funding for programs having religious transformation as their central goal is constitutionally impermissible. Other programs encompassed by the Charitable Choice initiatives may create environments within which constitutional violations are more likely to occur, but such programs can be conducted in a constitutionally appropriate fashion. Funding for programs like Teen Challenge and Prison Fellowship Ministries, however, would clearly seem to be funding *for* religion and—under decades of First Amendment jurisprudence—constitutionally prohibited. That is certainly the view of plaintiffs in several pending lawsuits challenging these prison ministries. In *Americans United for Separation of Church and State v. Mapes* (filed February 12, 2003, U.S. District Court, Southern District of Iowa), plaintiffs have challenged a rehabilitation program in the Iowa prisons run by InnerChange Freedom Initiative. (InnerChange is an affiliate of Prison Fellowship Ministries.) Among the lawsuit's allegations are that the state is financially supporting religious instruction, in violation of the First Amendment, that the program favors evangelical Christianity over other faith communities, and that the program creates incentives for prisoners to become evangelical Christians. At the time of publication, the District Court has ruled for the plaintiffs and struck down the program.

The prohibition on direct government funding need not be fatal to the participation of all faith-intensive programs; there are alternatives to direct government contracts with such agencies that would arguably be constitutionally permissible. In *Agostini v. Felton* (521 U.S. 203 [1997]), the Court (quoting from *Witters v. Washington Department of Services for the Blind*, 474 U.S. 481 [1986]) explained that in order to be constitutionally permissible, any public money earmarked for secular purposes that ultimately goes to pervasively religious institutions must do so "only as a result of the genuinely independent and private choices of individuals." In 2002, the Supreme Court resolved a number of uncertainties about the use of vouchers when it handed down its decision in *Zelman v. Simmons-Harris* (536 U.S. 639 [2002]). That case arose out of a Cleveland school choice experiment. The Court ruled that voucher programs passed constitutional muster *if*—and this is a critical *if* for Charitable Choice programs—the beneficiaries are provided with a genuine, meaningful choice between religious and secular programs.

A properly structured voucher program for social services allowing recipients to choose between religious and secular providers would be very likely to pass constitutional muster (Kennedy 2001; Minow 1999). If public dollars have been allocated for a secular purpose (e.g., nursing home care or drug treatment) and if there is a "genuinely independent and private" choice of service provider,

then—just as there is no constitutionally persuasive reason to prevent an elderly person seeking nursing home care from spending
her benefits in a nursing home run by her religious denomination—
there should be no reason to prevent a drug-dependent teen from
choosing to enroll in Teen Challenge. (This approach would not
save most prison ministries, for obvious reasons.) As the Court
struggles for neutrality in its application of the religion clauses,
as it searches for a formulation that neither burdens nor benefits
religious practice and belief, the exercise of intervening independent choice sufficient to insulate government from a charge of
endorsement would seem to be the fairest way to achieve even-
handedness.

Religious Tests for Employment

Of all the constitutional questions raised by Charitable Choice and
the president's Faith-Based Initiative, the issue that has been most
politically contentious has been the law's explicit exemption of religious contractors from federal and state antidiscrimination laws.
It has always been the case that religious organizations enjoy free
exercise rights that entitle them to an exemption from civil rights
laws to the extent that such laws conflict with their religious beliefs.[4] In most states, however, this exemption from civil rights laws
does not extend to programs funded by government contracts.
States making this distinction acknowledge that religious organizations have a First Amendment right to hire and fire based upon
religious principles when they are spending their own money, but
they draw the line when the use of government dollars is involved.
These states invoke the level playing field, saying, in essence, "Religious organizations don't have to take government money. If they
choose to do so, they will have to follow the same rules that apply
to all the other bidders."

Proponents of greater faith-based participation in government programs argue that this formulation discriminates against
strongly faith-based organizations, because many are unwilling to
participate under those circumstances. They see the religious provider's "freedom to select employees dedicated to their faith-based
mission" as critical to the protection of its institutional integrity

(Esbeck, Carlson-Theis, and Sider, 2004, 90). Critics respond that the exemption amounts to "special rights" for religious organizations, and they echo the argument made by the states, that organizations unwilling to abide by rules that are uniformly applicable to all contractors need not bid.

The Supreme Court's unanimous decision in *Norwood v. Harrison* (413 U.S. 455 [1973]), sometimes referred to as a leading case on this issue, may offer guidance. In *Norwood*, the Court considered the constitutionality of Mississippi's practice of "lending" school textbooks to private schools that practiced racial discrimination, and it ruled that the Constitution bars efforts by the state to aid private discrimination. It is "axiomatic that a state may not induce, encourage or promote private persons to accomplish what it is constitutionally forbidden to accomplish" (*Norwood v. Harrison*, 465). Proponents of the exemption dismiss those who cite *Norwood*, and they argue that the "eradication of racially segregated public schools is a duty of the state. . . . To permit faith-based organizations to staff on a religious basis undercuts no duty of the state to ensure that it refrain from religious discrimination" (Esbeck, Carlson-Theis and Sider 2004, 38). As Melissa Rogers has noted, it is more difficult to dismiss *Dodge v. Salvation Army* (WL 53857 [Southern District, Mississippi, 1989]), decided in 1989. In that case,

> The only court to have squarely faced this issue so far ruled in an unreported decision that, when an employment position within the religious organization was funded "substantially, if not exclusively" by the government, "allowing the [religious organization] to choose the person to fill or maintain the position based on religious preference clearly has the effect of advancing religion, and is unconstitutional." (Rogers 2005, 114)

Rogers suggests that, in light of existing case law, those who hire based upon the belief that the White House rule or the Charitable Choice exemption protects them are on "shaky legal ground" and will make "attractive targets for lawsuits."

Two even more recent cases raise squarely the constitutional propriety of contractor discrimination in hiring when the positions in question are funded by government. *Pedreira v. Kentucky Bap-*

tist Children's Home (U.S. District Court, Western Kentucky, 2000) and *Bellmore v. United Methodist Children's Home* (Georgia Superior Court, Fulton County, 2002) do not directly challenge Charitable Choice, but their resolution has clear implications for faith-based contractors. In *Pedreira,* a religious children's home discharged a highly qualified counselor; the organization was very candid that the only reason for terminating her was that she was a lesbian. That organization, the Kentucky Baptist Children's Home, receives the bulk of its budget from the State of Kentucky. In *Bellmore,* a facility receiving a majority of its support from the State of Georgia was sued for refusing to hire a highly qualified Jewish psychologist and for firing a lesbian employee. The *Pedreira* case has been mired in jurisdictional disputes for several years and to our knowledge has not been finally resolved, but the *Bellmore* case was settled in late 2003, when lawyers for the State of Georgia and the Methodist Children's Home agreed with attorneys for the plaintiffs that the First Amendment prohibited the use of religious tests for positions funded with tax dollars. It is important to note that settlements do not constitute precedents, and that the Supreme Court has not had occasion to rule on the constitutionality of the religious exemption.

The Court may or may not get such an opportunity in another case, *Lown v. Salvation Army* (filed June 21, 2004, U.S. District Court, Southern District of New York). That suit claims that the Salvation Army—a longtime partner in government antipoverty programs—has recently reinvigorated the religious content of its programming and in furtherance of its religious mission has made unlawful changes to its employment practices. Plaintiffs allege that Salvation Army employment forms now ask employees to disclose the last ten years of their church affiliations; require that employees waive the confidentiality of their private communications with clergy and authorize the disclosure of those communications to the Salvation Army; and ask employees for explicit commitments to support the organization's religious mission and to preach the gospel of Jesus Christ. The complaint also contains allegations that the new work environment is "religiously hostile," particularly to employees who believe they are being asked to compromise or breach their professional obligations to teenagers at risk for HIV, sexually transmitted diseases, or pregnancy (*Lown v. Salvation Army*).

This case squarely presents two of the most important issues raised by Charitable Choice: the presence or absence of state action, and the constitutionality of the religious employment exemption. As legal analysts have noted, the incoherence of current state action doctrine makes the ultimate resolution of this case difficult to predict (Lupu and Tuttle 2004, 62). If the Salvation Army is found to be a private actor, the courts will not rule on the propriety of the conduct. The only prediction that can be made with any confidence is that—whatever the legal resolution of the hiring issue—it will continue to be a subject of contentious political debate.

Other Constitutional Issues

Two other constitutional issues deserve mention: the manner in which the Bush Faith-Based Initiative has been implemented and the effect of state constitutional provisions in a federal system.

In 2004, the Roundtable on Religion and Social Welfare Policy issued a report titled "The Expanding Administrative Presidency: George W. Bush and the Faith-Based Initiative." The report detailed the aggressive advancement of the Faith-Based Initiative through "executive orders, rule changes, managerial realignment in federal agencies, and other innovative uses of the prerogatives of his office," and it concluded that the new regulations had marked "a major shift in the constitutional separation of church and state." Among the shifts identified in the report were rules allowing the use of federal job-training vouchers for religious training, suspension of a previous requirement by the Veterans' Administration that social service providers certify that they exert no religious influence, and changes allowing contractors to convert government-forfeited property to religious purposes (Farris, Nathan, and Wright 2004). Policy changes of this magnitude and significance are rarely made by administrative fiat in a system characterized by constitutional checks and balances. Americans expect major changes of this sort to be the subject of legislative decision making. Effecting substantive legal changes through administrative orders may be legally permissible, but it is a method of policymaking that runs afoul of time-honored public administration principles.

Executive branch administrative orders apply primarily to federal agencies and the programs they manage. Most social service programs, however, are administered by the states. That is why proponents and opponents of faith-based contracting watched closely when the Supreme Court decided *Locke v. Davey* (124 U.S. 1307 [2004]); the case promised to have very significant implications for Charitable Choice and the president's Faith-Based Initiative. *Locke* was a challenge to Washington State's refusal to award a scholarship to an otherwise eligible student who proposed to use the money to study for the ministry. The case was widely described as a challenge to Washington's "Baby Blaine Amendment," which bars the transfer of state funds or property to religious institutions. Thirty-seven states have such amendments, and ten of them prohibit not just direct funding of religious organizations but also the use of publicly funded vouchers at religious institutions (Lupu and Tuttle 2003).

"Blaine amendments" are named for Senator James Blaine of Maine, whose 1876 campaign for the presidency included a promise to add a similar amendment to the federal Constitution. Blaine and other nativists wanted to preserve the Protestant nature of America's public schools; they also wanted to prevent states from appropriating funds for the separate Catholic schools that were being established in response to the public system's Protestant character. Many legal commentators felt that the anti-Catholic animus that led to the adoption of many of these amendments would persuade the Court to rule against Washington in *Locke v. Davey*; this, however, did not occur. Lawyers for the state argued successfully that the constitutional provision at issue—an article titled "Religious Freedom"—was not their version of a Blaine amendment. The Court's ruling upheld the authority of the states to maintain their own policies of church/state separation, even when the provision in question requires a more stringent separation than is required under the establishment clause (Lupu and Tuttle 2004).

Constitutional Competence

If the constitutional issues involved in Charitable Choice seem complex even to legal scholars, what about the congregational leaders and other FBO managers who must perform under these contracts? What is the likelihood, first, that these individuals will be willing to enter into contractual relations with government agencies, and second, that they possess sufficient familiarity with First Amendment constraints to administer such contracts in a constitutionally appropriate fashion?

The latter question led us to administer a simple survey to one subset of faith-based managers, congregational leaders in South Bend, Indiana. (We chose South Bend because it is large enough and diverse enough to be representative but small enough to be manageable.) To assess the constitutional competence of congregational leaders, we developed an eleven-item instrument and used a simple three-option response format of agree, disagree, and don't know. Our goal was to have a simple instrument using clear language for very basic constitutional constraints attached to receiving and spending state and federal dollars. We also collected basic demographic data from the respondents with the hypothesis that race, gender, level of education, or religious affiliation might explain some of the differences in the scores.

The sample used was obtained through a collaborative arrangement with the United Religious Community [URC] of Saint Joseph County, Indiana. The URC has a list of 344 religious congregations representing a wide range of denominations, including mainline Protestant groups, Catholics, Jews, Muslims, and independents. With the endorsement of the URC Board, we mailed a survey (with a postage-paid return envelope) to each of the 344 congregations. The envelopes were coded to allow for a targeted mail follow-up and subsequent telephone calls to nonrespondents, asking them to return the instrument. We received 103 usable surveys, for a 30 percent response rate.

There was no clear statistical significance for most of the findings, and with a 30 percent response rate, it would be inappropriate to characterize the results as other than anecdotal. But we were able to draw at least one clear conclusion: Leaders of religious congregations are *not* well versed in the constitutional limitations that constrain the use of public funds for faith-based social services. If the federal government or state agencies continue their outreach to religious congregations for these purposes, the education of grantees will need to be a priority.

When the questionnaires were tallied by questions missed, certain widespread deficiencies in basic constitutional knowledge were startling. Of the 103 responses, for example, 75 disagreed with the statement "The First Amendment and other provisions of the Bill of Rights apply only to government action." This is disheartening. The concept of state action—the principle that the Bill of Rights constrains only action by agencies of government—is basic to any understanding of the operation of American constitutional principles. Even more troubling, given the context in which the question was asked, was the response of the 70 respondents who disagreed with the statement "If a congregation has a contract with government to provide services, the congregation may not include religious instruction or prayer as part of the services funded under the contract." Charitable Choice and the President's Faith-Based Initiative depend for their viability upon the ability of contractors to follow the constitutional rules. This question arguably goes to the very heart of these proposals.

Although no other question came close to the number of wrong answers elicited by the two described above, 49 respondents (almost half) disagreed with the statement "The First Amendment's separation of church and state means that tax dollars cannot be used to fund religion or religious expression." (In addition to a wrong response, several respondents wrote impassioned marginal notes to the effect that separation of church and state is not constitutionally required, that the concept was "an invention of the ACLU," and that they would feel no compunction using tax dollars to save souls.)

Fifty respondents reported either current receipt of government funding or a willingness to enter into a contractual relationship with a government agency. Of that group, nearly one-third (fifteen) had scores of six or below (out of eleven). Another twenty-three scored seven or eight. There were seven nines, two tens, and three perfect scores. Whatever the merits of Charitable Choice, whatever the capacities of FBOs to provide needed social services, these results should give us pause, because they suggest that a majority of congregational leaders (like a majority of American citizens generally) have a very tenuous connection to the principles that frame our legal system.

Public administrators have an obligation to ensure an adequate level of constitutional competence on the part of those we entrust with our tax dollars, just as they must insist upon appropriate fiscal controls. How that is to be accomplished raises still other questions. In a survey of state managers of faith-based programs, we found virtually no evidence that program officers were concerned with constitutional compliance, monitored for constitutional compliance, or even knew who (if anyone) in their state had responsibility for such matters.

Conclusion

If agencies of government are to continue providing services through third-party surrogates, it will be imperative to address and clarify the significant questions of constitutional accountability that are currently unresolved. As with so many of the issues that are debated in the public square as "either/or" propositions, such a paradigm is distinctly unhelpful. The constitutional question is frequently not whether, but how.

There are persuasive reasons to be troubled by the Faith-Based Initiative. As it has been implemented and justified by the Bush administration, it represents a substantial departure from former legal and political practices. At times, the administration has appeared to be deliberately challenging long-held, traditional American legal principles. As Lupu and Tuttle noted in 2003,

> It is no secret that the Bush Administration would like to create
> as welcome an environment as legally possible for faith-based
> organizations participating in government-financed service
> programs. Moreover, it is equally well-known that the Supreme
> Court is closely divided on these questions. In these circumstances,
> [federal] agencies have an incentive to imply a wider range of
> permissible government-financed religious activities than a careful
> review of the Establishment Clause law would indicate. From the
> agencies' perspective, "pushing the limits" of the constitutional
> doctrine may be attractive on policy and political grounds as a way
> to test whether or not Establishment Clause principles limiting the
> direct financing of services with religious content will change in
> the future. Our concern with this tactic lies not in its chances for

ultimate success or failure, but rather in its implicit invitation to
faith-based organizations to rely on norms that are highly vulnerable
to constitutional challenge—and to challenge that could easily
exhaust the resources and energies of such organizations. At the least,
a strategy of transparency, in which faith-based organizations could
assess their level of legal risk, would be far preferable to one resting
on ambiguity. (Lupu and Tuttle 2003, 11)

In *The Rule of Law in America*, Ronald Cass lists four constitutive
elements to the rule of law: "(1) fidelity to rules (2) of principled predictability (3) embodied in valid authority (4) that is external to individual government decision-makers" (Cass 2001, 4). Viewed through
the lens of those elements, Charitable Choice and the Bush Faith-
Based Initiative clearly raise a number of significant concerns.

Notes

1. Legal scholars have addressed several of these issues in more technical
detail. In particular, Ira Lupu and Robert Tuttle have produced an excellent
legal analysis of the First Amendment issues in particular, and readers desir-
ing to consult interpretations more closely grounded in disciplinary exegesis
should consult their work. This chapter is written primarily for nonlawyers,
and it is intended to be a more normative, less technical discussion of the issues involved.

2. For a description of that template, see chapters 4 and 5.

3. In August 2001, for example, the White House issued a report called *Un-
even Playing Field*, purporting to identify barriers to participation by FBOs,
and detailing what it described as the resulting underrepresentation of those
organizations. As Lupu and Tuttle have noted, however, the report was factually inaccurate in several respects; The U.S. Department of Housing and Development (HUD), for example, reported that no FBOs received funding under the Self-Help Homeownership Opportunity Program, although Habitat
for Humanity, an FBO, had in actuality received more than half that program's
$20 million in funding. HUD also reported that religious organizations were
"banned" from owning projects under the Section 202 Supportive Housing
for the Elderly Program, despite the fact that more than two-thirds of that
program's "sponsoring organizations" have been religious.

4. Melissa Rogers has written an excellent history and explanation of the
religious exemption offered under Title VII of the 1964 Civil Rights Act. See
"Federal Funding and Religion-Based Employment Decisions" (Rogers 2005).

PART III
Summing Up

Chapter 8

Talking Past Each Other

$\mathcal{A}$FTER NEARLY FOUR YEARS OF RESEARCH
AND STUDY, WHAT CAN WE FINALLY SAY
about Charitable Choice legislation and the president's Faith-Based
Initiative? Have these programs and approaches been successful?
Are faith-based efforts to alleviate poverty more or less effective
than secular ones? Are armies of compassion helping more poor
people achieve self-sufficiency? Or is the emphasis on faith-based
contracting diverting necessary resources from direct services and
eroding constitutional boundaries?

Can we even agree on what "success," "effectiveness," and "help"
(let alone "faith") mean? And—perhaps more fundamentally—is
the highly polarized discourse and conceptual incoherence that
characterize this particular policy arena simply another example
of the partisan nature of policymaking in the United States—a re-
minder of the truth of the old admonition not to look too closely
at the process of making either sausages or laws—or is this debate
a "special case," and if so, why? Our research suggests a number
of answers to those questions, some prosaic, others that implicate
very different conceptions of what it means to be an American. We
turn first to the prosaic.

Standards of Measurement

If a community development organization proposed building ten
units of affordable rental housing, we would measure its success by
counting the completed housing units and comparing the rents with
what is considered affordable in the relevant market. We might
also examine the quality of construction, the competence of property management (evaluated by service norms in the industry),

and similar indicators. When we attempt to assess the success of Charitable Choice legislation, we confront a very different landscape, because "faith-based organizations" (FBOs) and "success" mean different things to different people. Even among people who strongly support (or strongly oppose) faith-based initiatives, there is considerable dispute about the characteristics of an FBO and little agreement on the basic indicators against which "success" might be measured.

Two examples illustrate this dilemma. The first involves a case study with which some members of our research team were involved. The principal investigator on that study required a restrictive application of a very specific definition of "faith based" for purposes of categorizing the providers involved; the chosen definition required that religious affirmation or observance be an explicit element of programming in order to classify a provider as "faith based." Other studies—ours included—distinguish among religious providers along a continuum, using a number of dimensions, so that an organization founded upon certain religious tenets or by adherents of particular religions might be considered somewhat or moderately "faith based" (depending upon the factors described in chapter 4); organizations that include explicitly religious programming would be categorized as more strongly faith based. The presence of explicitly religious elements in program delivery certainly distinguishes some FBOs from others, and it has constitutional implications as well; but to use that dimension to *define* faith based would exclude even many programs operated by congregations and/or motivated by strongly sectarian beliefs. The adequacy of such a definition aside, it confirms a difficult problem with the comparability of research results; to the extent that different researchers are using different tests to determine whether any particular organization should be labeled "faith based," the results of these studies will not yield meaningful comparisons.

In the second example, a colleague who is a nationally respected expert on program evaluation was asked in 2001 to assist the White House Office of Faith-Based and Community Initiatives in establishing benchmarks for later evaluation of the President's Faith-Based Initiative. The people he spoke to in this office described their charge in very different terms. To some, the initiative was an effort simply to "level the playing field"; to others, it was a way to bring meaning and value to the lives of the poor; and to still others, it was an effort to break down bureaucratic barriers to new and innovative programs. Some focused upon the "street level" nature of the organizations to be targeted, believing the purpose was to increase government contracting with organizations closer to the communities being served. Others insisted that the focus was on the "faith factor"—these were the proponents who believed that "the power of faith" was the crucial element missing from anti-poverty programs. This multiplicity—and incommensurability—of goals confounds efforts at evaluation. The threshold question for an evaluator is always, "What is the standard against which we are measuring this program?" What, in other words, will success look like?

Critics of faith-based initiatives have been no more coherent than supporters. As we have noted in previous chapters, Charitable Choice elicited an immediate and hostile response from a wide variety of critics. Some opponents charged that the "real" legislative goal had less to do with "faith," however defined, than with load shedding—that what the George W. Bush administration was really trying to do was reduce spending on the most vulnerable and voiceless in the population, those who are least able to protect themselves politically. Civil libertarians detected a theocratic agenda, an effort to further erode the constitutional wall between church and state. Political cynics saw partisan political motivations; they believed that the president was both playing to his base and trying to "bribe" African American clergy with the promise of badly needed financial support. A number of religious leaders warned that it was an effort to co-opt religion's prophetic voice and turn the church into an arm of the state.

Scholars of welfare policy, practitioners who have been heavily involved in social service provision, and others who did not approach Charitable Choice with preconceived notions have often echoed the executive director of a faith-based provider we interviewed, who called Charitable Choice "a solution in search of a problem." In his view, the deficiencies of social welfare policy have more to do with inadequate resources than discrimination against religious providers or onerous reporting requirements. In the debates over the intent and efficacy of this particular policy, as with so many others, policymakers and stakeholders of various sorts have simply "talked past each other."

One Set of Results

This lack of consensus on what problem the policy was intended to solve makes productive deliberation difficult; it also poses significant challenges for research methodology and process. The foregoing chapters have detailed the various ways we resolved those difficulties, the definitions we employed, and the methodologies we chose. Our findings must be understood in the context of these choices and with recognition of the fact that we studied one type of social service in a limited number of settings.

Our findings must also be understood in the context of the response by religious providers to the invitation of Charitable Choice and the Faith-Based Initiative. To be blunt, there has been no dramatic (or even significant) change in the social welfare landscape. The hypothesized "armies of compassion" have thus far not materialized; in states where such information is available, it would appear that the composition of social service contractor pools has changed very little. What we cannot say with any degree of confidence is why. It seems reasonable to assume that fiscal realities have played a role; the states have been in fiscal crisis almost from the time the administration began encouraging them to find faith-based partners, and the lack of added federal funds for social services has prevented any expansion of social service programs.

To the contrary, in many cases, the scarcity of resources has resulted in the termination of programs not required by state or federal law, and fewer dollars for the programs that have survived. It has not been an auspicious time for new contractors to enter into the already tenuous mix of government, for-profit, and nonprofit organizations that make up America's tattered "safety net." Another possible disincentive is theological and/or cultural; many religious nonprofits and congregations, for a variety of reasons, look with suspicion on partnerships with government. Other small FBOs do not want the legal restraints and reporting burdens that accompany contractor status, while still others have been lured into a contract relationship and, after a brief time, determined that it was not in their interest to continue. It has also been suggested that those religious contractors that really had an interest in working with government on social welfare issues were already doing so. Whatever the reason, responses from religious organizations to Charitable Choice and the Faith-Based Initiative have been decidedly tepid.

Turning to the specific research questions we addressed, we can summarize our findings as follows:

- *Effects of federalism.* As hypothesized, different states did approach Charitable Choice implementation differently. Despite the centralized nature of the welfare system, and the regulations promulgated under the Personal Responsibility and Work Opportunity Reconciliation Act of 1996, chapter 3 details the myriad ways in which state approaches to implementation diverged and the ways in which those differences reflected local political cultures.

- *Comparative efficacy.* In our study, we found no evidence to support the contention that faith-based contractors are more effective than secular providers. Other research on effectiveness is under way, and it will either support our conclusions or come to different ones, but such research as has emerged thus far suggests that our results are not an anomaly. (One recent investigation found no difference in the "ethical considerations" motivating religious and secular providers, workers, and volunteers because "even secular programs have sacred roots"; Lockhart 2001, 12). Though different people define "effectiveness" differently, when we limit the definition to the programmatic goal of placing people in jobs that will allow them to achieve self-sufficiency, FBOs do not do a better job; and, on some dimensions, they do not do as well as their secular counterparts.

- *Effects on FBOs.* Critics of Charitable Choice, and even some supporters, worried about potentially deleterious effects on faith-based providers as a result of doing business with agencies of government. Those concerns ranged from the practical (cash flow problems, a lack of resources to adequately report and account for funds and clients) to the systemic (co-option of the "prophetic voice" of religious organizations, mission creep resulting from growing dependence upon government dollars). We found that the more strongly faith-based organizations were likely to include explicitly religious elements in programming, and as a result to experience more negative reactions from clients.

They were also more likely to provide services for which they were not being reimbursed. We found no positive correlation between faith and holistic service provision, although such a connection has been widely hypothesized. In addition, research by others supports the contention that contracting with government affects nonprofits' missions. Studies suggest that "sustaining the distinctive normative climates that ensure uniqueness and selectivity is increasingly difficult" (Lynn 2002, 58) for nonprofits (not just faith-based nonprofits) that contract with the government. These and similar findings lend strength to the hypothesis that there may be measurable outcome differences between faith-based services funded by private contributions and those provided by a faith-based government contractor.

These organizational research results underline certain of the conceptual difficulties with Charitable Choice. There are significant organizational differences between congregations and other faith-based nonprofits, and these differences deserve more recognition than current outreach efforts accord them. Congregations are—first and foremost—communities of worship. They are not formed to be social service providers, and some of the demands made upon them by the latter status are inconsistent with the mission of the former. Pastors and other congregation leaders are rarely equipped to deal with the multiple and difficult issues of poverty (Farnsley 2003). Furthermore, research does not support the assumption that congregations are more rooted in and familiar with their neighborhoods and communities. (Interestingly, members of African American churches are even less likely to live in the neighborhood where the church is located than are members of white churches; Farnsley 2003, 52.)

- *Constitutional accountability.* Critics of Charitable Choice have warned that faith-based contracting will invite wholesale constitutional violations, a concern that our study suggests is not entirely misplaced. Certainly, state-level agencies lack the resources—fiscal and human—to conduct even the most cursory monitoring for such violations, and our research demonstrates that no oversight mechanisms are in place. As chapter 7 details, constitutional concerns arise in several contexts. The pressure on state agencies to demonstrate that they are not discriminating against FBOs has led to accusations that they are erring in the other direction and are improperly favoring religious contractors. Allegations of proselytizing, of coercing clients into participation in religious rituals and observances, have begun to surface (although it is difficult to know whether these practices have become more common or whether the visibility of the Charitable Choice debate and thus of religious contracting has made people more alert to them; Pierce 2005; Fried 2004; Neary 2003; Sager and Stephens 2005). Few public managers or managers of small FBOs display a sound understanding of the First Amendment constraints that accompany tax dollars. Though it would not be accurate to characterize hiring practices based upon religious criteria as constitutional violations until and unless the Supreme Court rules on the Charitable Choice exemption from civil rights laws, such hiring practices raise numerous policy concerns. And in addition to the issues specific to the First Amendment, there are the broader constitutional concerns raised by third-party government in general.

What do these specific research findings tell us? First, they suggest certain concrete recommendations for policymakers, public managers, and religious nonprofit organizations considering whether to partner with government.

Policymakers need to consider whether a proposal—whatever its perceived merits—really requires action by the state, or whether it addresses an area best left to individual public managers or to private actors. If a new law is needed, care must be taken to define the terms of the legislation, including the specific goals to be achieved. And a good-faith effort must be made to assess all existing evidence relevant to a new initiative. ("It depends" may not make for a snappy bumper sticker slogan, but an appreciation of complexity is a necessary component of good policy.)

Public managers attempting to implement new policies must also clarify their objectives. In addition, they will need to understand the legal context of the new program, including the constitutional constraints that may give rise to liability, and consider how they will approach oversight and evaluation. In an area as contentious as this one, public managers at the state and local levels would be particularly well advised to familiarize themselves with the experiences of other states, both those reported in this book and those that will undoubtedly emerge in the future.

And finally, FBO *nonprofit managers* must carefully assess the pros and cons of doing business with government. This assessment should begin with an honest consideration of the organization's goals, strengths, and weaknesses, and it should include an appraisal of the transaction costs involved as well as the benefits that might accrue. Arguably, it is just these calculations that have led so many FBO managers to conclude that government contracting is not, on balance, appropriate for their organizations.

Aside from these practical recommendations for policymakers, public managers, and those who run FBOs, our study suggests a broader conclusion, applicable to all of them—a conclusion that is unavoidable for anyone familiar with the discourse and emerging literature on Charitable Choice and the Faith-Based Initiative: Attempts to understand the competing points of view involved are hampered if not made entirely futile by the fact that those engaged in the discussion frequently inhabit different realities. As noted above, participants in these discussions are in large measure talking past each other.

Toward a More Productive Discourse

Those who are heavily invested in the arguments over Charitable Choice at either end of the ideological spectrum will undoubtedly remain wedded to their perspectives. But that does not mean that a more engaged and productive discourse is impossible. It seems reasonable to consider what the outlines of such a discussion might look like.

To the extent possible, productive conversations should focus on "how" rather than "whether." It bears repeating that there is no reason—constitutional or prudential—that government should exclude (or favor) religious social service providers. Religious organizations have always been an important part of the social service contracting mix, and they will continue to be. Those who are opposed to—or leery of—a role for faith-based providers need to acknowledge that reality. For their part, those who favor an increased role for FBOs need to acknowledge that some FBOs and services they offer do fall outside the constitutional pale. Government can and does purchase secular services from religious vendors; but government is constitutionally prohibited from purchasing religious services or from entering into transactions that will have the effect of financially supporting or endorsing religion. Most Charitable Choice and other faith-based initiatives are neither "constitutional" nor "unconstitutional" per se; their propriety depends upon the manner in which they are implemented. If we can focus the national conversation on the appropriate questions, we stand a much better chance of getting useful answers.

Suggestions for reframing the discussion of Charitable Choice have begun to emerge. As David Campbell (2002) has suggested, treating contracting choices as a zero-sum game in which government and faith-related organizations represent alternatives is unproductive. Campbell suggests that we focus more on the difficult task of integrating fragmented services at the community level, improving communication and cooperation among the various grassroots organizations involved. A number of people have advocated for greater emphasis on capacity building for grassroots organizations—whether secular or faith based—and for the formation of umbrella organizations that would act as intermediaries between government agencies and small, grassroots providers. Such umbrella organizations could handle the accounting and legal compliance reporting that so many small organizations (whatever their faith component) find costly and burdensome, and they could also provide valuable assistance in integrating social service networks.

Once we refocus the discussion—if, indeed, that can be done—the need for credible, empirical data becomes clear. If we argue in the abstract, or from ideological perspectives, data are irrelevant; if we are genuinely concerned with concrete performance, we need to agree on basic definitions and on organizational and performance indicators. At the very least, we need to know:

- What organizational characteristics are most likely to produce successful program results?
- Are there measurable differences in program delivery that can be attributed to the religious character of the provider? If so, how do those differences correlate with the "religiosity" of the

provider? That is, if we determine that there are observable, de-scribable differences between religious and secular providers, how do we define and account for those differences, and how do we recognize and describe the organizations likely to display them?

- What do we mean by programmatic "success"? Clearly, the defi-nition of success will vary from program to program; we need to agree about the outcomes that will constitute success for vari-ous types of social services. This will undoubtedly require stud-ies of longer duration than ours; in the case of job training, for example, it would be highly relevant to know which programs produced the longest-term results: Were clients still employed one year or five years after their initial placement? Had they been able to achieve self-sufficiency? For those who had, what elements of the program, in retrospect, had been most and least helpful? Currently, no longitudinal data are available on such issues.

- Are different FBOs more successful in different areas, or with different populations? That is, are some religious providers more likely to succeed with certain types of problems or with particular types of clients? If so, why? Are the characteristics that correlate with such a finding (if made) different from the char-acteristics of their secular counterparts? If so, how?

- What are the long-term effects on FBOs that partner with gov-ernment? Are certain types of FBOs more likely to experience mission creep, or other changes to their organizational charac-ter, than others? Are these changes experienced as negative or positive? (We were surprised by the fact that several religious providers reporting an effect on their mission considered the effect a positive one—clearly, such changes can be experienced as either positive or negative.)

- Constitutionally, we need to know what is really happening "on the ground." Are religious providers impermissibly injecting re-ligious dogma into service delivery or requiring participation in religious observances? Are government agencies monitoring for constitutional compliance? Are they providing faith-based con-tractors with sufficient information to allow those contractors to avoid unconstitutional practices? Are certain kinds of services more apt to breach constitutional boundaries than others?

- Do government managers make contracting decisions on the basis of the religious character of the provider? This inquiry needs to go beyond the simple question of favoring or disfavoring undifferentiated "religious" bidders. Are some religious providers preferred over others? If so, which ones are preferred and why?
- Is the application of civil rights protections to jobs funded with tax dollars really a disincentive to participation by some religious providers? The issue of employment discrimination is easily the most contentious part of faith-based initiatives; defenders of these preferences argue that they are necessary because many FBOs will not participate otherwise. Thus far, there is no empirical evidence for that assertion, and several FBO managers we interviewed disputed it. If it should turn out that the requirement of nondiscriminatory hiring dissuades few potential contractors, a major conflict might be avoided.

Answering these questions will present significant methodological challenges and will require significant resources. Until we have at least preliminary answers to many of them, however, we will continue arguing about assumptions that may be true, untrue, or irrelevant. For those who support Charitable Choice and the Faith-Based Initiative because they want to improve the safety net available to those in need, replacing conjecture with evidence should be a priority. Similarly, if the common goal is to provide more help for our impoverished citizens, then the first—and presumably easiest—point of agreement should be the need to ensure that adequate resources are available to support programs that are found to be effective. In an article posted on the website Beliefnet in early 2005, David Koh, a former White House aide and ardent proponent of the Faith-Based Initiative, made precisely that point—"the faith-based initiative and compassionate conservatism" had been left at "precisely the place Gov. Bush pledged it would not go." He continued:

> It has done the work of praising and informing but it has not been given the "resources to change lives." In short, like the hurting Charities it is trying to help, the Initiative has been forced to make bricks without straw.... The Administration ... has pushed an

ambitious domestic agenda; three huge budgets have been submitted, each of which had billions of dollars for other domestic priorities but lacked any new money to pay for "compassionate agenda" promises, which are ever more in need of fulfillment. After all, there are now more poor Americans than ever before. (Koh 2005)

One of the reasons there has been so little evaluation of the efficacy of government-sponsored social services is that there are not even enough resources to provide the promised services to all who qualify—let alone funds for evaluation and proper program monitoring. If this seems penny wise and very pound foolish, it is; without the ability to evaluate providers and determine the outcomes and comparable merits of their programs, we have no way of knowing whether we are spending public dollars wisely or throwing good money after bad. In the absence of such information, it is much more likely that public managers will favor contractors with whom they are comfortable, or those whose beliefs (programmatic, religious, or other) they find compatible.

Finally, we need to assess faith-based contracting within the larger context of the continuing trend to privatization, understood as outsourcing and government "reinvention." We need a better understanding of the implications of America's move to what some have called government by proxy. When services are delivered by nonprofit organizations and FBOs, rather than by private for-profit companies, it is particularly critical that we know what effect that relationship has on the nonprofit or faith-based partner. The questions that we should be asking here will fall into the following broad areas:

- *Fiscal, constitutional, and political accountability.* If government is responsible for delivering a service, is there sufficient transparency in the arrangement to allow us to assess performance and to attribute this performance to the state? If funds are being wasted, constitutional safeguards breached, or friends or political allies being favored, will we know? Can we construct safeguards to prevent such problems? Can we impose remedies for abuses?
- *Does government by proxy affect social capital formation?* Voluntary organizations—nonprofits and FBOs—act as a buffer be-

tween the state and the individual citizen. The so-called third sector, composed of voluntary associations, is something other than the family unit, with its unique relationships, or govern-ment, with its monopoly on the legitimate exercise of coercive power. The networks of trust and reciprocity developed through participation in voluntary organizations are neither govern-mental nor individual; instead, these nonprofit organizations are "mediating institutions," facilitating and moderating the relationships between citizens and their formal governmental structures. The continued health of the voluntary sector is thus every bit as important to democratic governments as it is to in-dividual citizens. The nonprofit sector is where citizens acquire human capital, defined as the skills needed for effective com-munity participation, and it is the arena in which they build social capital—those connections that enable them to use those skills in concert with others to influence political and commu-nity decision making. In an era of privatization (or, more ac-curately, outsourcing), the ability of government contractors to deliver social services will depend to a considerable degree upon the extent of their social capital. What if the increasing use of nonprofit and faith-based agencies to deliver social services is changing the character of those agencies in a way that is eroding their ability to generate that social capital?

- *If we are building social capital, is it the right kind?* Govern-ment benefits from bridging social capital, but there is reason to worry that a proliferation of faith-based providers, especially those subject to selection by prospective clients holding govern-ment vouchers, could instead produce bonding social capital, hastening a process of balkanization, channeling people into communities of the like-minded, and discouraging broader in-teraction with people who are different. It may well prove more effective in the short term to send people to service providers with whom they share ethnic or religious beliefs; the question for the broader society is whether, in the long term, such segre-gation of client populations helps or hinders socialization into the American mosaic.

- *Does outsourcing represent a more cost-effective use of tax dollars?* In the early days of privatization and the "reinvention of govern-ment," contracting was said to be both cheaper and more efficient than government service delivery; private for-profit companies were driven by market forces and could be expected to deliver better services for less money. Though that assertion neglected certain inconvenient facts—the cost to government of developing contracts, monitoring performance, and generally managing the relationship, for example—the fiscal purpose of the outsourcing relationship was quite clear. Nonprofit organizations and FBOs, unlike private commercial ventures, have not been disciplined by market forces, and the reasons for contracting with such entities are rarely fiscal. Though this does not mean that contracting with nonprofit partners is less beneficial, it does mean that we need to distinguish between types of outsourcing relationships and to clarify when and why government partnerships with nonprofit organizations and FBOs are desirable.

Although many of these questions are difficult, at least they are issues that careful scholarship can illuminate and help to resolve. Yet it is impossible to conclude this chapter—or this book—without also recognizing the larger, less tractable conflicts that Charitable Choice policies implicate. As we pursued our research, we came to see the larger, "big picture" debates identified in chapter 1—the definitional and evidentiary incoherence, arguments over the relative priorities of faith and funding, and constitutional and management concerns—as evidence of a significant and troubling disconnect between conflicting worldviews.

Law, Language, and Religion

Religion and law are two of the frames through which people perceive the world. "Like other modes of thought—science and art, for example—they are frames of reference, ideational and affective approaches to subjects both in and beyond their literal domains" (Dane 1999, 114). Even when policy debates are couched in what John Rawls (e.g., 1993) would call "public reasons," the intractability of some perennially difficult issues comes not merely from differences about these public reasons—differences that might be compromised, or resolved, by empirical investigation—but also in deeper disagreements rooted in beliefs about the existence and nature God, the role of humans in the universe, and fundamental concepts such as justice, charity, and responsibility.

Even our definitions of what beliefs should be considered "religious" are incommensurate: Winnifred Sullivan, a member of the Advisory Committee for the research project on which this book is based, reminds us that "the traditional American evangelical Protestant definition of religion as chosen, private, individual and believed" now shares space in a pluralist culture in which many other traditions define religion as "given, public, communal and enacted" (W. Sullivan 2004, 257). Facile political references to a "Judeo-Christian" Americanism ignore or trivialize those profound distinctions. People who share a political community may nevertheless inhabit different realities, which are rooted in different religious traditions leading to divergent worldviews and normative assumptions; as a result, they literally do "talk past" each other.

Even those who operate within the basic constraints of the Enlightenment liberal construct often do so for very different reasons. Howe (1965) has reminded us that separation of church and state was the result of two quite different traditions: rationalist anticlericalism, which feared religion's potential for division and even tyranny, and radical Baptist theology, which feared the corrupting influence of the state. Dividing jurisdiction of the church from that of the state was thus a common solution to two quite different concerns—concerns that continue to inform political discourse. Liberals, adopting variants of Enlightenment rationalism, tend to view the state as a *means* to civic peace and order. They believe that the threshold question about the propriety of government action is, "Who decides and how?" Communitarians, conversely, believe that the state should be more concerned with *ends*.

Saint Augustine criticized Rome in *City of God* for its failure to create a "true" republic, on the grounds that it had not established the right sort of human community. John Winthrop, one of the early Puritans who has "been taken as exemplary of our beginnings" (Bellah et al. 1996, 28) spoke of the "City on the Hill," in which liberty would be understood not as the freedom to do as one might wish but rather as the liberty to do that "which is good, just and honest" (p. 29)—presumably as Puritans defined goodness, justice, and honesty. Contemporary political philosophers often characterize Enlightenment liberalism's "Who shall decide?"

as a "thin" procedural inquiry, and they describe the Communitarian question "What is to be decided?" as "thick"—a distinctly unhelpful framework. Labeling one approach as "thick" and one as "thin" mischaracterizes these important differences and fails to recognize that the dispute reflects different, equally "thick," conceptions of the good.

These disputes do not just involve "religion" or "religious beliefs"—difficult as those are to define. They also involve religiously rooted ways of seeing the world that, as Hunter has noted (1991, 2004), are often no longer experienced as religious or theological in nature. As a result, these conflicts no longer fit into the (not so) neat categories we have created for questions of church and state. Martin Marty has described ours as a polity in which "citizens in their various competitive groups do inhabit incommensurable universes of discourse" (1997, 72). George Marsden nicely captured the nature of such "incommensurable universes" in a passage describing the famous conflict between William Jennings Bryan and Clarence Darrow over the Scopes trial: "Each considered the other's view ridiculous, and wondered aloud how any sane person could hold it" (Marsden 1980, 213).

This inability to communicate in any meaningful sense has characterized discussion of Charitable Choice ever since passage of Section 104 of the Personal Responsibility and Work Opportunity Reconciliation Act of 1996. Some of the more striking examples include the following:

- Proponents clearly meant the term "faith based" to be equivalent to "religious." It was probably an effort to be inclusive, although the notion that "faith" is the central defining feature of religiosity betrays a narrowly Protestant conception of religion. Many religions, including Judaism and Catholicism, are considered "works based." The very language of these efforts sent a message to adherents of non-faith-based religions, and it was undoubtedly not the message that was intended by those who coined the term.
- Opponents suspected that Charitable Choice and the Faith-Based Initiative were really efforts to privilege certain (evangelical) religious providers over others and to erode the constitutional separation of church and state. From their perspective,

such suspicions were confirmed when congressional supporters of Charitable Choice responded dismissively to reminders of the participation of government's long-term religious partners on the grounds that these providers had become "secularized"— defined as their adoption of professional norms and their provision of services in which "faith" is not a central element.

- Opponents criticized the legislation for incorporating assumptions that were unsupported by any evidence; to supporters, such criticisms betrayed a lack of understanding of the nature of "faith" and were thus irrelevant. This insistence on the transformative nature of faith in turn ignored the very real constitutional barriers that prevent government from purchasing spiritual transformation (but not food or job training) from sectarian providers.

- A primary purpose of Charitable Choice, according to its advocates, was the need to ensure a level playing field. They charged that government's contracting processes had discriminated against religious organizations, a charge that appears to rest (at least in part) on the belief that holding FBOs to the same standards as secular ones is discriminatory. Critics respond that performance can only be evaluated through the application of relevant professional standards. That definition of performance "effectiveness" is in turn rejected by those who believe that the poor "need the internal pressure to [as Booker T. Washington said], live honored and useful lives modeled after our perfect leader, Christ'" (Chernus 2001, quoting Marvin Olasky). They see individual transformation as the only way to end poverty, because poverty, in their worldview, is a result of individual moral inadequacy, the lack of proper values and internalized norms—and (while few would articulate this belief so baldly) they believe that organizations that do not equate poverty with a failure of what are euphemistically referred to as "middle-class" values are neither authentically "faith based" nor effective. (As Arthur Farnsley has pointed out, those who hold this position take as a given the ability of FBOs, especially congregations, to impart values and effectuate that transformation—an assumption for which there is no empirical evidence, and much reason to question; Farnsley, conversation with the author). Empirical studies comparing job placement rates of secular organizations and FBOs are beside the point to those who approach poverty issues through this particular lens.

It is very important to emphasize that the highly ideological positions described above are much more characteristic of politicians, policymakers, and pundits than of the people working with either religious or secular providers, or of government welfare officials. These are people who *do* talk to each other. The vast majority of those who actually work in these agencies, public and private, faith based and secular, understand the dimensions and complexity of the challenges they face, and they tend to be far less invested in rigid political or religious perspectives. They are simply trying to do their jobs. For them, the pressing questions are much more practical, and the lack of consensus, continuity, and clear direction that are an inevitable consequence of ideological policymaking are unnecessary barriers to performance and are sources of real frustration.

Summing Up

All policymaking is "messy." Stakeholders have interests they want to protect, politicians have constituencies they want to please, and advocates and experts have policy goals they want to advance. That the debates over Charitable Choice legislation reflect these political realities is nothing new. On the basis of our conversations and research, however, we believe that there is something more than "politics as usual" at work here.

One scholar who has studied Charitable Choice extensively recently remarked that, given the paucity of the actual changes that had occurred, there has been "much more smoke than fire." At risk of unduly burdening the metaphor, we would suggest that the fire may not be burning in the antipoverty programs—rather, that the smoke we see is weapons fire from the culture wars. As another scholar put it, in a discussion of political polarization generally, issues do not explain the partisan divide. The question is how to govern in an age when people do not inhabit the same reality. That, of course, is the central question raised by our liberal democratic paradigm—a worldview that sees government and religion as different, if related, life spheres and defines modernity in large measure by the secular nature of the state. The questions we confront are foundational: What sort of moral consensus is necessary to sustain Western liberal society? In so diverse a society, is such a consensus possible?

Certainly, there are those who are not themselves "culture warriors" who are nevertheless perfectly happy to use cultural "wedge" issues for political advantage, and Charitable Choice has become one such issue. There are also sincere proponents and opponents of the Faith-Based Initiative whose policy preferences are not outgrowths of metaphysical commitments. It would be a mistake to generalize too broadly about the genesis of any particular policy debate. That said, however, Charitable Choice arguments implicate deeply held and often opposed realities. The issue truly is one of "faith," understood not simply as a set of particular theological or religious beliefs but also as an investment in particular conceptual paradigms. Alasdair MacIntyre framed the dilemma in *After Virtue*: "From our rival conclusions we can argue back to our rival premises; but when we do arrive at our premises argument ceases and the invocation of one premise against another becomes a matter of pure assertion and counter-assertion" (quoted in Marty 1997, 72).

The term "culture wars" became popularized after the publication of a book with that title by James Davison Hunter (1991). In a more recent reflection, Hunter suggested that an unaccountable information technology has become a powerful contributor to cultural conflict. "The dominant voices and platforms through which public discourse presently takes place are notably conducive to reaching mass audiences but not at all conducive to substantive deliberation. . . . The technological nature of these practices holds no inherent moderating capability" (Hunter 2004, 28). The ease with which such contemporary communication techniques can be used to solidify one's political "base" and generate passion from those who share one's worldview makes their use for such purposes too tempting for many to ignore.

The bottom line is that religiously rooted worldviews, broadly understood, frame legal and policy discussions in ways that are too infrequently recognized and appreciated. Questions like "What is the state, and what is its jurisdiction?" "From where does the state derive its authority?" and "How far does that authority extend?"

grow out of conflicting beliefs about the source of law's authority, the nature of human community, and the definition of liberty.
As numerous political philosophers have noted, the fundamental
challenge to liberal democratic regimes comes from those unwilling to "privatize" hegemonic ideologies. If the goal of the law in liberal regimes is to achieve neutrality among differing conceptions
of the good, how should society deal with those whose beliefs require that they be imposed as the law of the land and who consequently experience government neutrality between different moral
visions as discrimination?

An honest discussion of that dilemma should begin by recognizing what our American devotion to equality sometimes ob-
scures: that the achievement of strict neutrality is not what our
constitutional architecture was intended to provide. The First
Amendment's establishment clause—indeed, the entire Bill of
Rights—clearly privileges certain concepts of the good over others. The contemporary secular state does not represent an absence
of a conception of the good, as some assert. It represents a choice
of one particular conception of the good. The neutrality required
under our system is equal treatment among those willing to accept
that original choice and to operate within the confines of laws that
flow from it.

Ultimately, the debate over the importance of "faith" in addressing poverty is a debate over whose fundamental beliefs will shape
American policy. The issue is not whether religiously affiliated organizations should provide social services—it is *which ones*. It is
an effort to privilege certain worldviews over others, and the fault
line is not between religious and secular providers, even assuming that such a line could be conveniently drawn. This larger conflict is about power, about who gets to define America. Whatever
other political, programmatic, or policy debates may be involved,
the controversy over Charitable Choice and the Faith-Based Initiative is yet another example of the conflict Hunter outlined so
starkly in 1991. It seems appropriate to conclude by quoting that
description:

> The divisions of political consequence today are not theological and
> ecclesiastic in character but the result of differing worldviews. That is

to say, they no longer revolve around specific doctrinal issues or styles of religious practice and organization but around our most cherished assumptions about how to order our lives—our own lives and our lives together in this society. Our most fundamental ideas about who we are as Americans are now at odds. (Hunter 1991, 42)

Appendix A

Methodology and Data

This appendix contains tables displaying data and statistical findings that are discussed in detail in chapters 5 and 6.

Data and Findings for Chapter 5

We begin with tables A.1 and A.2. Table A.1 shows the simple correlations between the variables used in this chapter. In table A.2, we begin the detailed analysis of the management challenges of the organizations in our study. We examined the management challenges shown in table A.2 using the following logic: We first determined the percentage of providers by faith orientation that had identified specific management challenges (the second, third, and fourth columns of the table). To discover where faith differences might be related to those management challenges, we identified challenges where we found a substantial percentage difference (defined as 19 percent or more in the fifth column of the table) between "strongly faith-based" and "non-faith-based" organizations. For example, this would include among others: "achieving our mission" (–19 percent), "recruiting/keeping effective board" (32 percent), "managing board/staff relations" (26 percent), and "strategic planning process" (25 percent). We then computed a correlation between the 0–8 faith-based scale and the management challenges (sixth column of the table). We used these and partial correlations (seventh and eighth columns of the table) to examine the extent to which age or size appeared to be related to the management challenges. For example, if a partial correlation between faith influence and a management challenge, controlling for size, is much smaller than the original faith influence–management challenge correlation, we concluded that size is likely a factor in that particular management challenge. This type of pattern can be seen in "delivering high-quality services," where the simple correlation with faith influence is 0.222 and the partial correlation controlling for size is 0.115. We conclude here that size (in addition to faith influence) is also a factor in the delivery of high-quality services.

Table A.1. Correlations of Management Challenge Indices and Other Variables

Index or Variable	External Relations	Internal Operations	Size (log)	Age	Received Technical Assistance	Faith-Based Index (0–7)	Years Contracting with IMPACT	Director Tenure
Mission and governance	0.409	0.518	−0.151	−0.333	0.162	0.043	−0.249	−0.212
External relations		0.717	−0.192	0.161	0.007	0.025	0.087	0.029
Internal operations			0.041	0.144	−0.086	−0.165	0.090	0.058
Size (log)				0.429	−0.078	−0.374	0.110	0.184
Age					−0.003	−0.294	0.479	0.440
Technical assistance						0.098	−0.190	0.043
Faith-based index							−0.236	−0.330
Years contracting with IMPACT								0.263

Source: Indiana IMPACT Provider Survey.

We do not, however, know exactly how size is related to service delivery. Do smaller organizations have a greater problem delivering high-quality services, or is this more of a problem for larger organizations?

To further analyze the effects of age and size on management challenges (in addition to faith influence), we computed the partial correlation between size or age and the management challenge, this time controlling for faith influence. These calculations are shown in table A.3. These calculations allowed us to determine the direction of the size/age–management challenge relationship. In other words, if there is a size or age relationship, is it larger or smaller organizations, or younger or older organizations, which experience more management challenges?

Table A.3 shows that among the management challenges which were "significantly" related to faith influence (shown in the fifth column of table A.2), "recruiting/keeping effective board," managing board/staff relations," "attracting new clients," and "managing our programs" were also influenced by the organization's age, as shown by the difference between the simple correlation (second column of the table) and the partial controlling for age (third column of the table). For example, for "recruiting/keeping effective board," the simple correlation is 0.193 and the partial controlling for age is 0.113. The fifth column of the table shows the direction of the age effect (independent of the faith-influence effect) for these management challenges. For example, the negative partial correlation for "recruiting/keeping effective board" (–0.252) shown in the fifth column of the table indicates that younger organizations have more difficulty in this regard, independent of their faith status.

In addition, "delivering high-quality services," "attracting new clients," and "using information technology effectively" were also influenced by organizational size (as shown by the change between the simple correlation and the partial controlling for size, in the fourth column). For example, for "delivering high-quality services," the simple correlation is 0.222 and the partial correlation controlling for size is 0.115. The table's sixth column shows the direction of the size effect (independent of the faith-influence effect) for these management challenges. For example, the negative partial correlation in the sixth column for "delivering high-quality services" (–0.270) indicates that smaller organizations have more difficulty in this regard, independent of their faith status.

Data and Findings for Chapter 6

Our rationale, and the process we used for the analyses in chapter 6, are as follows. We begin with table A.4.

Table A.2. Faith Influence and Management Challenges, Controlling for Age and Size

Management Challenge	Faith Influence (percent)			Difference: SFB − NFB	Pearson Correlation with Faith Orientation	Partial Correlation (controlling for age)	Partial Correlation (controlling for size)
	NFB	MFB	SFB				
Mission and governance					0.043	−0.067	−0.014
Clearly defining our mission	12	0	17	5	−0.019	−0.090	−0.085
Achieving our mission	35	17	17	−19	−0.212	−0.225	−0.333
Recruiting/keeping effective board	18	0	50	32	0.193	0.113	0.167
Smoothly functioning board	12	0	17	5	−0.019	−0.126	0.029
Managing board/staff relations	24	0	50	26	0.190	0.101	0.179
External relations					0.025	0.080	−0.050
Obtaining adequate information	59	17	50	−9	−0.123	−0.172	−0.176
Identifying & targeting results	47	33	33	−14	−0.046	−0.005	−0.133
Strategic planning process	41	33	67	25	0.171	0.205	0.118
Implementing plans	41	33	33	−8	−0.022	0.073	−0.060
Delivering high-quality services	24	17	50	26	0.222	0.254	0.115
Meeting the needs of current clients	53	33	67	14	0.093	0.230	0.039
Attracting new clients	53	50	83	30	0.167	0.105	−0.007
Enhancing visibility and reputation	65	0	67	2	−0.116	−0.112	−0.060
Developing/maintaining good relations with other organizations	29	0	17	−13	−0.139	−0.057	−0.077
Measuring program outcomes	35	33	17	−19	−0.069	−0.038	−0.047

Table A.2. Continued

Internal operations					−0.165	−0.131	−0.163
Recruiting/keeping qualified administrators	12	0	0	−12	−0.211	−0.271	−0.233
Recruiting/keeping qualified staff	35	0	50	15	0.060	0.024	0.054
Recruiting/keeping qualified and reliable volunteers	29	33	33	4	0.125	0.163	0.117
Managing human resources	35	0	33	−2	−0.045	0.013	−0.169
Managing our programs	35	17	17	−19	−0.145	−0.106	−0.117
Communicating internally	53	33	17	−36	−0.288	−0.239	−0.213
Developing and using teamwork	41	0	33	−8	−0.101	−0.126	−0.099
Developing/sustaining good working relationships in the organization	47	17	17	−30	−0.280	−0.256	−0.277
Dealing with disputes in the organization	24	0	33	10	0.083	0.022	−0.014
Reorganizing structure if needed	35	17	33	−2	0.096	0.132	0.117
Anticipating financial needs	59	33	33	−25	−0.182	−0.127	−0.205
Obtaining funding or other financial resources	88	50	67	−22	−0.225	−0.186	−0.263
Financial management and accounting	35	0	33	−2	−0.078	−0.029	−0.128
Managing the facilities/space	24	17	50	26	0.222	0.276	0.253
Using information technology effectively	53	33	33	−20	−0.159	−0.156	−0.036
Using technology for service provision	53	17	17	−36	−0.361	−0.360	−0.328

Note: NFB = non-faith-based

MFB = moderately faith-based

SFB = strongly faith-based

Source: Indiana IMPACT Provider Survey.

Table A.3. Age and Size Effects on Select Management Challenges

Management Challenge	Pearson Correlation with Faith-Based	Partial Correlation (controlling For age)	Partial Correlation (controlling for size)	Partial Correlation with Age (controlling for faith)	Partial Correlation with Size (controlling for faith)
Recruiting/keeping effective board	0.193	0.113	0.167	−0.252	−0.037
Managing board/ staff relations	0.190	0.101	0.179	−0.283	0.006
Delivering high-quality services	0.222	0.254	0.115	0.140	−0.270
Attracting new clients	0.167	0.105	−0.007	−0.188	−0.443
Managing our programs	−0.145	−0.106	−0.117	0.109	0.052
Using information technology effectively	−0.159	−0.156	−0.036	−0.013	0.313

Source: Indiana IMPACT Provider Survey.

We used dummy variables (0, 1) for caseworkers as the instruments. That is, we assumed that the predisposition of caseworkers affecting assignment to faith-based versus secular providers would drive systematic differences in assignments of clients to each type of provider but that the caseworkers would have no direct impact on the potential outcomes for the clients. This assumption is plausible because of the quasi-random assignment of clients to caseworkers and the relative lack of involvement of caseworkers once a client begins the job training program. Ideally, we would have liked to estimate the average treatment effect (ATE), which is the causal effect of the treatment on outcomes. However, except in special cases like constant treatment effects and certain types of randomized trials, the standard exclusion assumptions of instrumental variables (IV) are not sufficient to determine ATE, even in the population subject to treatment (e.g., see Angrist 2001; Angrist and Evans 1998).

Instead, the IV assumptions identify treatment effects on "compliers," which Angrist, Imbens, and Rubin (1996) define as the subpopulation of treated individuals whose treatment status can be influenced by the instruments. In our case, the extent to which IV estimates determine ATE depends on the ability of caseworkers (instruments) to assign clients (treated individuals) to faith-based providers instead of secular providers

Table A.4. Summary Statistics of Variables Used in the Analysis of Job Outcomes

		Including All Faith-Based Providers			Excluding New Faith-Based Providers		
Variable	Definition	N	Mean	St. dev.	N	Mean	St. dev.
Placed	= 1 if the client was placed into a job; 0 otherwise	5,683	0.397	0.489	4,910	0.396	0.489
Full-time (35 hours)	= 1 if the client worked 35 or more hours per week	2,258	0.445	0.497	1,942	0.456	0.498
Full-time (40 hours)	= 1 if the client worked 40 or more hours per week	2258	0.354	0.478	1,942	0.360	0.480
Hourly wage	wages in $ per hour	2,252	6.875	1.928	1,939	6.877	1.949
Health insurance	= 1 if the client has health insurance from the employer; 0 otherwise	2,231	0.057	0.233	1,916	0.057	0.233
Provider faith degree	= provider score on an eight-point faith-influence scale	5,683	1.516	2.147	4,910	1.101	1.959
Marion County	= 1 if the client lived in Marion County; 0 if the client lived in Lake County	5,683	0.371	0.483	4,910	0.416	0.493
Female	= 1 if the client was female; 0 otherwise	5,683	0.770	0.421	4,910	0.770	0.421
White	= 1 if the client was White, Non-Hispanic; 0 otherwise	5,683	0.202	0.402	4,910	0.222	0.416
High school diploma	= 1 if the client has a high school diploma only; 0 otherwise	5,683	0.521	0.500	4,910	0.506	0.500
Beyond high school	= 1 if the client has some education beyond a high school diploma	5,683	0.069	0.253	4,910	0.067	0.250
Fiscal year 2001[a]	= 1 if the record is from October 1 to September 30, 2001; 0 otherwise	5,683	0.356	0.479	4,910	0.358	0.480
Fiscal year 2002[a]	= 1 if record is from October 1 to December 1, 2002; 0 otherwise	5,683	0.077	0.266	4,910	0.059	0.236

[a]Fiscal year 2000, if record is from October 1 to September 30, 2000, is the omitted category.

Source: Data from Indiana Family and Social Service Administration.

of job training. Given that our population consists of individuals who are already seeking training, we decided that it was reasonable to believe that most clients would not refuse training if they were assigned to a faith-based provider, or vice versa, nor are most clients likely to insist on one type of provider over another. Therefore, our estimates are likely to determine ATE reasonably well for the subpopulation of individuals on welfare who choose to enroll in job training programs.

Our calculations of employment outcome results were performed in the following way:

- *First-stage regression:* Ordinary least squares regressions are used to estimate the determinants of assignment to faith-based providers for the entire sample. This is the first-stage regression implied by the IV procedure. In addition to the client characteristics described in table A.4, the models we used contained dummy variables for fifty-four caseworkers. There were considerably more caseworkers in our sample, but we created dummy variables only for those caseworkers with frequencies of at least 0.5 percent (i.e., caseworkers who had assigned at least twenty-eight clients). All other caseworkers are grouped together in the baseline (omitted) category. (Regression coefficients showing the effects of the independent variables on provider assignment are reported in table A.5). We did not report estimates for individual caseworker variables because these are not interpretable, and in any event, this was not the purpose of the analysis. The important finding was that the estimates of caseworker effects are jointly significant. The statistics rebut the hypothesis that all caseworkers will be identical in their propensities to assign clients to faith-based providers. That is, caseworkers are not homogeneous: they do differ in their propensities to assign clients to faith-based providers. (Note that our model treats caseworkers as a black box so it is not possible to learn anything about why they differ.) Women and minorities were significantly more likely to receive job training services from religious providers. Clients with more education were also more likely to be assigned to faith-based providers. As compared to fiscal year 2001, clients were progressively more likely to be assigned to faith-based providers in fiscal years 2002 and 2003.
- *Second-stage regression:* We next estimated IV regressions for labor market outcomes for both samples. This is the second stage of the IV regression procedure. Parameter estimates from these models are shown in the chapter in table 6.1 for the "including all faith-based providers" sample and table 6.2 for the sample "excluding new faith-based providers."

Table A.5. Regression (Instrumental Variable First Stage): Assignment to a Faith-Based Job Training Provider[a]—All Faith-Based Providers

Marion County	−0.053**
	(0.016)
Female	0.043**
	(0.015)
White	−0.116**
	(0.015)
High school diploma	0.056**
	(0.013)
More than high school	0.049**
	(0.025)
Fiscal year 2001	0.070**
	(0.014)
Fiscal year 2002	0.461**
	(0.020)
F-test of caseworker effect	4.120**
D.F. for F (v_1, v_2)	54, 5621
R^2	0.132

Note: Robust standard errors are in parentheses.

[a]The dependent variable is the provider's score on the faith-influence scale. The analysis was also performed using whether the provider was faith-based or not (0, 1). The results were substantially similar.

* Statistically significant at the 5 percent level.

** Statistically significant at the 1 percent level.

Source: Data from Indiana Family and Social Service Administration.

Appendix B

The Indiana IMPACT Provider Survey Questions

This appendix contains questions from the provider questionnaire. The responses to these questions are discussed in detail in chapters 4 and 5.

1. Is your organization nonprofit, for-profit, or a government agency?

   ☐ Nonprofit (If they ask, that means exempt from corporate taxes.)

   ☐ For-profit

   ☐ Government:
      CHECK ONE: ☐ federal ☐ state ☐ city ☐ county

2. In what year was your organization founded? _____

3. What is your total number of full-time paid employees? _____
   Part-time _____

   Of these employees, what is the full-time equivalent (FTE) number of employees who are dedicated to the following tasks?

   Administering/supporting the IMPACT contract? _____

   Providing service under the IMPACT contract? _____

4. How long has your executive director been with the organization? _____

5. Does your organization use any volunteers, other than those who serve on the board of directors?

   ☐ yes ☐ no ☐ don't know

   IF YES:

   Approximately how many people performed volunteer work for your organization this year up to August 30? (not including board members) _____

   Were any of your volunteers involved in providing IMPACT services?

   ☐ yes ☐ no ☐ don't know

   IF YES, how many, and what did they do?

6. What is the geographic area currently served by your organization? Please estimate the percentage of your clients that come from these geographic areas.

	Percent of Clients
Neighborhood (within 1 mile)	_____
Your area of the city (1–5 miles)	_____
Outside your area of the city (more than 5 miles)	_____
Don't know	_____

7. Please provide the following information for your organization for the most recently completed fiscal year. (WRITE "0" IF NONE.)

Total revenues	$ _____
Total expenditures	$ _____
Total assets	$ _____
Total liabilities	$ _____

8. Please check all of the services that your organization PROVIDES DIRECTLY under its current IMPACT contract.

Job Training
- ☐ Vocational Training
- ☐ Computer Skills Training

Job Readiness
- ☐ Problem Solving
- ☐ Conflict Resolution
- ☐ Workplace Expectations
- ☐ Cultural Diversity
- ☐ Anger Management
- ☐ Communication
- ☐ Time Management
- ☐ Budgeting/Money Management
- ☐ Customer Service Skills
- ☐ Social Skills
- ☐ Personal Hygiene/Grooming
- ☐ Self-Image
- ☐ Stress Management

☐ Drug Treatment

☐ Alcohol Treatment

☐ Mental Health Treatment

Job Search, Development, and Placement

☐ Steps in Job Search Process

☐ Expectations of Job Search Process

☐ Telephone Etiquette

☐ Resume Preparation

☐ Assistance with Job Application

☐ Where to Search for Jobs

☐ Provide Access to Job Search Materials (computer, newspaper, magazines)

☐ Job Fairs

☐ Interview Techniques

☐ Work Experience Site Placement

Assessment

☐ Education

☐ Work Experience

☐ Skills and Interests

☐ Family Problems

☐ Health

☐ Chemical Dependency

☐ Barriers

☐ Life Skills

☐ Personality

Education

☐ Basic Education

☐ English as a Second Language (ESL)

☐ GED Preparation

Case Management

☐ Coordination of Additional Services for Client (transportation, childcare, housing, heath, education)

Miscellaneous

☐ Teen Pregnancy Prevention

☐ Small Business Assistance

☐ Homeownership Assistance

☐ Mediate Conflicts between Employers and Clients

☐ Parenting

☐ Others (please specify)

9. Does your organization provide IMPACT clients with any other services besides those specified in the contract?

   ☐ yes ☐ no ☐ don't know

   IF YES,

   b. What types of services?

   c. Are these reimbursed in some way?

   ☐ yes ☐ no ☐ don't know

   IF YES, by whom are they reimbursed?

10. As part of your IMPACT services, do you promote values?

    ☐ yes ☐ no ☐ don't know

    IF YES, which services? _____

    What values? _____

11. Besides finding employment, are there any other goals you would like the IMPACT clients in your program to achieve?

    ☐ yes ☐ no ☐ don't know

    IF YES, what are they?

12. Please list below the organizations that you routinely interact with to deliver IMPACT services. Check the column that indicates the type of interaction for each. If you need more room, please attach a separate sheet.

    Specify: Nonprofit, for-profit, government agency, religious organization.

    Specify: give or receive funding, service provision, competitor, policy or regulatory issue, subcontractor.

13. Has contracting with IMPACT led to any other community involvements?

    ☐ yes ☐ no ☐ don't know

    IF YES, what are these involvements?

Has contracting with IMPACT changed your organization's relations with other organizations or groups? (PLEASE CHECK ONE.)

☐ yes ☐ no ☐ don't know

IF YES, how?

14. Have you received information or technical assistance in carrying out your contract from the state or county?

☐ yes ☐ no ☐ don't know

IF YES, describe.

15. Have you contracted with IMPACT before this contract year?

☐ yes ☐ no ☐ don't know

IF YES, for how long?_____

16. To what extent do the following types of activities currently pose significant challenges for your organization AND/OR your IMPACT program?

Activity	Major organization challenge	Minor organization challenge	IMPACT challenge	Not a challenge	Don't know
Clearly defining our mission	☐	☐	☐	☐	☐
Achieving our mission	☐	☐	☐	☐	☐
Obtaining adequate information	☐	☐	☐	☐	☐
Identifying and targeting results	☐	☐	☐	☐	☐
Strategic planning process	☐	☐	☐	☐	☐
Implementing plans	☐	☐	☐	☐	☐
Delivering high-quality program/ services	☐	☐	☐	☐	☐
Meeting the needs/ interests of current clients	☐	☐	☐	☐	☐
Attracting new clients	☐	☐	☐	☐	☐

Activity	Major organization challenge	Minor organization challenge	IMPACT challenge	Not a challenge	Don't know
Enhancing our visibility and reputation	☐	☐	☐	☐	☐
Developing/ maintaining good relations with other organizations	☐	☐	☐	☐	☐
Recruiting/keeping effective board members	☐	☐	☐	☐	☐
Having a smoothly functioning board	☐	☐	☐	☐	☐
Recruiting/keeping qualified administrators	☐	☐	☐	☐	☐
Recruiting/keeping qualified service staff	☐	☐	☐	☐	☐
Recruiting/keeping qualified and reliable volunteers	☐	☐	☐	☐	☐
Managing human resources (staff and volunteers)	☐	☐	☐	☐	☐
Managing or improving board/ staff relations	☐	☐	☐	☐	☐
Managing our programs	☐	☐	☐	☐	☐
Measuring program outcomes	☐	☐	☐	☐	☐
Communicating internally	☐	☐	☐	☐	☐
Developing and using teamwork	☐	☐	☐	☐	☐

Developing/sustaining good working relationships in the organization	☐	☐	☐	☐	☐
Dealing with disputes in the organization	☐	☐	☐	☐	☐
Organizing or reorganizing our structure when we need to	☐	☐	☐	☐	☐
Anticipating financial needs	☐	☐	☐	☐	☐
Obtaining funding or other financial resources	☐	☐	☐	☐	☐
Financial management and accounting	☐	☐	☐	☐	☐
Managing the facilities/ space we use	☐	☐	☐	☐	☐
Using information technology effectively	☐	☐	☐	☐	☐
Using technology for service provision	☐	☐	☐	☐	☐

RELIGIOUS ORGANIZATIONS ARE INCREASINGLY BECOMING INVOLVED IN SERVICE DELIVERY. WE'D LIKE TO ASK SOME QUESTIONS REGARDING YOUR ORGANIZATION'S INVOLVEMENT WITH RELIGION.

17. Is your organization affiliated with any religious organization or faith tradition?

    ☐ yes (SPECIFY_____)

    ☐ no ☐ don't know

18. Does the organization desire, request, or require that staff and volunteers share the same religious belief or faith?

    ☐ IF YES, is it ☐ desired, ☐ requested or ☐ required? (CHECK ONE)

19. Do you provide funds or any other support to any religious organizations?

    ☐ yes ☐ no ☐ don't know

    IF YES, which organizations and what kind of support?

20. Is religion or faith a part of any of the services that you provide?

    ☐ yes ☐ no ☐ don't know

    IF YES, which services? _____

    IF YES, how is it a part?_____

21. When making organizational decisions, is your organization guided by prayer or religious texts such as the Bible or Koran or other religious documents, periodicals, or reports?

    ☐ yes ☐ no ☐ don't know,

22. Are any religious or faith criteria used to assign staff to positions?

    ☐ yes ☐ no ☐ don't know

23. (FBO) In light of your receipt of government funds, indicate whether your agency either (1) does it, (2) would like to do it but feel you legally cannot do it, (3) has no desire to do it.

Practice	Do this	Would like to do but feel you cannot do it legally	Has no desire to do it
a. Have a religious leader (pastor, rabbi, imam, etc.) on staff	1	2	3
b. Staff that are members of the congregation	1	2	3
c. Religious symbols/pictures in facilities	1	2	3
d. Voluntary religious exercises for clients	1	2	3
e. Required religious exercises for clients	1	2	3
f. Spoken prayers at meals for clients	1	2	3
g. Informal references to religious ideas by staff in contact with clients	1	2	3
h. A generalized spirit or atmosphere of service/concern/love among your staff	1	2	3
i. Only hiring staff who agree with your religious orientation	1	2	3

j. Giving preference when hiring staff to
those in agreement with your religious
orientation   1   2   3

k. Efforts to encourage clients to make
personal religious commitments   1   2   2

l. Giving preference when accepting
clients to those who agree with your
religious orientation   1   2   3

24. (FBO) Are there any other religious practices you feel you have had
to curtail or eliminate because you receive government funds?

☐ yes ☐ no ☐ don't know

IF YES, please specify which ones.

25. (FBO) Have any government officials ever questioned any of your
religious-based practices or brought pressure to bear on you to
change any of them?

☐ yes ☐ no ☐ don't know

IF YES, please explain.

26. (FBO) Have you received any other criticism or pressure or lawsuits
because of any of your religious-based practices?

☐ yes ☐ no ☐ don't know

IF YES, please explain.

27. (FBO) Have you had any issues with clients related to being a faith-
based organization?

☐ yes ☐ no ☐ don't know

IF YES, what were they?

28. (FBO) Have any of your IMPACT clients attended congregational
activities or services, or joined the congregation?

☐ yes ☐ no ☐ don't know

29. (FBO) Is religion or faith integrated into IMPACT services?

☐ yes ☐ no ☐ don't know

IF YES, how?

IF YES, what services?

30. (FBO) Have there been any consequences for your congregation
because of your involvement with IMPACT?

☐ yes ☐ no ☐ don't know ☐ not applicable

IF YES, what were they?

References

Alexander, J., R. Nank, and C. Stivers. 1999. Implications of Welfare Reform: Do Nonprofit Survival Strategies Threaten Civil Society? *Nonprofit and Voluntary Sector Quarterly* 28, no. 4:452–75.

Alexander, Jennifer. 2000. Adaptive Strategies of Nonprofit Human Service Organizations in an Era of Devolution and New Public Management. *Nonprofit Management and Leadership* 10, no. 3:287–303.

Althauser, R. P. 1990. Paradox in Popular Religion: The Limits of Instrumental Faith. *Social Forces* 69, no. 2:585–602.

Amar, Akhil Reed. 1998. *The Bill of Rights: Creation and Reconstruction.* New Haven, Conn.: Yale University Press.

American Jewish Committee. 1990. *Report of Task Force on Sectarian Social Services and Public Funding.* New York: American Jewish Committee.

Angrist, J. 2001. Estimation of Limited Dependent Variable Models with Dummy Endogenous Regressors: Simple Strategies for Empirical Practice. *Journal of Business and Economic Statistics* 19:2–16.

Angrist, J., and W. E. Evans. 1998. Children and Their Parents' Labor Supply: Evidence from Exogenous Variation in Family Size. *American Economic Review* 88:450–77.

Angrist, J., G. Imbens, and D. B. Rubin. 1996. Identification of Causal Effects Using Instrumental Variables. *Journal of the American Statistical Association* 91:444–55.

Bane, Mary Jo, Brent Coffin, and Ronald Thiemann. 2000. *Who Will Provide? The Changing Role of Religion in American Welfare.* Boulder, Colo.: Westview Press.

Bartkowski, J. P., and H. A. Regis. 1999. *Religious Organizations, Anti-Poverty and Charitable Choice: A Feasibility Study of Faith-Based Welfare Reform in Mississippi.* Arlington, Va.: PricewaterhouseCoopers Endowment for the Business of Government.

Bellah, Robert N., Richard Madsen, William Sullivan, Ann Swidler, and Steven M. Tipton. 1996. *Habits of the Heart: Individualism and Commitment in American Life.* Berkeley: University of California Press. (Orig. pub. 1985.)

Bielefeld, W., L. Littlepage, and R. Thelin. 2002. The Role of Faith-Based Providers in a Social Service Delivery System. Working Paper, Center for Urban Policy and the Environment, Indiana University–Purdue University, Indianapolis.

Blake, R. N. 2005. The Black Church: Now More Than Ever. *Black Commentator*, June 23.

Bloom, H. S., L. L. Orr, S. H. Bell, G. Cave, F. Doolittle, W. Lin, and W. Bos. 1997. The Benefits and Costs of JTPA Title II-A Programs: Key Findings from the National Job Training Partnership Act. *Journal of Human Resources* 32:549–76.

Brest, Paul. 1982. State Action and Liberal Theory. *University of Pennsylvania Labor Review* 130, no. 6:1296–1330.

Brinckerhoff, P. C. 1999. *Faith-Based Management: Leading Organizations That Are Based on More Than Just Mission.* New York: John Wiley & Sons.

Brown, D. M., and E. McKeown. 1997. *The Poor Belong to Us: Catholic Charities and American Welfare.* Cambridge, Mass.: Harvard University Press.

Brownstein, Alan E. 1999. Interpreting the Religion Clauses in Terms of Liberty, Equality, and Free Speech Values: A Critical Analysis of "Neutrality Theory" and Charitable Choice. *Notre Dame Journal of Law, Ethics & Public Policy* 13:243–84.

Buis, M. 1998. The Limits of Welfare Reform: Implementation of TANF in Massachusetts. Paper presented at Annual Meeting of New England Political Science Association, May 1–2, Worcester.

Campbell, David. 2002. Beyond Charitable Choice: The Diverse Service Delivery Approaches of Local Faith-Related Organizations. *Nonprofit and Voluntary Sector Quarterly* 31 (June): 207–30.

Carlson-Theis, S. W. 2000. *Charitable Choice for Welfare and Community Services.* Washington, D.C.: Center for Public Justice.

Cass, Ronald A. 2001. *The Rule of Law in America.* Baltimore: Johns Hopkins University Press.

Chambré, S. M. 2001. The Changing Nature of "Faith" in Faith-Based Organizations: Secularization and Ecumenism in Four Aids Organizations in New York City. *Social Service Review* 75, no. 3:435–55.

Chaves, M. 1993. Denominations as Dual Structures: An Organizational Analysis. *Sociology of Religion* 54:147–69.

———. 1999. Religious Congregations and Welfare Reform: Who Will Take Advantage of Charitable Choice? *American Sociological Review* 6:839–46.

———. 2003. Debunking Charitable Choice: The Evidence Doesn't Support the Political Left or Right. *Stanford Social Innovation Review* 1, no. 2:28–36.

Chaves, M., and W. Tsitsos. 2001. Congregations and Social Services: What They Do, How They Do It, and with Whom. Working paper, Aspen Institute, Washington, D.C.

Chernus, Ira. 2001. http://spot.colorado.edu/~chernus/ Newspaper%20Columns/The%20Bush% 20Aadministration/ Olaskyand19th%20Century.htm/.

Choi, Gil, and Terry Tirrito. 1999. The Korean Church as a Social Service Provider for Older Adults. *Arete* 23, no. 3:69–83.

Cnaan, Ram A., and Stephanie C. Boddie. 2002. Charitable Choice and Faith-Based Welfare: A Call for Social Work. *Social Work* 47, no. 3:224–35.

Cnaan, Ram A., Robert J. Wineburg, and Stephanie C. Boddie. 1999. *The Newer Deal: Social Work and Religion in Partnership*. New York: Columbia University Press.

Conlan, Timothy, and François Vergniolle de Chantal. 2001. The Rehnquist Court and Contemporary American Federalism: The Challenge of Dual Sovereignty. *Political Science Quarterly* 116, no. 2:253–75.

Coontz, S. 1992. *The Way We Never Were: American Families and the Nostalgia Trap*. New York: BasicBooks.

Crew, Robert E. 2003. Faith-Based Organizations and the Delivery of Social Services in Florida: A Case Study. In *Roundtable on Religion and Social Welfare Policy*, ed. Rockefeller Institute of Government. Albany, N.Y.: Rockefeller Institute of Government.

Dane, Perry. 1999. Constitutional Law and Religion. *A Companion to Philosophy of Law and Legal Theory*, ed. Dennis Patterson. New York: Blackwell Publishing.

De Vita, C., and P. Palmer. 2004. Church–State Partnerships: Some Reflections from Washington, D.C. *Charting Civil Society* 14 (Center on Nonprofits and Philanthropy).

Demerath III, N. J., P. D. Hall, T. Schmitt, and R. H. Williams, eds. 1998. *Sacred Companies: Organizational Aspects of Religion and Religious Aspects of Organizations*. New York: Oxford University Press.

Desmond, D. P., and J. F. Maddux. 1981. Religious Programs and Careers of Chronic Heroin Users. *American Journal of Drug and Alcohol Abuse* 8, no. 1:71–83.

Diekman, K., A. Tenbrunsel, and M. Bazerman. 1997. Fairness, Justification, and Dispute Resolution. *Workplace Dispute Resolution: Directions for the 21st Century,* ed. S. E. Gleason. East Lansing: Michigan State University Press.

Ebaugh, Helen Rose. 2003. The Faith-Based Initiative in Texas: A Case Study. *Roundtable on Religion and Social Welfare Policy.* Albany, N.Y.: Rockefeller Institute of Government.

Ebaugh, Helen R., Paula F. Pipes, Janet S. Chafetz, and Martha Daniels. 2003. Where's the Religion: Distinguishing Faith-Based from Secular Social Service Agencies. *Journal for the Scientific Study of Religion* 42:411–26.

Edin, K., and L. Lein. 1998. The Private Safety Net: The Role of Charitable Organizations in the Lives of the Poor. *Housing Policy Debate* 9, no. 3:541–73.

Elazar, Daniel J. 1994. The Political Subcultures of the United States. *The American Mosaic: The Impact of Space, Time, and Culture on American Politics.* Boulder, Colo.: Westview Press.

Esbeck, Carl H., Stanley W. Carlson-Theis, and Ronald Sider. 2004. *The Freedom of Faith-Based Organizations to Staff on a Religious Basis.* Washington, D.C.: Center for Public Justice.

Farnsley, Arthur Emery. 2000. *Ten Good Questions about Faith-Based Partnerships and Welfare Reform.* Indianapolis: Polis Center of Indiana University School of Liberal Arts and Indiana University–Purdue University, Indianapolis.

———. 2001. Can Faith-Based Organizations Compete? *Nonprofit and Voluntary Sector Quarterly* 30:99–111.

———. 2003. *Rising Expectations: Urban Congregations, Welfare Reform and Civic Life.* Bloomington: Indiana University Press.

Farris, Anne, Richard P. Nathan, and David J. Wright. 2004. *The Expanding Administrative Presidency: George W. Bush and the Faith-Based Initiative.* Roundtable on Religion and Social Welfare Policy. Albany, N.Y.: Rockefeller Institute of Government.

Fried, Bill. 2004. Good Faith and Bad Faith. *Boston Globe,* August 6.

Fried, Charles. 2004. *Saying What the Law Is: The Constitution in the Supreme Court.* Cambridge, Mass.: Harvard University Press.

Frumkin, Peter. 2002. *On Being Nonprofit: A Conceptual and Policy Primer.* Cambridge, Mass.: Harvard University Press.

Gais, T., and C. Burke. 2004. *Funding Faith-Based Services in a Time of Fiscal Pressures.* Report of Roundtable on Religion and Social Welfare Policy Annual Conference. Albany, N.Y.: Rockefeller Institute of Government.

Gartner, J., T. O'Connor, D. Larson, K. Wright, and M. C. Young. 1990. Final Report on Year One: Prison Fellowship Research Project, Prison Fellowship Ministries, Washington, D.C. Unpublished research project internal report prepared by Institute for Religious Research, Loyola College.

Gibelman, M., and S. R. Gelman. 2002. Should We Have Faith in Faith-Based Social Services? Rhetoric versus Realistic Expectations. *Nonprofit Management and Leadership* 13, no. 1:49–65.

Gilmour, R. S., and L. S. Jensen. 1998. Reinventing Government Accountability: Public Functions, Privatization, and the Meaning of "State Action." *Public Administration Review* 58:247–58.

Goggin, Malcolm L., and Deborah A. Orth. 2002. How Faith-Based and Secular Organizations Tackle Housing for the Homeless. *Roundtable on Religion and Social Welfare Policy.* Albany, N.Y.: Rockefeller Institute of Government.

Green, John C., and Amy L. Sherman. 2002. *Fruitful Collaborations: A Survey of Government-Funded Faith-Based Programs in 15 States.* Indianapolis: Hudson Institute.

Grettenberger, S. 1997. Churches as a Resource for Human Services and Social Capital Development. Ph.D. diss., Michigan State University.

Grønbjerg, K. 1997. Transaction Costs in Social Service Contracting: Lessons from the USA. In *The Contract Culture in Public Services: Studies from Britain, Europe, and the USA*, ed. Perri [*sic*] 6 and J. Kendall. Brookfield, Vt.: Arena Publishing.

Guislain, Pierre. 1997. *The Privatization Challenge: A Strategic, Legal, and Institutional Analysis of International Experience.* World Bank Regional and Sectoral Studies. Washington, D.C.: World Bank.

Handler, J., and Y. Hasenfeld. 1997. *We the Poor People: Work, Poverty, and Welfare.* New Haven, Conn.: Yale University Press.

Harris, M. 1998. *Organizing God's Work: Challenges for Churches and Synagogues.* New York: St. Martin's Press.

Harvey, T. J. 1997. *Government Promotion of Faith-Based Solutions to Social Problems: Partisan or Prophetic.* Washington, D.C.: Aspen Institute.

Heckman, J. J., R. J. Lalonde, and J. A. Smith. 1999. The Economics and Econometrics of Active Labor Market Programs. *Handbook of Labor Economics*, ed. O. Ashenfelter and D. Card. Amsterdam: Elsevier Science, North-Holland.

Heinrich, C. J. 2000. Organizational Form and Performance: An Empirical Investigation of Nonprofit and For-Profit Job Training Service Providers. *Journal of Policy Analysis and Management* 19:233–61.

Hodgkinson, V. A., M. S. Weitzman, A. D. Kirsch, S. M. Noga, and H. A. Gorski. 1993. *From Belief to Commitment: The Community Service Activities and Finances of Religious Congregations in the United States, 1993 Edition.* Washington, D.C.: Independent Sector.

Howe, Mark DeWolfe. 1965. *The Garden and the Wilderness: Religion and Government in American Constitutional History.* Chicago: University of Chicago Press.

Hunter, James Davison. 1991. *Culture Wars: The Struggle to Define America.* New York: BasicBooks.

———. 2004. The Discourse of Negation and the Ironies of Common Culture. *Hedgehog Review: Critical Reflections on Contemporary Culture,* Fall.

Indiana Department of Public Welfare. 1985. *The Evolution of Indiana's Public Welfare System.* Indianapolis: Indiana Department of Public Welfare.

Jeavons, T. H. 1994. *When the Bottom Line Is Faithfulness: Management of Christian Service Organizations.* Bloomington: Indiana University Press.

———. 1998. Identifying Characteristics of "Religious" Organizations: An Exploratory Proposal. In *Sacred Companies: Organizational Aspects of Religion and Religious Aspects of Organizations,* ed. N. J. Demerath III, Peter Dobkin Hall, Terry Schmitt, and Rhys H. Williams. New York: Oxford University Press.

Jensen, Laura. 2003. Interim Report on the Implementation of Charitable Choice in Massachusetts. In *Charitable Choice: First Results from Three States,* ed. Sheila Suess and Wolfgang Bielefeld. Indianapolis: Center for Urban Policy and the Environment, Indiana University–Purdue University, Indianapolis.

Jensen, L. S., and S. S. Kennedy. 2005. Public Ethics, Legal Accountability, and the New Governance. In *Ethics in Public Management,* ed. H. George Frederickson and Richard K. Ghere. Armonk, N.Y.: M. E. Sharpe.

Johnson, B. R., R. B. Tompkins, and D. Webb. 2002. *Objective Hope: Assessing the Effectiveness of Faith-Based Organizations—A Review of the Literature.* Philadelphia: Center for Research on Religion and Urban Civil Society, University of Pennsylvania.

Kearns, K. P. 1994. The Strategic Management of Accountability in Nonprofit Organizations: An Analytical Framework. *Public Administration Review* 54, no. 2:185–92.

Kearns, K., C. Park, and L. Yankoski. 2005. Comparing Faith-Based and Secular Community Service Corporations in Pittsburgh and Allegheny County, Pennsylvania. *Nonprofit and Voluntary Sector Quarterly* 34:206–31.

Kennedy, S. S. 2001. When Is Private Public? State Action in the Era of Privatization and Public–Private Partnerships. *George Mason University Civil Rights Law Journal* 11:203–23.

———. 2003. Tilting the Level Playing Field: Public Administration Meets Legal Theory. *Brooklyn Journal of Law and Policy* 11, no. 2:495–523.

———. 2006. The Poor You Always Have with You: The Case of the "Sturdy Beggar." In *A History of Indiana Law.* Athens: Ohio University Press.

Kennedy, S. S., and W. Bielefeld. 2002. Government Shekels without Government Shackles? The Administrative Challenges of Charitable Choice. *Public Administration Review* 62, no. 1:4–11.

Kettl, Donald. F. 1988. *Government by Proxy: (Mis?)Managing Federal Programs.* Washington, D.C.: CQ Press.

———. 1993. *Sharing Power: Public Governance and Private Markets.* Washington, D.C.: Brookings Institution Press.

———. 1999. Governor Rehnquist. *Governing,* August.

Klacik, Drew, and Dana Jones. 2001. The Quest for the Holy Grail. Presentation, Annual Meeting, Association for Research on Nonprofit Organizations and Voluntary Associations, Miami, November.

Koh, David. 2005. Please, Keep Faith. *Beliefnet.* http://www.beliefnet.com/story/160/story_16092_1.html.

Kramer, F. D., D. S. Nightingale, J. Trutko, S. Spaulding, and B. S. Barnow. 2002. Faith-Based Organizations Providing Employment and Training Services: A Preliminary Exploration. Working paper, Urban Institute, Washington, D.C.

Kramer, Fredericka, Carol De Vita, and Kenneth Finegold. 2005. Faith-Based Organizations, Federal Social Programs, and Local Services. In *Assessing the New Federalism: Eight Years Later,* ed. Olivia Golden. Washington D.C.: Urban Institute Press.

La Barbera, P. A. 1991. Commercial Ventures of Religious Organizations. *Nonprofit Management and Leadership* 1, no. 3:217–34.

Lenkowsky, Leslie. 2001. Funding the Faithful: Why Bush Is Right. *Commentary* 111, no. 6:19–24. http://www.commentarymagazine.com/0106/lenkowsky.htm.

Lockhart, William H. 2001. Getting Saved from Poverty: Religion in Poverty-to Work Programs. Ph.D. diss., University of Virginia.

Lowi, T. 1995. *The End of the Republican Era.* Norman: University of Oklahoma Press.

Lupu, Ira C., and Robert W. Tuttle. 2003. *The State of the Law 2003: Developments in the Law Concerning Government Partnerships with Religious Organizations.* Roundtable on Religion and Social Welfare Policy. Albany, N.Y.: Rockefeller Institute of Government.

———. 2004. *The State of the Law 2004: Developments in the Law Concerning Government Partnerships with Religious Organizations.* Roundtable on Religion and Social Welfare Policy. Albany, N.Y.: Rockefeller Institute of Government.

Lynn, Laurence E., Jr. 2002. Social Services and the State: The Public Appropriation of Private Charity. *Social Service Review.*

MacIntyre, Alasdair C. 1981. *After Virtue: A Study in Moral Theory.* Notre Dame, Ind.: University of Notre Dame Press.

Marone, James A. 2003. *Hellfire Nation: The Politics of Sin in American History.* New Haven, Conn.: Yale University Press.

Marsden, George M. 1980. *Fundamentalism and American Culture: The Shaping of Twentieth Century Evangelicalism, 1870–1925.* New York: Oxford University Press.

Marty, Martin. 1997. *The One and the Many: America's Struggle for the Common Good.* Cambridge, Mass.: Harvard University Press.

McCarthy, J., and J. Castelli. 1999. *Religion-Sponsored Social Service Providers: The Not-So-Independent Sector.* Washington, D.C.: Aspen Institute.

Mead, Lawrence M. 2004. State Political Culture and Welfare Reform. *Policy Studies Journal* 32, no. 2: 271–96.

Merrow, Katherine B. 2003. *Faith-Based Organizations and Social Service Delivery in New Hampshire.* Roundtable on Religion and Social Welfare Policy. Albany, N.Y.: Rockefeller Institute of Government.

Milbank, Dana. 2001. Bush Assails Faith-Based Critics. *Washington Post,* June 6.

Miller, Paul. 2003. *The Challenges of Implementing Faith-Based and Community Initiatives in Montana.* Roundtable on Religion and Social Welfare Policy. Albany, N.Y.: Rockefeller Institute of Government.

Milofsky, C. and R. Cnaan, eds. 1997. Special Issue: Small Religious Nonprofits. *Nonprofit and Voluntary Sector Quarterly* 26.

Milward, H. Brinton. 1994. Nonprofit Contracting and the Hollow State. *Public Administration Review* 54, no. 1 (January–February): 73–77.

Minow, Martha. 1999. Choice or Commonality: Welfare and Schooling after the End of Welfare as We Knew It. *Duke Law Journal* 49:493–559.

Monsma, S. V. 1996. *When Sacred and Secular Mix: Religious Nonprofit Organizations and Public Money.* Lanham, Md.: Rowman & Littlefield.

———. 1998. *Government Cooperation with Social Ministries: Happy or Dysfunctional?* Washington, D.C.: Center for Public Justice.

———. 2005. *Putting Faith in Partnerships: Welfare-to-Work in Four Cities.* Ann Arbor: University of Michigan Press.

Monsma, Stephen V., and Carolyn Mounts. 2002. *Working Faith: How Religious Organizations Provide Welfare-to-Work Services.* Philadelphia: Center for Research on Religion and Urban Civil Society, University of Pennsylvania.

Moos, R. H., B. Mehren, and B. Moos. 1978. Evaluation of a Salvation Army Alcoholism Treatment Program. *Journal of Studies on Alcohol* 39, no. 7:1267–75.

Muñoz, Vincent Phillip. 2003. James Madison's Principle of Religious Liberty. *American Political Science Review* 97, no. 1:17–32.

Nank, R., and C. Stivers. 2001. Nonprofit Capacity Building for What? Lessons Learned from a Two-Year Effort under Welfare Reform. Paper presented at American Political Science Association Annual Meeting, August 31, San Francisco.

Neary, Lynn. 2003. Profile: Faith Partners, a Church-Run Social Service Program for Welfare Mothers in Colorado. *National Public Radio Weekend Edition*, November 1.

Neibuhr, Reinhold. 1993. *The Nature and Destiny of Man*. Louisville: Westminster John Knox Press.

Netting, F. E. 1982. Secular and Religious Funding of Church Related Agencies. *Social Service Review* 56, no. 4:586–604.

———. 1984. Church-Related Agencies and Social Welfare. *Social Service Review* 58, no. 3:404–20.

New York Times. 2005. Judge Halts Grants over Religion. January 16.

Nilsen, Sigurd R. 2002. *Charitable Choice: Overview of Research Findings on Implementation*. Washington, D.C.: U.S. General Accounting Office.

Nitterhouse, D. 1997. Financial Management and Accountability in Small, Religiously Affiliated Nonprofit Organizations. *Nonprofit and Voluntary Sector Quarterly* 26:S101–21.

Oates, M. J. 2003. Faith and Good Works: Catholic Giving and Taking. In *Charity, Philanthropy, and Civility in American History*, ed. L. J. Friedman and M. D. McGarvie. New York: Cambridge University Press.

Orr, L. L., H. S. Bloom, S. H. Bell, F. Doolittle, W. Lin, and G. Cave. 1996. *Does Training for the Disadvantaged Work?* Washington, D.C.: Urban Institute Press.

Pierce, Neal. 2005. Pioneering Minister Blows Whistle on Bush's Faith-Based Initiative. *Washington Post*, March 13.

Pirog, Maureen, and David A. Reingold. 2002. *Has the Social Safety Net Been Altered? New Roles for Faith-Based Organizations*. Perspectives 8. Bloomington: School of Public and Environmental Affairs, Indiana University.

Poole, Dennis L., Miguel Ferguson, Diana DiNitto, and A. James Schwab. 2002. The Capacity of Community-Based Organizations to Lead Local Innovations in Welfare Reform: Early Findings from Texas. *Nonprofit Management and Leadership* 12, no. 3:261–76.

Porterfield, A. 2003. Protestant Missionaries: Pioneers of American Philanthropy. In *Charity, Philanthropy, and Civility in American History*, ed. L. J. Friedman and M. D. McGarvie. New York: Cambridge University Press.

Prinz, T. J. 1998. Faith-Based Service Providers in the Nation's Capital: Can They Do More? *Charting Civil Society* 2.

Queen, E. L., II. 2000. *Serving Those in Need: A Handbook for Managing Faith-Based Human Service Organizations*. San Francisco: Jossey-Bass.

———. 2003. *Federalism and Charitable Choice Implementation: Some of the Effects of Charitable Choice*. Indianapolis: Center for Urban Policy and the Environment, Indiana University–Purdue University, Indianapolis.

Railey, John, and Kevin Begos. 2003. Board Did Its Duty, Quietly. *Winston-Salem Journal*, http://extras.journalnow.com/againsttheirwill/parts/one/storybody4.html.

Rawls, John. 1993. *Political Liberalism*. New York: Columbia University Press.

Richard, A. J., D. C. Bell, and J. W. Carlson. 2000. Individual Religiosity, Moral Community and Drug User Treatment. *Journal for the Scientific Study of Religion* 39, no. 32:240–46.

Richie, I., and S. S. Kennedy. 2001. *To Market, To Market: Reinventing Indianapolis*. Lanham, Md.: University Press of America.

Rogers, Melissa. 2005. Federal Funding and Religion-Based Employment Decisions. In *Sanctioning Religion? Politics, Law and Faith-Based Public Services*, ed. David K. Ryden and Jeffrey Polet. Boulder, Colo.: Lynne Rienner.

Romzek, B. S., and J. M. Johnston. 2001. State Contracting, Social Service Networks, and Effective Accountability: An Explanatory Model. Paper presented at American Political Science Association Annual Meeting, August 31, San Francisco.

Rosin, Hannah. 2000. Two Arrested in Texas Child Abuse Case: Supervisors Were Part of Faith-Based Program Supported by Gov. Bush. *Washington Post*, April 11. A5.

Ryden, D. K. 2000. Black Churches' Involvement in "Charitable Choice" Programs: The Promise and the Peril. Paper presented at American Political Science Association Annual Meeting, September 3, Washington.

Sager, Rebecca, and Laura Susan Stephens. 2005. Serving Up Sermons: Clients' Reactions to Religious Elements at Congregation-Run Feeding Establishments. *Nonprofit and Voluntary Sector Quarterly* 34, no. 3:297–315.

Salamon, L. M. 1993. The Marketization of Welfare: Changing Nonprofit and For-Profit Roles in the American Welfare State. *Social Service Review* 67:16–39.

———, ed. 2002. *The Tools of Government: A Guide to the New Governance*. New York: Oxford University Press.

Scott, R. D. 2003. *The Scope and Scale of Faith-Based Social Services, 2nd Edition.* Roundtable on Religion and Social Welfare Policy. Albany, N.Y.: Rockefeller Institute of Government.

Sharp, Brett S. 2003. *Great Expectations and Recent Frustrations: Oklahoma's Continuing Quest to Partner with Faith-Based Organizations.* Roundtable on Religion and Social Welfare Policy. Albany, N.Y.: Rockefeller Institute of Government.

Sherman, A. L. 2003. Faith in Communities: A Solid Investment. *Society,* January–February, 19–26.

Skocpol, T. 2000. Religion, Civil Society, and Social Provision in the U.S. In *Who Will Provide? The Changing Role of Religion in American Social Welfare,* ed. Mary Jo Bane, Brent Coffin, and Ronald Thiemann. Boulder, Colo.: Westview Press.

Smith, S. R., and M. Lipsky. 1993. *Nonprofits for Hire: The Welfare State in the Age of Contracting.* Cambridge, Mass.: Harvard University Press.

Smith, S. R., and M. R. Sosin. 2001. The Varieties of Faith-Related Agencies. *Public Administration Review* 61:651–70.

Smith, S. R., and Judith Smyth. 1996. Contracting for Services in a Decentralized System. *Journal of Public Administration Research and Theory* 6, no. 2:277–96.

Stillman, F. A., L. R. Bone, C. Rand, D. M. Levine, and D. M. Becker. 1993. Heart, Body and Soul: A Church-Based Smoking Cessation Program for Urban African-Americans. *Preventative Medicine* 22, no. 3:335–49.

Stone, G. R., L. M. Seidman, C. R. Sunstein, and M. V. Tushnet. 1991. *Constitutional Law,* 2nd ed. Boston: Little, Brown.

Stone, M. M., and M. M. Wood. 1997. Governance and the Small, Religiously Affiliated Social Service Provider. *Nonprofit and Voluntary Sector Quarterly* 26: S44–61.

Sullivan, A. 2004. Faith without Works. *Washington Monthly,* October.

Sullivan, Winifred Fallers. 2004. The State. In *Themes in Religion and American Culture,* ed. Philip Goff and Paul Harvey. Chapel Hill: University of North Carolina Press.

Thelin, Rachel. 2003. Interim Report on the Implementation of Charitable Choice in Indiana. In *Charitable Choice: First Results from Three States,* ed. Sheila Suess and Wolfgang Bielefeld. Indianapolis: Center for Urban Policy and the Environment, Indiana University–Purdue University, Indianapolis.

Thomas, S. B., S. C. Quinn, A. Billingsley, and C. Caldwell. 1994. The Characteristics of Northern Black Churches with Community Health Outreach Programs. *American Journal of Public Health* 84:575–79.

Tirrito, T., and T. Cascio, eds. 2003. *Religious Organizations in Community Services: A Social Work Perspective.* New York: Springer.

U.S. Congress. 1997. Testimony of Spencer Abraham. *Congressional Record,* 105th Cong., 1st sess., vol. 141, no. 156:S12119–33.

U.S. Senate, Committee on the Judiciary. 2001. Faith-Based Solutions: What Are the Legal Issues? Hearing Before the Senate Judiciary Committee. 107th Cong., 1st sess., June 6.

Wallin, B. A. 1997. The Need for a Privatization Process: Lessons from Development and Implementation. *Public Administration Review* 57:11–20.

Wallsten, P. 2004. Faith-Based Chief Cites "Culture War." *Los Angeles Times,* June 2.

Walsh, A. D. 2000. *Religion, Economics, and Public Policy: Ironies, Tragedies, and Absurdities of the Contemporary Culture Wars.* Westport, Conn.: Praeger.

Weisbrod, B. A. 1989. Rewarding Performance That Is Hard to Measure: The Private Nonprofit Sector. *Science* 244:541–46.

White House. 2001. Rallying the Armies of Compassion. http://www.whitehouse.gov/news/reports/faithbased.html.

Wilson, P. 2003. Faith-Based Organizations, Charitable Choice, and Government. *Administration & Society* 35:29–51.

Wineburg, Bob. 1994. A Longitudinal Case Study of Religious Congregations in Local Human Services. *Nonprofit and Voluntary Sector Quarterly* 23:159–69.

———. 2000. Faith Community Coordinators: An Emerging Model to Handle Welfare Reform in North Carolina. Paper presented at Association for Research on Nonprofit Organizations and Voluntary Associations, November 16–18, New Orleans.

———. 2001. *A Limited Partnership.* New York: Columbia University Press.

Wofford, Harris, et al. 2002. Finding Common Ground: 29 Recommendations of the Working Group on Human Needs and Faith-Based and Community Initiatives. Paper prepared by Working Group on Human Needs and Faith-Based and Community Initiatives, Search for Common Ground, Washington.

Index